The Virtues
We Need Again

The Virtues
We Need Again

21 Life Lessons from the Great Books of the West

by

Mitchell Kalpakgian

A Crossroad Book
The Crossroad Publishing Company
New York

Acknowledgments

While several of these essays are entirely new for this volume, a number of them have appeared in earlier, differently edited versions, and they are being reprinted here with permission. I am most appreciative and grateful to the editors.

The following essays were published by *New Oxford Review:* "Simplicity" appeared in the March 2006 issue as "The Ideology of Diverse Families"; the chapter "Leisure" appeared as a "A Cold, Commercial World" in the November 2005 issue; the chapter "Wisdom" appeared as "Universal Knowledge: The Secret of Human Happiness" in the April 2005 issue; and the chapter "Generosity" appeared as "The Christian Art of Christmas Spending" in the December 2010 issue.

Two essays were published in *Saint Austin Review:* "Gratitude" appeared as "The Theology of Food" in the January/February 2009 issue, and "Grace" appeared as "The Virtue of Graciousness in the Poetry of Gerard Manley Hopkins" in the November/December 2010 issue.

Some essays were published in *Catholic Men's Quarterly:* "Humility" appeared as "The Comedy of Money in Folktales" in the Spring/Summer 2007 issue; "Playfulness" appeared as "The Windows of Life" in the Fall/Winter 2006 issue; and "Serendipity" appeared as "The Divine Mystery of Luck: Gambling or Fishing?" in the Winter/Spring 2006 issue.

Three essays were published in *Homiletic and Pastoral Review:* "Moderation" appeared as "Balance: The Genius of the Catholic Faith" in the December 2004 issue; the essay "Love" appeared as "The Rhythm of Love" in the December 2011 issue; and the essay "Obedience" appeared as "The Generosity of God " in the April 2008 issue.

One essay was published by *Faith & Reason: "Pietas"* appeared as "The Ideological Attack on the Family in Orwell's *1984* and Huxley's *Brave New World* in the Winter 2001 issue.

The Crossroad Publishing Company
www.crossroadpublishing.com

Printed in the United States of America.
The text of this book is set in Sabon.
The display face is Sabon.

Library of Congress Cataloging-in-Publication Data
Kalpakgian, Mitchell.
The virtues we need again : 21 life lessons from the great books of the West / by Mitchell Kalpakgian.
p. cm.

ISBN 978-0-8245-2655-9
1. Virtues in literature. 2. Literature and morals. 3. Books and reading--Moral and ethical aspects. I. Title.
PN49.K27 2012
809'.93353--dc23
2012032726

Books published by The Crossroad Publishing Company may be purchased at special quantity discount rates for classes and institutional use. For information, please email sales@crossroadpublishing.com

ISBN 978-0-8245-2655-9

Dedication

In memory of my wife Joyce, a miraculous gift of a woman, and my parents Khatchig (Archie) and Meline Kalpakgian, the most devoted of parents.

In memory of Dr. Dennis Quinn, the greatest and the most inspiring of teachers.

To my children and grandchildren, the purest of joys and the richest of gifts.

Table of Contents

I. Why Read Old Books?

If some evil genius or demon wished to inhibit the transmission of wisdom from old age to youth, what would he do? The first thing might be to replace reading books with watching movies, even movies made from classic books. The film creates the illusion of knowledge, and viewing the movie creates the spell of authentic learning. Reading becomes optional or unnecessary if movies are the primary medium for transmitting education. If youth can become addicted to watching films as the quintessential form of recreational and educational experience, then the habit of reading and the cultivation of the intellect from good books suffer. A poem that will never become a film perfectly illustrates this point.

In Robert Frost's "The Mountain," a young traveler arrives at the small town of Lunenburg, population sixty according to the latest census, to visit a famous mountain known as Hor and to climb to the top. Meeting an old man driving a slow oxcart, the traveler asks, "Is that the way to reach the top from here?"[1] The old man notes that many in the past ("those that *have* been up") have used a trail five miles away. The old man admits that he has never felt any keen desire to ascend to the mountaintop: "It doesn't seem much to climb a mountain/ You've

---

1   *The Poetry of Robert Frost*, ed. Edward Connery Lathem (New York: Holt, Rinehart and Winston, 1967), 40.

worked around the foot of all your life." The answer perplexes the tourist. Although the old man has traveled around the mountain many times and explored the sides in his deer hunting and trout fishing, he has never shown the curiosity to mount the heights or investigate the unknown. For him, the world below is a school and universe in itself.

In their conversation the young traveler not only learns about trails that lead to the pinnacle of Mount Hor but also gathers all the lore about the mountain that the old man volunteers: a brook originates somewhere on the mountain, a stream that is, amazingly, "cold in summer, warm in winter." The old-timer guesses that the spring must be near the top if not "on the very top." It is possible to walk around the mountain, he explains, and still remain in the town of Lunenburg, which is not a village, "only scattered farms." Throughout the poem the young visitor, impressed by the old man's fund of knowledge, poses the same question several ways:

> You've never climbed?
> You never saw it?
> You've lived here all your life?

How can someone know so much about the top of the mountain when he has only traveled below on the sides? How can anyone who moves so leisurely ("so slow/ With white-faced oxen in a heavy cart") appear so well traveled, so well versed, about paths leading to the top, about deer and trout on the sides, and about brooks cold in summer and warm in winter? The young tourist remains puzzled by the wit and wisdom of his

older companion, who remarks, " 'T wouldn't seem real
to climb for climbing it," and does not understand why
someone going around the mountain in the course of
a lifetime would not venture to the top by the quickest
path. The young man romanticizes the notion of climbing
to the top and beholding a panoramic view of the wide
world below: "There ought to be a view around the
world/ From such a mountain." Driving a slow-moving
oxcart around the base of the mountain, by comparison,
appears inglorious and unadventurous, humdrum and
uneventful. What does the old man know that the young
traveler does not grasp? "As above, so below," as the
proverbial saying goes.

In the poem, Frost contrasts the young and the old,
knowledge and wisdom, surface and depth, information
and mystery. The young man's desire to reach the top of
the mountain in the most direct and quickest way leads
him to knowledge: the path most people travel is "five
miles back," the old man reports. However, the view from
the top does not reveal the trout streams and the deer's
hiding places on the side or the mystery of the brook
above that steams in winter "like an ox's breath." The
tourist discovers the surface and height of the mountain
but does not penetrate the hidden, mysterious places,
because he is in a rush and seeks the shortest and fastest
route; he does not have time to go around the mountain
several times. In the dialogue between the young man
and the old-timer, the traveler is asking the questions,
and the elderly man who has always lived in Lunenburg
all his days is handing down wisdom from a lifetime of
experience. The visitor knows so little, and the lifetime
resident so much. To go leisurely around and around a

mountain in an oxcart offers advantages that a straight, hasty course to the peak does not allow. Recognizing the effects at the bottom of the mountain, the old man knows the cause behind the effect, for invisible things are known by the things that are visible, as St. Paul said. Living around the mountain all his life instead of being a tourist for a day, the old man possesses a profound knowledge of the mountain in all four seasons, both its interior and exterior. His knowledge is extensive and deep, not superficial. As an ancient philosopher said, "The way up is the way down."

The curious traveler's approach to knowledge in "The Mountain" corresponds to the great temptation of youth: to seek short cuts to truth and ignore the slow, arduous process of acquiring wisdom by discovering the perennial truths of the past. It is commonplace today to hear high school and college students assert that they would rather see the movie adaptation of a book rather than read the story, and it is all too typical for high school English teachers to show a film and then assign an essay on the movie rather than require the students to read the book. A two- or three-hour film or video, of course, is direct and swift compared to the slow, interrupted pace of leisurely reading a novel. The movie, however, no matter how well adapted, remains superficial compared to the original novel or story itself. It is impossible to explore the sides of the mountain or detect the cool spring in the summer if the primary object is simply to reach the top in the most expeditious manner. Likewise, it is impossible to appreciate the power, beauty, eloquence, and art of words and to penetrate to the depths of a great story in all its universality through a film version. Even filmed versions of plays offer a palpably different experience than viewing a live production.

Modern students (and adults) complain that life is too short, and therefore reading is too time consuming, an onerous activity that interferes with the life of excitement and pleasure. It spoils the passionate desire, in Walter Pater's famous words, "to burn always with this hard gem-like flame." Because reading is as leisurely and as unspectacular as the old man slowly driving his oxcart around the mountain, it encourages reflection and contemplation, the art of being still and recollected and the ability to experience wonder and to behold a miracle or touch a mystery. Reading cultivates the interior life and develops the imagination, making present what is absent and translating the author's words into pictures. Reading sensitizes the mind, heart, and conscience in a way that the sensations, images, and music in films fail to move the soul. Movies—for all their devices, technical effects, and cinematography—may stir the passions and move the emotions, but they do not plumb the depths of the person like a literary work of art. Most movies today (there are exceptions, of course, like *The Passion of the Christ* and some classic films like *Babette's Feast*) simply provide a momentary relief from boredom—from the modern malaise that stems from the absence of a vital intellectual, spiritual, or family life. The chronic non-reading moviegoer is listless and craves excitement. Sensationalism is equated with action, drama, violence, and forbidden knowledge, and real life is expected to imitate art, that is, to copy Hollywood—its style, language, manners, and morals. As Oscar Wilde illustrates in *The Picture of Dorian Gray*, aestheticism is the philosophy that attempts to make daily, humdrum life imitate art (always full of thrills) instead of imitating nature or reality, as Aristotle argued in the *Poetics*. To the young intoxicated with movies and to the aesthete longing to burn with a "hard gem-like flame," going around and around the mountain is unromantic, unpoetic, and unadventurous. Reading the classics page after page appears tedious and lackluster, unlike the flashiness of films.

Students lament that reading is laborious, almost implying that reading is an unnatural activity compared to the ease of watching videos. However, learning to swim and learning to ride a bicycle are also time-consuming and demanding, as opposed to, say, playing video games. Just as it is easier to make one trip to the top of the mountain than to circle around the base many times, watching films does not require the effort, concentration, or patience that the exercise of reading prescribes. In short, people nowadays are tempted to believe that seeing the movie is tantamount to reading the book; some even judge the film a greater work of art than was the original novel. They fail to discern that viewing a film amounts to a tourist's ephemeral experience of one part of the great Mount Hor, never the old man's lifetime of wisdom about the whole. Especially when one is young, it is easy to confuse the ephemeral with the substantive, the superficial with the essential, and naively equate film watching with true education and high art.

In Aldous Huxley's *Brave New World*, everyone is addicted to the drug "soma" and to the film entertainment called "the feelies" as books disappear and the classics are prohibited because "We haven't any use for old things here," as the book's Controller says. An Indian called

Savage protests that "Othello's better than those feelies." Exasperated, he demands of his addicted contemporaries: "But do you like being slaves? ... Do you like being babies?"[2] They have no answer. They have never learned to understand such questions. Instead, as the Controller explains, they have grown up on a diet of "agreeable sensations" dictated by "Emotional Engineers." Because old things perpetuate the culture of the past and transmit the wisdom of earlier ages, they threaten the zeitgeist of the modern age. In Orwell's *1984*, old things have been banished from Oceania. The hero Winston nevertheless finds a pawn shop with antiques like a mahogany bed, an old-fashioned glass clock, and a coral paperweight in the shape of a rose, and they evoke a sense of wonder for the beauty of traditional art: "[T]he room had awakened in him a sort of nostalgia, a sort of ancestral memory." Later in the novel, when Winston reads "the forbidden book" that states the ideology of Big Brother, he discovers a radical agenda:

> The alteration of the past is necessary for two reasons, one of which is subsidiary and, so to speak, precautionary. The subsidiary reason is that the Party member, like the proletarian, tolerates present-day party conditions partly because he has no standards of comparison. He must be cut off from the past, just as he must be cut off from foreign countries, because it is necessary for him to believe that he is

---

2   Alduous Huxley, *Brave New World* (New York: Harper & Row, 1989), 225, 226, 218.

better off than his ancestors and the average level of material comfort is constantly rising.[3]

Thus the past must be censored because it provides "standards of comparison" to judge the contemporary and the fashionable, or the past must be erased because the brainwashed person must think that "he is better off than his ancestors"—that is, wiser, bolder, more emancipated, more enlightened, and less puritanical.

In short, everyone is better off watching modern films than reading old books: so we have learned to think. When the film watching of contemporary movies supplants the reading of good books, then the young lose an awareness of normative, universal experience. As Russell Kirk explains in *Enemies of the Permanent Things,*

> Every major form of literary art has taken for its deeper themes what T.S. Eliot called "the permanent things"—the very norms of human nature. Until very recent years, men took it for granted that literature exists to form the normative consciousness: that is, to teach human beings their true nature, their dignity, and their rightful place in the scheme of things.[4]

Given the nature of too many Hollywood productions—with their penchant for violence, prurience,

---

3 George Orwell, *1984* (New York: Signet Classic, 1989), 82, 175.
4 Russell Kirk, *Enemies of the Permanent Things* (New Rochelle, New York: Arlington House, 1969), 41.

sensationalism, and banality—the common standard of culture degenerates to the level of the lowest common denominator, while exciting aberrations and perverse forms of cruelty begin to seem almost normal. In a culture ruled by the dictatorship of relativism, no moral consensus, authority, tradition, or religion has a right to judge "the normative consciousness." Institutions hallowed by time, such as fatherhood, church, and the traditional family, are dipped in the acid bath of postmodern skepticism—and few survive fundamentally unchanged. Again, Orwell prophesies the impending evil: "And when memory failed and written records were falsified . . . there did not exist, and never again could exist, any standard against which it [propaganda] could be tested" (79).

As contemporary movies assume a predominant cultural influence in the formation of young minds and sensibilities, they subvert traditional norms and moral ideals. Older classics pale in comparison with the previews of upcoming films. Even in the Hollywood production of *The Lord of the Rings*, the movie becomes the work of art, the novel a secondary version of the film. The addiction to light and sound erodes the docility of the student who expects learning always to be thrilling, dramatic, colorful, and emotional. What teacher or book can compete with the images, colors, music, and glamor that appear on the screen? How can the serenity of a Homer, a Chaucer, or an Austen compete with the shock and sensationalism of Hollywood fare? The consumption of movie after movie habituates the young mind into associating learning with passivity and effortlessness instead of discipline and willpower. In *The Scholemaster*, Roger Ascham, a famous teacher of the sixteenth century, describes one of the essential virtues of the student: *philoponos*, an aptitude for learning. Such a student "[i]s he, that hath a lust to labor, and a will to take paines." Instead of seeking to labor and discover knowledge through discipline and the patience to overcome difficulties, the moviegoer expects knowledge to be served in sweet and satisfying snack-food portions. Stephen King is easy to read, but Charles Dickens is ponderous, J. K. Rowling, author of the Harry Potter series, is fascinating; Jane Austen, boring. The moviegoer, in short, does not realize that he is being indoctrinated, desensitized, pandered to, and "dumbed down" to the point where he cannot discriminate between the excellent and the banal, the beautiful and the flashy, the universal and the bizarre, what is noble and what is vulgar. While the moviegoer's eyes are being glutted, his mind is starved and deadened. While his mind feasts on novelties and oddities, it never transcends to the universal and eternal. There is only one standard—the one low enough to sell sufficient tickets.

In his essay "On the Reading of Old Books," C. S. Lewis warns of the dangers of reading only new books: "It is a good rule, after reading a new book, never to allow yourself another new one until you have read an old one in between." Acknowledging that every age needs correction of its own particular forms of blindness, Lewis sees an effective cure to these prejudices: "And that means the old books. . . . The only palliative is to keep the clean sea breeze of the centuries blowing through our minds, and this can be done only by reading old books."[5] Lewis's distinction between old and new books does not even hint at the enormous gulf between old books and modern films. If reading only new books intensifies what Lewis calls "chronological snobbery"— the presumption that everything modern is ipso facto superior to everything traditional—modern films teach people that error even more quickly. Without authentic standards of comparison, quality and excellence give way to style and trendiness; the shocking, the avant-garde, and the risqué determine the norm. There is no "normative consciousness" without the perennial wisdom of the past and the universal truths passed on to us in print. The young person who learns to treasure such ancient things is depicted in Chaucer's portrait of the true scholar in the Prologue of *The Canterbury Tales*, the Clerk of Oxenford: "He would rather have twenty volumes of Aristotle and his philosophy, bound in black or red, at the head of his bed than rich robes, or a fiddle, or a gay psaltery."[6]

One of the habits of mind the ancient world cultivates is *equanimity*, the virtue that Matthew Arnold attributed to Homer and the Greeks: "to see things steadily and as a whole." Cardinal Newman in *The Idea of a University* also identified this ability as the crowning achievement of liberal education at its best: "true enlargement of mind which is the power of viewing many things at once as one whole" and "the clear, calm, accurate vision

---

5   C.S. Lewis, *God in the Dock* (Grand Rapids, Michigan: Wm. B. Eeerdmans Publishing Co., 1970), 200 ff.

6   Geoffrey Chaucer, *The Canterbury Tales*, ed. R. M. Lumiansky (New York: Modern Library, 1954), 8.

and comprehension of all things." This poise Newman compares to "the repose of faith, because nothing can startle it; it has almost the beauty and harmony of heavenly contemplation, so intimate is it with the eternal order of things and the music of the spheres."[7] The old man in "The Mountain" epitomizes this repose, equanimity, and clear vision of seeing the entire mountain as a whole from the top to the bottom and from the exterior to the interior. Because of this self-possession he is not in a state of bustle to climb to the top. The young traveler, on the other hand, is impulsive and impatient, desiring the sensation of reaching the heights immediately. Restless by nature and prone to *Sturm und Drang*, the young do not need the overstimulation of the senses, passions, and appetites that the film industry indulges. Without the counterpoise of old people, old books, and old-fashioned manners and morals, the young will learn to live only for instant gratification and the excitement of sensation. No one is born appreciating the importance of serenity and the value of contemplation, qualities that apprehend the eternal and the universal. The old man's slow repetitious travel around the mountain does not tap into the thrill of the moment or the drama of the unknown. All great art and true education order the passions, achieve a temperance and moderation of the emotions, and instill a repose in the mind. As Newman explains, a liberal education forms this balance: "A habit of mind is formed which lasts through life, of which the attributes are freedom, equitableness, calmness, moderation, and

---

7   John Henry Newman, *The Uses of Knowledge*, ed. Leo L. Ward (Wheeling, Illinois: Harlan Davidson, Inc., 1948), 40, 42.

wisdom"(10). Corrupt art and false education, on the other hand, arouse the passions and agitate and confuse the mind—a view that L'Abbe Dubos in *Reflections on Poetry and Painting* (1719) summarized as follows: "[N]othing is in general so disagreeable to the mind as the languid, listless state of indolence into which it falls upon the removal of all passion and occupation."[8] That is, the mind is always bored and hence demands arousal—not equanimity or repose. It craves what it does not need: a new movie instead of an old book.

Old men and old books speak with conviction and authority and transmit a perennial wisdom of the ages: there is nothing new under the sun. Many new movies and new books, however, teach that constant change is the only reality and that nothing is universally true or right for all people in all times and in all places. In C. S. Lewis's *The Screwtape Letters*, the devils concur that the strategy of "inflaming the horror of the same Old Thing" in humans actually captures souls for hell. As Screwtape informs Wormwood, "Finally the desire for novelty is indispensable if we are to produce Fashions or Vogues." [9] Modern films are notorious for inciting revolutionary changes in manners, morals, language, and good taste— which is precisely why Christians reacted to them in the 1930s with organizations like the Legion of Decency and guidelines like the Production Code. While such institutions are widely derided today, in fact they proved

---

8   Quoted by David Hume, "Of Tragedy," in *Criticism: The Major Texts* (New York: Harcourt, Brace & World, Inc., 1952), 193.
9   *The Screwtape Letters* (New York: The Macmillan Company, 1969), 116, 117.

a prudent and partly effective measure for restraining the amoral, sometimes propagandistic power of cinema. Not incidentally, they forced filmmakers to resort to a subtlety in expressions of violence and sexuality that even made for better movies: hence Hollywood's "golden age."

When students read only new authors like Stephen King or J. K. Rowling, or when the re-creation of films replaces the reading of classics, both Screwtape and Big Brother taste victory. The devils agree that "it is most important thus to cut every generation off from all others; for where learning makes a free commerce between the ages there is always the danger that the characteristic errors of one may be corrected by the other" (129). Tyrants of every sort take satisfaction that students and "great scholars are now as little nourished by the past as the most ignorant mechanic who holds that 'history is bunk.' "

While the young traveler in "The Mountain" was skeptical of the old man's knowledge of a mountain he had never climbed to the top, the youth nevertheless showed curiosity and asked questions. The old man was no fool but a sage who piqued the interest of the tourist in the greatness and wonder of the mountain. A student who only watches movies instead of reading will not pause to listen to such old men. He has been taught that "real life" in all its moral relativism, brutal honesty, base vulgarity, and frank sexuality is learned from modern films and best-seller books—not from the past. The classics are the works of "dead white men," mere idealistic nonsense, or works in some dead language. In fact, they are what Edmund Burke in *Reflections on the Revolution in France* calls "the collected reason of ages" and "the general bank and capital of nations, and of ages." It is true that old books do not provide "the myriad sensations" or "the fiery colored life" of Oscar Wilde's Dorian Gray, who aspired to make his life a dramatic production. Rather, like the old man in "The Mountain," the classics slowly travel around a subject and behold its many facets, exploring the outside and the inside and penetrating to the heart of reality. Without exaggeration or distortion, old books reveal the nature of things and the mysteries of life. Without spectacular sensationalism, they penetrate the human heart and the depths of spirituality. The way up is the way down and around. No film can equal Homer as he teaches the profound truth that life goes on ("rose-fingered rose once again") no matter how horrific or heartbreaking the tragedy. No movie can illuminate the truth about "the tears of things"—the inherent sadness that permeates all of life because of the inevitability of loss and death—as well as Virgil does in the *Aeneid*. No Hollywood romance can teach the hard truths about marriage—its economic, social, moral, and romantic aspects—as intelligently or as elegantly as Jane Austen does in *Pride and Prejudice* when Elizabeth falls in love with Darcy: "She respected, she esteemed, she was grateful to him, she felt a real interest in his welfare."[10] No Hollywood version of the relationship between the sexes approaches Tolstoy's depiction of "real life" in *Anna Karenina*, a life grounded in married love, extended family, and the blessing of children. As Tolstoy writes of Levin, the noblest man in the novel, "He could not

---

10 Jane Austen, *Pride and Prejudice* (New York: Penguin Books, 1996), 216.

imagine the love of woman without marriage. . . . [F]or Levin it was the chief thing in life, on which the whole happiness of life depended."[11] No Walt Disney version of "The Snow Queen" captures the magic and innocence of childhood as eloquently as Hans Christian Andersen in his description of little Gerda's childlike power to melt hearts. As an old woman says of the girl who charms everyone in her search for her lost companion,

> I can't give her greater power than she has already! Can't you see how great that is? Can't you see how she makes man and beast serve her, and how well she's made her way in the world on her own bare feet? She mustn't know of her power from us—it comes of her heart, it comes of her being a sweet innocent child.[12]

The task in this collection of insights gleaned from a wide array of old and great books is to help modern readers employ the wisdom of the ancients to free themselves from the tyranny of the moment and recover a measure of such blessed innocence for themselves.

---

11 Leo Tolstoy, *Anna Karenina* (New York: Oxford University Press, 1998), 94.

12 *Fairy Tales: A Selection* (New York: Oxford University Press, 2009), 264.

II. Grace:
The Poetry of
Gerard Manley Hopkins

There is a virtue that has largely fallen out of use in today's purpose-driven, results-oriented world. Not entirely by coincidence, it shares a name with a central theological concept for Christians, the prayer some of us still say before meals, the extra time granted a debtor out of courtesy, and the Italian word for "thank you" (*grazie*). It can refer, in varied contexts, to the tone of a young girl's voice or the movement of a muscled athlete, to the dignity of an elderly queen or the way a soldier comports himself under pressure. That word is *grace*. And the whole range of meanings suggested by this rich, multifaceted word is illustrated in the work of a single nineteenth-century poet and priest, Gerard Manley Hopkins.

Hopkins's poem "As Kingfishers Catch Fire" depicts grace as one of the forms of beauty in the world. Just "As kingfishers catch fire" and "dragonflies draw flame," thus leaving a streak of color and light in their trail as they flash through the air, all gracious actions create an aftereffect and leave an imprint. The golden flash of the kingfisher as the bird moves through the sky charges the atmosphere with a glow and brilliance that dazzle. The sparks of the dragonflies illuminate the darkness of the night with fire and radiance that suggest a trail of glory.

Gracious gestures, courteous actions, and beautiful movements also leave behind powerful impressions that linger and abide, effects that energize and transform an atmosphere. Hopkins compares the afterglow of the flight of the kingfisher and the flash in the wake of fireflies to the echo of moving water:

As tumbled over rim in roundy wells
Stones ring; like each tucked string tells, each hung bell's
Bow swung finds tongue to fling out its broad name.[1]

Stones that create waves of concentric circles in wells, resonating with sound, and bells that peal in their succession of notes provide another image of grace— beautiful sounds, sweet music, and lyrical songs that continue to ring and reverberate. Likewise, human beings also leave a trail of glory, a sound of music, and an afterglow of joy as they act, move, and speak with grace.

For Hopkins, each person is created to be a source of saving grace to others by the way he moves, speaks, and acts—by the way he reflects Christ's actions, embodies Christ's words, and transfigures the world in his coming and going:

Each mortal thing does one thing and the same:
Deals out that being indoors each one dwells;
Selves—goes itself (129).

---

1   *Gerard Manley Hopkins: The Major Works* (New York: Oxford University Press, 2002), 129.

The fire of love, the music of joy, the glow of happiness, and the overflow of goodness that reside in Christlike hearts ("that being indoors each one dwells") must express themselves and leave trails and resonate in visible, audible ways. One who "deals out that being indoors" and "selves—Goes itself" is doing what God created it to do—to be a source of grace to others, to be a grace-filled source of light, a spark of life, and a voice of truth and happiness. When man honors the moral law and obeys the Commandments, he lives a life of justice:

I say more: the just man justices;
Keeps grace; that keeps all his goings graces (129).

Thus all good deeds and just actions emit grace, God's presence in the world brings light into the darkness, His voice brings music to the ears, and His word transfigures the world. Grace charges an atmosphere and renews the face of the earth. When each person—whatever his station or vocation in life—"Acts in God's eye what in God's eye he is," that is, a source of grace to others, then the world revels with joy, for "Christ plays in ten thousand places" through His creatures imitating Him as they fill each other's lives with beauty and music, mirth and warmth, and love and goodness. In this hidden, mysterious way, God is everywhere:

Lovely in limbs, and lovely in eyes not his
To the father through the features of men's faces (129).

Like youth, lithe and lovely in limbs, grace moves in effortless, natural motions and reflects the playfulness

19

of God, His surprising appearances taking a myriad of forms.

Grace smiles, plays, sings, dances, and revels; it does not move in ponderous, awkward motions. It jumps or tumbles rather than proceed in methodical, prescribed steps. It flashes and sparkles with the splendor of color, relieving the monotony of regimentation and dullness. Grace is youthful, energetic, and ebullient, lifting the spirits and rejoicing the heart. As the Bl. Mother Teresa once said: "Every time you smile at someone, it is an action of love, a gift to that person, a beautiful thing." Courteous words, unexpected compliments, and delightful conversation also transform the quality of daily life from humdrum to joyous and fill the air with the sounds that signify happiness: laughter and jollity. The hospitality that welcomes guests and celebrates the simple pleasures of company and friendship refreshes the weary soul and renews the inner life.

Grace is a divine energy, God's life-giving spirit that brings joy out of sorrow and brightness out of gloom, and Hopkins refers to the ringing, swinging, flinging, and playing manifestations of grace. Grace gives savor and relish to human existence, a salt and spice that dispel the bland tastelessness of monotonous routine. Mysterious as God's grace is, it expresses itself throughout all creation in the movements, sounds, colors, words, gestures, and actions of all things that come and go—the invisible things of God being known by the visible things, in St. Paul's famous words (Hebrews 1:20).

In this grace-filled world bursting, overflowing, and sparkling with divine light and sound, men and women are the primary sources of this goodness and beauty.

They must "deal out that being indoors each one dwells," that is, release the enormous potential of love locked in man's heart so that its dynamic power can exalt the world. What is the catalyst for this explosion? Hopkins's poem begins with the little things and mounts to the greater. Progressing from the motion of kingfishers and dragonflies to the rush of water, to the resonance of music, to the beating of the heart "crying *What I do is me: for that I came*," Hopkins captures the essence of grace: it abounds in the world in inexhaustible supply, ever giving and replenishing itself. Waiting to erupt in each person's soul so that it may "selve" or unleash itself in an outpouring, grace is God's constant activity in the world, Christ's playing "in ten thousand places" in small ways and big ways—from beautiful smiles and joyous affability to gracious civility and gifts of love.

Every time someone receives a personal letter, the surprise of a gift, or a friendly visit, *a kingfisher catches fire*. Each time a person radiates a smile, initiates friendship, extends hospitality, or sends invitations for festive occasions, *dragonflies draw flame*. Whenever gentle words, sweet sounds of music, or inspired eloquence move the heart, *a tolling bell echoes and awakens the spirit*. When one beholds the beauty of art in dance, painting, poem, or architecture, splendor illumines daily life. When great musicians perform or gifted athletes excel, they evoke our wonder. When good people perform the works of mercy, grace abounds as their inmost being "selves—goes itself" in its generous charity. These are some of the ordinary comings and "goings" that are graces, leaving behind their powerful aftereffects in their display of divine energy.

This exciting movement of God's grace in "As Kingfishers Catch Fire" that reflects itself in color, light, beauty, music, joy, goodness, and love resembles His dynamic actions in Hopkins's poem "God's Grandeur":

> The world is charged with the grandeur of God.
> It will flame out, like shining from shook foil;
> It gathers to a greatness, like the ooze of oil
> Crushed (128).

Again Hopkins compares the eruptions of grace in the world to electric energy flaming and shining in explosive flashes. The force of grace collects itself and converges until its power is irresistible and then discharges its spiritual energy in bursts. Despite the age and decay of the world, an ancient home in need of repair and a place where

> Generations have trod, have trod, have trod;
> All is seared with trade; bleared, smeared with toil;
> And wears man's smudge and shares man's smell . . .
> (128)

God's grandeur (grace) suddenly breaks through the faded, decrepit, exhausted world to revitalize and refresh it:

> And for all this, nature is never spent;
> There lives the dearest freshness deep down things (128).

Like a hidden spring, the water of grace rushes from hidden sources to renew the face of the earth. The aged world becomes a new creation, a dying body reinfused with life. No matter how dead or depleted the world appears, no matter how foreboding the gloom, "Oh, morning, at the brown brink eastward, springs." Grace bursts, explodes, penetrates. These galvanizing effects of grace manifest themselves with surprising flashes from the depths to reveal the ever-present nearness of God constantly recharging, refreshing, and refilling the world with love's energy. The movements all resemble one another: lightning darting across the sky, water erupting from an underground spring, daylight springing from the darkness. These natural motions from an invisible source to the light of day capture the mystery of grace's workings in daily life:

Because the Holy Ghost over the bent
World broods with warm breast and with ah! bright
wings (128).

Like a mother rushing to her offspring and a bird flying with instant speed, grace races, runs, jumps, plunges, and dashes from place to place, from up to down and from down to up.

In "Brothers," Hopkins captures the nature of the grace-filled hearts of two siblings:

How lovely the elder brother's
Life all laced in the other's,
Love-laced! (151)

In the poem, the younger brother John is chosen for a part in a play at the parish hall. Henry watches his brother's acting from offstage. While "roguish" Jack, described also as "brass-bold," shows no nervousness about appearing on stage and acts with perfect confidence, his older brother Henry suffers stage fright, bashfulness, and jitteriness as he watches his brother perform. How to explain the fact that the older brother who has no lines to memorize feels more anxiety about the play than his daredevil brother who does? It is Henry who blushes and bites his lip, who clutches his hands and clasps his knees, who drops his eyes and dares not look, whereas Jack, "young dog," awaits his cue with poise and aplomb. Their relationship as brothers is "love-laced," that is, intricately bound and delicately united by the many threads of love that entwine the hearts of family members. As brothers they are so close, their grace-filled hearts so intertwined, that the two become one in happiness and sorrow. When Jack finally makes his appearance on stage, Henry is so thrilled that he cannot contain his tears of joy, "His tear-tricked cheeks of flame" streaming out of the fullness of his joy. Thus the heart in its release of tears "Deals out that being indoors each one dwells"—an outpouring of grace, a burst of love's kinetic energy generating more grace. Just as lace reflects the intricate skill of designing human hands, so the human heart reveals the drama of grace's sudden entrances—its outbursts of happy tears.

Without realizing it, Henry's heartfelt affection for his younger brother captures the attention of the parish priest himself (Hopkins) who notices the "tell tale" sign of Henry's tears, one of "truth's tokens" that reminds him of the depth of human love and the mystery of the grace-filled heart. As Henry is watching his brother act on stage, the priest is watching Henry's reactions, "making my play / Turn most on tender byplay." There are really *two* performances occurring simultaneously—Jack's acting on stage that the audience witnesses and Henry's reaction that only the priest observes. As Henry is moved to tears by Jack's talent and "the imp's success," the priest is touched by Henry's affection for his brother—"the tear-tricked cheeks of flame" that issue from the grace that abounds in his heart. In fact, the priest is so melted by the older brother's weeping for joy that he is brought to tears:

> Ah nature, framed in fault,
> There's comfort then, there's salt;
> Nature, bad, base, and blind,
> Dearly thou canst be kind;
> There dearly then, dearly,
> I'll cry thou canst be kind (152).

The tears, then, are "that being indoors each one dwells": the sensitive, love-laced kindness of the pure heart whose outbursts of goodness prove once more that "there lives the dearest freshness deep down things" and that grace flashes, springs, and flames out, secretly gathering into a greatness and then dynamically exploding in a passion of love.

These flashes, bursts, surges, and eruptions of grace in the beauty of creation and in the rhythms of the human heart reflect the passion of Christ, the source of all grace. In *The Wreck of the Deutschland*, a long meditative poem on the tragedy of a German ship that capsized in the North Sea in 1875, Hopkins depicts the sinking of the *Deutschland* as a terrifying accident that destroys many human lives—but also as a metaphor of a fallen world devastated by original sin: a violent world infused with grace that overpowers the fury of the storm, just as Christ calmed the sea when the storm alarmed the disciples on Lake Genesareth. The tempest at sea in *The Wreck of the Deutschland* becomes a microcosm of the deadly effects of original sin in the universe: "And after it almost unmade, what with dread / Thy doing." The fear unleashed by the vehemence of the sea evokes the dread of God's punishment for sin, "His lightning and lashed rod" and "the hurtle of hell." The death of the Franciscan nuns who perish in the storm recalls the constant decay and impermanence of man's mortal life, which Hopkins symbolizes in an hourglass marking our progression from birth to death:

> I am soft sift
> In an hourglass—at the wall
> Fast, but mined with a motion, a drift,
> And it crowds and it combs to the fall . . . (111)

However, in the crashing of the ship into the iceberg, in the wailing of the women, and in "the crying of the child without check," another voice penetrates the din, the cry of one of the Franciscan nuns, "a sister calling / A master, her master and mine!" In the midst of the frenzy and destruction,

> . . . she rears herself to divine
> Ears, and the call of the tall nun
> To the men in the tops and the tackle rode over the storm's brawling (114).

In this clash of the elements of wind and water in the raging of the storm, an even more formidable force contends with the mighty sea. The tall nun beholds the hand of almighty God in the horror of the storm:

> She to the black-about air, to the breaker, the thickly
> Falling flakes, to the throng that catches and quails
> Was calling 'O Christ, Christ, come quickly':
> The cross to her she calls Christ to her, christens her
> wild-worst Best (116).

In the darkest hour, Christ's grace-filled heart clashes with the violence of the tempest and the forces of darkness: "Thou art lightning and love, I found it, a winter and warm." The rage of the storm does not compare with the Passion of Christ. The fallen world's furious destruction cannot annihilate God's omnipotent love that overpowers the fury of death, for Christ's shedding of His blood on the cross is an explosion of rivers of grace.

Like a juicy, ripe plum that releases all its juices upon being tasted, Christ's heart also flows with abounding graces in the crucifixion:

> . . . How a lush-kept plush-capped sloe
> Will, mouthed to flesh-burst,
> Gush!—flush the man, the being with it, sour or sweet,
> Brim, in a flash, full!—Hither then, last or first,
> To hero of Calvary, Christ's feet— (112)

Ever giving, endlessly streaming, constantly outpouring, always emptying Himself of every drop of His precious blood, Christ in His passion is fire, lightning, energy, power, even explosion—more formidable than all the elements that rage in the shipwreck's wanton chaos. All this reserve of love, all this concentration of divine energy, erupts from the center of Christ's being, His burning furnace of charity that Hopkins describes as "Our hearts' charity's hearth's fire, our thoughts' chivalry's throng's Lord."

Centered within the largeness of the heart is love, which burns in the hearth, inside of which is the source of grace itself—the fire that warms the hearth that enkindles the love that inflames the heart that leaps and bursts. Christ's grace inspires chivalrous action, which forms noble minds that do not cower before the dread of death and the shock of tragedy, as the courageous nun faces her cross with the knowledge of Christ's presence. Thus God's grace in its copiousness overfills the heart and makes of frightened nuns heroes.

The poems of Hopkins, then, illuminate not only the sufficiency of God's grace but also its superabundance and greatness. This grace explains both the "love-laced" hearts of affectionate brothers and the courageous hearts of the nuns who perish in the storm. It traces both the flight of the kingfisher drawing flame and the lightning hurling its bolt. It paints the plain, pied beauty of nature's infinite variety and the awe-full power of God's grandeur gathering to a greatness. This grace is inexhaustible—an ocean of love, a sun of energy, a furnace of charity, a treasure trove of beauty, an eternal dance, an omnipotent and omnipresent God who plays "through the feature of men's faces," bringing smiles, laughter, joy, love, and beauty into a dying world in dire need of the "dearest freshness deep down things" to renew the face of the earth.

III. Leisure: Melville's "Bartleby the Scrivener"

Americans in the workforce do not generally enjoy the one-month summer vacation that the French welcome as *les grandes vacances*. In fact, we mostly sneer at the very idea of such a long absence from the office, taking pride in working harder, longer hours than Europeans do. And we start early: college graduates entering the corporate world commonly expect to work a sixty-hour week in order to reap high salaries, climb the ladder of success, and receive other perquisites. Many women who hold full-time jobs outside the home also assume the role of homemaker and manage all the domestic activities of cooking, cleaning, and shopping. In continuing-education programs, adult students who work full time and have families encumber themselves with evening courses, thus adding a third responsibility to their demanding schedules. Given the contemporary penchant for shopping on the Sabbath, the day of rest has assumed the nature of just another commercial day.

While St. Paul did warn that he who does not work should not eat, one can take the work ethic too far. And many of us have. The obsession with productivity and attendant workaholism can lead to a desensitizing, deadening, and dehumanizing of the human spirit. Is the overwork characteristic of modern life heroic or tragic? Is it humanizing or dehumanizing? Is it necessary or neurotic?

Books like *The Overworked American* by Juliet Schnor and *Take Back Your Time: Fighting Time Poverty in America*, edited by John de Graaf, depict the many social ills that obsession with work causes: the neglect of children, the increase in divorce, the loss of health, the decline in voter participation, and the loneliness of the elderly. Such research is important because it reminds us of what we already know; literary classics long ago have pointed the way to wisdom.

Herman Melville's short story "Bartleby, the Scrivener: A Story of Wall Street," a study of the grave effects of overwork, depicts the life of a young man employed by a law firm as a copyist, or scrivener. As an employee, Bartleby is punctual, industrious, and steadfast, laboring diligently long hours day and night to the great satisfaction of his employer. He embodies all the virtues of the Protestant work ethic that Benjamin Franklin acknowledged in his *Autobiography*, qualities like "silence," "order," "frugality," "resolution," and "industry." However, despite Bartleby's work ethic, the lawyer who oversees his work regrets Bartleby's silent, private, morose disposition: "I should have been quite delighted with his application, had he been cheerfully industrious. But he wrote on silently, palely, mechanically."[1] Isolated by a screen from his fellow employees, Bartleby copies, copies, and copies without protest, complaint, or weariness.

As he continues his work as scrivener at the law firm, Bartleby soon manifests his idiosyncrasies. Whenever asked to proofread copy, collate copies of the same

---

1   Herman Melville, *Billy Budd and Other Stories* (New York: Penguin Books, 1986), 12.

document, or do errands, his one constant reply is "I would prefer not to" (13)—with no explanation or apologies. Exasperated by Bartleby's "passive resistance" and obstinate refusal to perform all the tasks required of him at the office, the lawyer notices other eccentricities. The scrivener never leaves the office for any reason, never takes time for relaxation, never leaves his task for refreshments or dinner, and never engages in conversation. He neither receives visitors nor mingles in company, apparently having no family, friends, or relatives: "He was a perpetual sentry in the corner" (16). One fellow copyist remarks, "He's a little *luny*," and another scrivener comments, "I think I should kick him out of the office" (14, 13). Devoid of emotions, passions, and appetites, Bartleby does not seem to experience pangs of hunger, moments of anger, or the delights of pleasure. His diet consists only of ginger nuts; his one reaction to the threats, warnings, and indignation of his employer is apathetic indifference; and he revels in no rejuvenating pastimes or leisurely recreations. To all his colleagues, Bartleby, in his "great stillness" and "unalterableness of demeanor," resembles a lifeless ghost. Overwork dehumanizes a person and kills his spirit so that he becomes a shell of a human being, an apparition.

After attending worship services on a Sunday morning, the lawyer decides to visit his office, assuming of course that none of his copyists would be at the law firm laboring on the Sabbath. To his great consternation he discovers that Bartleby is in the office even on Sunday morning. In fact, Bartleby has never left the office since he accepted his position. The evidence of someone who has been sleeping on the sofa; the signs of a basin, soap, and towel; and the remains of some morsels of ginger nuts and cheese prove beyond a doubt that " . . . Bartleby must have ate, dressed, and slept in my office, and that, too, without plate, mirror, or bread" (22).

Overwork hardens and desensitizes a person. Bartleby's employer concludes that Bartleby is not just eccentric but abnormal and unnatural in his behavior and habits. Bartleby never speaks, never reads anything other than his copy, never eats at a restaurant, never travels or visits a single person, never takes a walk, and never drinks a beer. The workplace has become Bartleby's home and the office his entire world. Overwork kills the human spirit and deadens the capacity for joy. The scrivener has lost sight of the true end of man's life and the perennial truth that man works in order to play; to enjoy the higher things and finer feelings associated with leisure; to appreciate the arts, friendship, hospitality, games, conversation, and mirth; and to contemplate the true, the good, and the beautiful. These humanizing activities and liberal pursuits nurture the human spirit. One-sided and alienated, Bartleby does not live a balanced life in tune with nature's laws and rhythms. Lacking home-cooked food, fresh air, exercise, a life of the mind, the delight of the beautiful, the enjoyment of a social life, and a knowledge of God, Bartleby has developed into a monomaniac, a "workaholic" who lives and exists only to work. The result of this obsession with work is not only lifelessness but also loneliness and spiritual deprivation. The lawyer remarks on Bartleby's "solitude, how horrible!" and that "it was his soul that suffered, and his soul I could not reach" (25).Work unrelated to any vocation or higher calling, work divorced from the ideal of service, the support of a family, or the contribution to the common good, degenerates into perfunctory, stultifying activity that starves the soul.

Feeling a mixture of emotions, from frustration at Bartleby's recalcitrance to pity for his loneliness, the lawyer resolves to offer Bartleby a sum of money and to terminate his employment. Without recourse to "vulgar bullying" or "choleric hectoring," the lawyer congratulates himself for his "masterly management in getting rid of Bartleby"—only to discover that the scrivener continues to work and reside at the office the following day, "a fixture in my chamber." Ashamed to carry Bartleby out of the office by force or to summon the police to evict him, the lawyer finally begs Bartleby to leave—only to hear the familiar refrain "I would prefer *not* to quit you." The lawyer concludes that, rather than displace Bartleby, he has no further recourse but to move his office to another location: "Since he will not quit me, I must quit him" (37). Bidding farewell to Bartleby and moving all his furniture to a new building, the lawyer continues to be haunted by Bartleby, who now torments the new occupant of the office, another lawyer who makes the complaint that Bartleby refuses to work. The landlord grouses that the scrivener haunts the building and sleeps in the doorway. As a last resort, Bartleby's former employer invites the scrivener to his own home in a gesture of hospitality, but Bartleby's response remains the same: "No; at present I would prefer not to make any change at all" (41). Thus Bartleby does not move, think, adapt, adjust, or change. Stolid, inflexible, passionless, and taciturn, Bartleby has turned into a virtual pillar of salt. He evinces none of the sentiments of the heart—loyalty, courage, friendship, joy, love, or magnanimity. Devoid of creativity and joy, Bartleby works as a drudge and lives as a jade. His standard hackneyed response, "I prefer not to," reflects the narrowness of his emotional range. Overwork robs a person of a refined sensibility and deprives him of the cultivated sentiments of a gentleman: tact, thoughtfulness, courtesy, and nobility.

Eventually, the new landlord of Bartleby's office has him apprehended as a vagrant. When the lawyer visits Bartleby at an almshouse, he first finds him "preferring" not to eat. The outcome is inevitable. Shortly after Bartleby's funeral, a report circulates a revealing piece of information about Bartleby's past: in his previous employment, he worked as a clerk in the Dead Letter Office in Washington, D.C. The lawyer naturally draws the obvious conclusion:

> Dead letters! Does it not sound like dead men? Conceive a man by nature and misfortune prone to a pallid hopelessness, can any business seem more fitted to heighten it than that of continually handling these dead letters, and assorting them for the flames? (46)

The explanation, then, for Bartleby's strange antisocial, perverse, insensitive, abnormal behavior is the nature of his work. In the Dead Letter Office, letters designed to communicate never reach their destination. Good news is never received, a love letter is never read, letters that contain gifts fail to bring joy, and personal letters bringing hope, reconciliation, and apologies never gladden the hearts of their recipients. The Dead Letter

Office represents meaningless work: writing letters that serve no purpose, opening letters to burn them rather than to read them, sending gifts that are never received, sending good news that no one ever hears. Vanity of vanities! Meaningless, unrewarding work motivated only by money, lacking dignity or vocation, causes the worker to decline into apathy, then passivity, then silence, then death.

Thus Melville indicts the nature of work in the modern world as dehumanizing. Bartleby's coldness and dullness result from the mechanical, futile, and drab nature of his work. What a person does daily on a habitual basis is either life giving or death dealing and has effects on body, mind, and soul. Bartleby does not die of starvation, natural causes, or old age. His premature death follows from the absence of all the life-sustaining, rejuvenating, invigorating activities that relieve the tedium and dreariness of work as an end in itself. Living in his office day and night and sitting always at his desk, Bartleby is divorced from nature's laws and rhythms. He does not work and play, concentrate and relax, go to work and come home, marry and beget, or sow and reap. There is in his life no daytime and nighttime, no day of rest. Alienated from family and friends, Bartleby does not belong to society. Starved of intellectual and spiritual food, Bartleby lives no life of the mind. Because of the strange nature of his work in the Dead Letter Office and his bizarre occupation as a scrivener, Bartleby has no time or energy to play, socialize, read, visit, pray, or love. In short, he has no time for life, for the quintessential activities that distinguish a man from a mule. Deformed by his work, Bartleby has lost his identity and personality and lacks any vestige of charm, graciousness, liveliness, or affability. He is merely eccentric, an individualist in his own private world that excludes the larger realities of family, nature, and God.

A man without a family, Bartleby lacks all social skills, from the art of conversation to the grace of good manners. Unappreciative of his employer's goodness and kindness, he never says "Thank you" or returns a favor. Alienated from nature's balanced rhythms, Bartleby lives a rigid, regimented life. Melville's portrait of Bartleby, then, is not a caricature of a lovable eccentric but a satire of modern man twisted and malformed by the business he performs and the long hours he works. Bartleby works too much, labors at meaningless or tedious tasks with no relief, and exerts effort only to earn a livelihood for himself. As Stefan Cardinal Wyszynski writes in *All You Who Labor*, "Work must make way for the other tasks of the day. Man must have time for prayer, for rest, for conversation with his family, for his hobbies, and for helping his neighbor. When work is over, man must remain a man, that is to say, a social being."[2] Because Bartleby's compulsion for work does not allow him time for any of these normal human activities, he does not remain a man or a social being but rather turns into an automaton.

Contrast Bartleby with the craftsman renowned for his talent as a furniture maker cited in Ruth Sawyer's literary history, *The Way of a Storyteller*. One month each year he and his fellow artisans in the village take a

---

2   Stefan Cardinal Wyszynski, *All You Who Labor: Work and the Sanctification of Daily Life* (Manchester, New Hampshire: Sophia Institute Press, 1995), 170.

leave of absence from their work to stage and perform in an amateur opera. A frustrated patron frets that the interruption of the musical production would leave her plans for a new sofa behind schedule. It was inconceivable to her that serious men of business would allow an opera to take precedence over pleasing wealthy customers who paid handsomely for these custom-made pieces of furniture. The carpenter addresses the complaint of his patron with this extraordinary insight:

> All the goodness, the lift of the heart that we got out of playing in those operas, we would put back into our work—in the draperies and tapestries we hung, in the cabinets we made. Nothing was lost. That is how it should be when you have experienced something great and beautiful. *Gnädige Frau*, something of these operas will go into your sofa.[3]

Work that is never renewed by the mirth of play or rejuvenated by the wonder of beauty results in lackluster performance, shoddy workmanship, and halfhearted effort. Without the deep sources of joy inspiring labors of love, work assumes the deadly tedium and oppressive dreariness of Bartleby's mindless copying. Man is neither a mere hand that mechanically copies nor a mere eye that stares into a monitor. Work becomes human only when the heart and soul inform the mind and the body to produce sofas with "something of the opera" in them

---

3   Ruth Sawyer, *The Way of a Storyteller* (New York: Viking Press, 1962), 25.

because workers have tasted "something great and beautiful." How can one experience something great and beautiful if overwork provides no leisure for worship, for the contemplation of beauty, for the cultivation of friendship, for the love of play, or for the enjoyment of conversation and learning? Bartleby never left the office to behold the glory of nature; never attended a play, a musical, or an opera; never joined a club or enjoyed a sport; never entertained friends and family with hospitality; and never worshiped on Sunday. Without the spiritual nourishment of contemplation, work becomes humdrum, impersonal, and perfunctory. Thus Wyszynski writes, "In other words, work has a human character only when all of our faculties are joined together in it." He explains further: "Our mind, will, feeling, and physical strength share in work . . . . The upsetting of this balance will always be detrimental to a man and even to his work itself" (28, 26).

A human life demands more than the Protestant work ethic that Benjamin Franklin extols and the virtues it inculcates: diligence, frugality, prudence, temperance, and industriousness. As Franklin writes in his *Autobiography*, he religiously avoided any form of diversion or recreation that distracted him from his goal of financial success: "Reading was the only amusement I allowed myself. I spent no time in taverns, games, or frolics of any kind; and my industry in my business continued as indefatigable as it was necessary."[4] With no music in his soul or laughter in his heart, Franklin's single-minded earnestness about

---

4   Benjamin Franklin, *Autobiography and Selected Writings*, ed. Larzer Ziff (New York: Holt, Rinehart and Winston, 1967), 80.

work leads to the self-absorption of taking himself too seriously: " 'For the industry of that Franklin,' says [Dr. Baird], 'is superior to anything I ever saw of the kind; I see him still at work when I go home from club, and he is at work again before his neighbors are out of bed' " (61). Bartleby's ponderous sobriety and Franklin's weighty self-importance deprive them of the lightheartedness that allows for transcendence—what Chesterton calls the "levitation" and "levity" of the saints.

In their gravity and incapacity for transcendence, both Bartleby and Franklin ignore the significance of the Sabbath as a day of rest. In the *Autobiography*, Franklin writes: "I early absented myself from the public assemblies of the sect, Sunday being my studying day,"(81) while Bartleby, to the shock of his employer, is busy at the office on Sunday morning. In Franklin's list of moral virtues essential to the Protestant work ethic and life of success, he enumerates such virtues as moderation, order, frugality, and industry, explaining the meaning of industriousness as follows: "Lose no time; be always employed in something useful; cut off all unnecessary actions" (84). Bartleby reflects the same attitude, receiving praise for his diligent "application" and "incessant industry." In short, for Bartleby, Franklin, and too many modern workers, play, beauty, friendship, and worship are unnecessary, useless, and unproductive. Sunday as a day of rest and recreation and as a time for family, friends, and hospitality is a waste of time, and those pastimes that are loved for their own sake, as ends in themselves—like the cabinetmaker's pure delight in the music of the opera—serve no purpose in the march toward financial success.

The Church has always defended the necessity of the Sabbath as an essential day of rest and as a holy day for worshipping and honoring God—a time to uplift the spirit (*sursum corda*, "Lift up your hearts"), abstain from all unnecessary work, and transcend the prosaic routine of work to glimpse the divine. The Second Vatican Council in its Constitution on the Liturgy states that "Sunday is the first of all feast days . . . a day of gladness and a rest from work." Obsession with work as the be-all and end-all destroys the capacity for the contemplation of truth, goodness, beauty, and nobility, and the life without true leisure never participates in "something great and beautiful"—like the sublimity of art, music, and poetry that the opera represented to the cabinetmaker. While the industrialized and secularized world trivializes Sunday, leisure, and play as unessential and useless to the real business of life, the Church in her wisdom knows that the unessential, the unnecessary, and the useless are the most practical, useful, and powerful instruments in elevating man's spirit and leading his soul to God. Bl. John Henry Newman in *The Idea of a University* explains why the cabinetmaker's vacation from work to participate in the joy of an opera makes such extraordinary common sense, even though it would remain unintelligible to Bartleby or Franklin:

Good is not only good, but reproductive of good; this is one of its attributes; nothing is excellent, beautiful, perfect, desirable for its own sake, but it overflows, and spreads the likeness of itself all around it. Good is prolific; . . . A great good will impart great good.[5]

This is exactly what the cabinetmaker meant when he said, "*Gnädige Frau*, something of those operas will go into your sofa."

---

5   John Henry Newman, *The Uses of Knowledge* (Wheeling, Illinois: Harlan Davidson, Inc.), 64

IV. Serendipity: Izaak Walton's *The Compleat Angler* and Machiavelli's *The Prince*

Why is it that often when we do succeed, we were not trying very hard in the first place? Why does fortune favor the brave? What is beginner's luck? Why are fools and children the most common beneficiaries of luck in books of proverbs? Why is winning the favor of Lady Luck very similar to a man courting a woman in love? Why is fishing the sport most frequently associated with luck— and while we are at it, why did Jesus choose as His apostles so many fishermen?

Perhaps that choice was not an accident. Perhaps good fortune (or "serendipity") is not as random or meaningless as we might think. Since the earliest Western myths, Fortune has appeared as one of the great mysteries of human experience and been associated with the power of the gods. In Greek literature, Hermes is both the messenger god and the lord of luck who carries opportunities that intelligent men seize. The Greek word for such opportune time is *kairos*—and the poet Ion praises it as "the youngest child of Zeus," or the latest god-given gift. For this reason, athletes pray to Hermes for victory in the arena. Classical scholar S. H. Butcher describes the appearance of this god of luck and opportunity: "His hair is long in front and bald behind; he must be grasped, if at all, by the forelock . . . . It is *kairos* who seizes the lucky moment in the wrestling bout; *kairos* who with his chariot-wheels closely grazes the goal; *kairos* to whom men offered sacrifice as they entered the stadium."[1] Thus luck is a manifestation of the presence, intervention, and power of the divine in human affairs—which brings surprising victories in both athletics and war to the brave who recognize the opportune moment and pray for divine intercession. Without serendipity, strength and knowledge alone do not guarantee victory.

Athletic and warlike Romans alike paid their homage to luck, but as a goddess. Fortuna had a temple all her own in Rome, and competitors from generals down to gladiators avoided impiety by sharing the credit for victories with her. The Anglo-Saxons answered impossible questions and decided irresolvable conflicts by turning them over to the gods—and casting lots. Medieval painting and literature are full of references to the Wheel of Fortune, whose erratic turns spin out our fates in life's ups and downs. Nor were these Christian artists merely regurgitating an undigested lump of paganism; rather, by acknowledging how man's plans are subject to Fortune, they pointed to a higher power than human prudence and bowed before the intertwined mysteries of divine providence and God's permissive will in a fallen world.

Throughout folk literature and in many proverbs, the mystery of good fortune appears in the form of the luck of

---

1   S. H. Butcher, *Harvard Lectures on The Originality of Greece* (BiblioBazaar Reproduction Series), 119 ff.

the fool, good fortune coming often to those who do not try too hard: "His net caught fish though he were asleep" is one of many proverbs that relate the paradox of luck to the absence of effort and industry. In many folktales (such as the Grimms' "The Table, the Ass, and the Stick"), the fortunate son is often the simpleton, the youngest of three children, not the ambitious or enterprising older sons. In the eighteenth-century novels of Henry Fielding, Fortune is the handmaiden or nickname of divine providence. Acknowledging Cicero's wisdom in attributing divinity to the power of Fortune, Fielding writes, "and certain it is, there are some incidents in life so very strange and unaccountable, that it seems to require more than human skill and foresight in producing them." In the twentieth century, G. K. Chesterton carried on this tradition when he quipped, "The more coincidental things seem, the less coincidental they are." Throughout the ages, wise men have intuited that Fortune's role in human life is the daily expression of something eternal: the mysterious, paradoxical, and providential Reality that is otherwise unseen.

But there have been, at least since the Renaissance, men who saw things differently—whose attitude toward the permanent things was much more aggressive and self-confident. The philosopher of opportunism, Niccoló Machiavelli, demoted Fortuna from a goddess to a timid, hapless maiden prone to rape. As he wrote in *The Prince*: "I certainly think that it is better to be impetuous than cautious, for fortune is a woman, and it is necessary, if you wish to master her, to conquer her by force."[2] Instead

---

2 Niccolo Machiavelli, *The Prince* (New York: New American Library, 1952), 123.

of acknowledging man's dependence on providence and vulnerability to the unpredictable, Machiavellian politicians pretend that they can tame events to their will with the cunning of the fox and the power of the lion. The ideal ruler was a man whose will to power and passion for cunning would overcome the fickle wills of men or even God's sovereign will. Enlightenment thinkers relegated the whole concept of Fortune to superstition and ignorance. In a grandiose political gesture, Cardinal Richelieu boldly crossed out the word *unfortunate* from his dictionary, since bad luck resulted from poor judgment and imprudent thinking—not the will of God or some other inscrutable mystery.

Such men as Machiavelli did not think like fishermen, but like gamblers. Traditional proverbs ("Throw a fool into a sewer and he will come up with a fish in his mouth") and folklore link serendipity with the paradox of the fortunate fool or the comedy of beginner's luck. But the modern idea of luck attributes good fortune to the boldness of a card sharp or the skill of a master of chess. While fools and children in their innocence have no cunning schemes to acquire power or win wealth, gamblers and chess players seek to outwit and outmaneuver their opposition through shrewdness. As Machiavelli wrote, the politician who exercises power must practice the arts of deception and "appear to be good" while having no scruples of conscience; the prince's success owes nothing to fate and everything to policy.

With the march of science and technology, this picture of man's interaction with nature has come to dominate not just politics but every aspect of our lives—from our farming to fertility. Most of us take Machiavelli's attitude for granted now, not realizing that it is a very recent, aggressive, and risky creed that callously shrugs off millennia of hard-won human wisdom.

In the traditional view of Fortune as a goddess or lady, man must woo her and win her favor. She cannot be conquered, only courted. How does one court Lady Luck or win the favor of the goddess Fortuna? Why are fools, fishermen, beginners, and children known for their luck? Simpletons in folktales have no guile, fishermen do not weigh the odds or study the statistics, amateurs do not take themselves too seriously, and children epitomize innocence. The mystery of luck is strangely related to these attributes of simplicity, lightheartedness, and purity—qualities that Izaak Walton in *The Compleat Angler* attributes to fishermen: "God never did make a more calm, quiet, innocent recreation than Angling."[3]

Those blessed by luck are not those who seek victory by trickery or calculation in their pursuits of self-interest; the lucky are not those who are obsessed with a particular mania that consumes them, depriving them of openness to life's many opportunities; the lucky are not those who are paralyzed with caution and fearfulness, the circumspect who never take risks or trust chance. The fortunate know how to court Lady Luck by respecting her power and dignity, proving themselves worthy of her favor by their honorable intentions. They neither disdain her as a superstition, nor imagine they can rape her. Just as a woman wooed in love surrenders when she is assured that her suitor sincerely loves her with noble intentions,

---

3 Izaak Walton, *The Compleat Angler* (New York: Oxford University Press, 1982), 113.

Lady Luck offers her favors to those who respect her mystique—those who do not flatter her, pretend to figure her out, or attempt to manipulate her for their own ends. The fact that Fortune is feminine teaches us the right way for mankind to approach her: as a suitor. Man should only *invite* luck just as he should only *woo* a woman. Man cannot rightly demand Fortune's favors any more than he can force a woman's hand in marriage. This is Henry Fielding's theme in his great and neglected novel *Tom Jones*. Perhaps the luckiest character ever written, Tom wins the hand of the beautiful Sophia (or "wisdom") because he honored her dignity as a woman—unlike her many suitors who wished to marry her for her money or seduce her.

As the modern world becomes more mechanized, computerized, and micromanaged, the feminine power and mystique of Fortune disappears. As baseball managers climb out of the dugout with their computerized data on Blackberries, as boats carrying fishermen locate schools of fish for extermination using radar, as courtship assumes the aspect of online dating, as opinion polls prognosticate the results of elections, and as statistics presume to predict the population of the world and the limits of the food supply, the idea of fortune and even of providence lose credibility. As historians explain events in terms of anonymous economic forces, a sense of the marvelous or of miraculous events recedes.

But these men are missing something. Most recently, the best political analysts failed to predict the collapse of Communism. History is rife with such surprises, like the British defeat of the French at Agincourt and the stunning Christian victory against the Turks at Lepanto. It is wiser to see in such events the hand of providence, which wears the glove of luck. Indeed, proverbial literature consistently refers to luck as the "nickname" we use for divine providence.

To understand luck requires a sense of playfulness, the pure enjoyment of fun, not intensity or concentration. The professionalism of sports with its obsession on winning and profits misses the point. Luck requires childlikeness, the spontaneity of a child in a game. Calculating the odds, taking bets, and studying trends detract from pure enjoyment for its own sake and can even inhibit performance. Luck requires boldness, a willingness to take chances and risks—the daring of an athlete on the field or the courage of a soldier in the heat of battle. Those who think they can conquer Fortune are more likely to prove either foolishly rash or overcautious.

Luck requires courtship, modeled on the chivalrous man wooing his beloved through noble, self-sacrificing deeds. This is a world apart from the modern ethos of sex for pleasure rendered "safe" through careful planning. Luck requires guilelessness, like that of a simpleton who catches fish while he sleeps because he is not trying too hard—not the strategy of the chess player or gambler who restlessly calculates and desperately worries.

Without a sense of leisure, playfulness, romance, and mystery, modern man never discovers the wonder of luck. The Puritan work ethic overlooks the fact that "fairy favors" and gifts are magically given during the secrecy of the night when man is not striving or laboring. The loss of innocence and the premature initiation of the young into adulthood rob them of the imaginative life that marvels at St. Nicholas throwing bags of gold into chimneys in the silence of the night and at the elves who finish the shoemaker's shoes. The disappearance of chivalry renders courtship a lost art, so that women no longer illuminate for men the mystique of Lady Luck, who refuses to be conquered or manipulated. When men demystify history and Eros, turning God into a cipher and woman into a Playmate, they can no longer see fortune as a paradox to be honored. All of life, indeed, is a puzzle that those with high IQs know how to solve.

The best introduction to the mystery of luck is the art of fishing. As Izaak Walton writes in *The Compleat Angler*: "I and my companion have had such fortune a fishing this day" and "come drink, and tell me what luck of fish"(180, 184). In Walton's book, fishing is an art based on hope and patience, the ability to wait, to be silent, and to be receptive. Walton contrasts the angler who cultivates leisure to partake of "the sweet content" of recreation with the harried owner of a large estate burdened with several lawsuits. Walton distinguishes the fishermen, "meek quiet-spirited-men," from the restless spirits of worldly men "tost in boisterous Seas" and in "the vexatious World." Fishermen who are enjoying their favorite recreation are living the contemplative life, in which the mind is capable of wonder, beholding the vision of the earth's abundance and beauty and marveling at the goodness of creation. Walton quotes from the poetry of an angler who relates the leisure of the sport to meditative prayer. Beholding the green meadows, the fresh rivers, the verdant flowers, and the lofty woods, the angler-poet writes,

> All these, and many more of his Creation,
> That made the Heavens, the angler oft doth see,

Taking therein no little delectation,
To think how strange, how wonderful they be;
Framing thereof an outward contemplation,
To set his heart from other fancies free;
And whilst he looks on these with joyful eye,
His mind is rapt above the starry Skie (56).

Anglers, Walton explains, are simple, childlike, mirthful, humble men whom Christ saw fit to be His followers. They are not "serious grave men" obsessed with "money-getting" whose lives follow a frantic pace, "a hodge podge of business and money, and care, and money, and trouble." Walton describes the contented fisherman as amiable, quiet, civil, and innocent, unwilling to trade his peace for riches. Fishermen epitomize the blessed whom Christ praises in the Beatitudes: "the poor in spirit" who will inherit the kingdom of heaven and "the meek" who shall inherit the earth. "Rich in self-contentedness," the angler delighting in his sport resembles the innocent child reveling in his play. Enjoying the carefreeness that fishing encourages, the angler resembles the fool of proverbial and folk literature who is not dominated by anxiety. Contemplating the beauty of the outdoors, the angler marvels at the reality of Divine Providence by beholding the prodigious variety and number of fish. Relishing in the pure love of the sport for its sheer fun—as an end in itself, as well as a means—the angler resembles the lover who woos his beloved with pure intentions.

Luck, then, pertains not to gambling but to fishing. The man who honors it rightly seeks not to rape it but to court it. He favors play over work. He does not worry over the odds but takes a chance. He is not anxious and restless but rather he hopes and trusts. The more that modern man loves plans and schedules more than rhythm and leisure, preferring the casino to the stream, the unluckier he will feel. Unable to see the hand of providence in his affairs, he will grasp at technological, political, and population control. As his efforts to tame the world to his appetites crash and fail, he will begin to feel that he is cursed. He will learn at last what our forefathers already taught us, that fortune humbles the clever and exalts the pure of heart.

V. Playfulness: *A Midsummer Night's Dream, Orthodoxy,* **and** *At the Back of the North Wind*

In the midst of these explorations of how the Great Books can inspire us to embrace forgotten virtues, it might seem odd to encounter some praise of playfulness, silliness, even nonsense. Literary classics, it is true, lift the mind to a contemplation of the true, the good, and the beautiful. That is the main reason we keep on reading them, century after century. But they serve another, equally vital purpose when they bless the humbler, animal aspect of our existence in the form of comedy. The words *human, humor,* and *humility* all derive from the Latin word for dirt or soil—*humus*. Playful accounts of comic events remind man of his origins in the dust, pierce us when we become puffed up or pompous, and sometimes literally bring us down to earth. In *The Canterbury Tales*, Chaucer portrays the proverbial stargazing philosopher who, in searching the heavens, loses himself in abstraction and tumbles into a ditch. That is a fine depiction of what occurs when readers afflicted by self-importance or scrupulosity encounter a passage like this one from Shakespeare's *Twelfth Night:*

When that I was and a little tiny boy,
With hey, ho, the wind and the rain,

A foolish thing was but a toy,
For the rain it raineth every day.[1] (5.1.398–401)

What do those words mean? On the literal level, not a thing. They are, in fact, stark nonsense, as silly as Mother Goose's nursery rhymes: "Hey diddle, diddle / the cat and the fiddle! / The cow jumped over the moon." Does that mean we can safely skip over them, to get on with absorbing the "important" themes of the artwork in question—or even dismiss entirely works whose essence is playfulness and whose method is the judicious use of nonsense? Given that Christ called on us to be "born again" and to "become as little children," we do so at our own risk.

In a famous line, Wordsworth wrote, "The Child is father of the Man." In *A Child's Garden of Verses*, Robert Louis Stevenson writes as if in answer: "The world is so full of a number of things, / I think we should all be as happy as kings." Our lives begin in childhood, where we revel in play, wonder and imagine, gape at the world's great adventure, and fall in love with life. In Stevenson's poems, the child is always playing, indoors and out, daytime and night, both in the company of friends and in the quiet space of his imagination. The child plays all through the year, delighting in birds' nests and eggs in the spring, romping in the loft in the summer ("The happy hills of hay!"), and playing in the leaves of autumn. Stevenson writes in "Autumn Fires":

---

1   *The Major Plays of Shakespeare*, ed. G. B. Harrison (New York: Harcourt Brace Jovanovich, Publishers, 1968) , 879 .

Sing a song of seasons!
Something bright in all!
Flowers in the summer,
Fires in the fall![2]

While childhood must pass, the spirit of childhood—
playfulness, laughter, and lightheartedness—forms each
of us in our humanity. When parents and grandparents
enter children's realm of play, their own sleeping memories
awake, and (in the best sense) they regress. As Stevenson
writes in "To Willie and Henrietta":

"Time was," the golden head
Irrevocably said;
But time which none can bind,
While flowing fast away, leaves love behind.

One need not lose nor forget the magic of childhood,
a precious experience that leaves "love behind" so that it
can be remembered and cherished, and so flow from one
generation to the next. As Alyosha remarks to a group of
schoolboys in *The Brothers Karamazov*:

Remember that nothing is nobler, stronger, more
vital, or more useful in future life than some happy
memory, especially one from your very childhood,
from your family home. A lot is said about
upbringing, but the very best upbringing, perhaps,
is some lovely, holy memory preserved from one's

---

2   Robert Louis Stevenson, *A Child's Garden of Verses* (Racine,
     Wisconsin: Whitman Publishing Company, 1931), 77.

childhood. If a man carries many such memories with him, they will keep him safe throughout his life.[3]

In search of that playful spirit that can keep alive in our hearts the part that is always young, let us look to three great comic writers—George MacDonald, G. K. Chesterton, and William Shakespeare—whose works serve as a golden thread we can follow back to the innocent world of wonder.

George MacDonald's *At the Back of the North Wind* affirms the positive wisdom of nonsense. Diamond, the main character, is a young boy who delights the baby in the family with his improvised rhymes, which are nonsense to his mother but bring irrepressible smiles to his infant brother. Whenever Diamond sings these nursery rhymes, the entire atmosphere of the home is transformed from a place of gloom and anxiety to a realm of play and lightheartedness. The infant bursts with laughter as Diamond sings:

And baby's the bonniest
And baby's the funniest
And baby's the shiniest
And baby's the tiniest
And baby's the merriest

Diamond's playfulness with baby and his silly entertaining verses prompt his mother to remark, "I

---

3   Fyodor Dostoevsky, *The Brothers Karamazov* (New York: Oxford University Press, World Classics, 1998), 972.

declare a body would think you had been among the fairies." When Diamond begs his mother to read from a collection of nursery rhymes they accidentally find on the sand, the mother complains about the "nonsense" of the poem because "it would go on forever":

> I know a river
> whose waters run asleep
> run run ever
> sleeping so deep
> and all the swallows
> that dip their feathers
> in the hollows
> or in the shallows
> are the merriest swallows of all.[4]

To his mother's complaint that the poem seems to ramble forever, Diamond replies by pointing out that it's quite realistic: "That's what it did," he says, of the gurgling river he saw at the back of the North Wind— the heavenly world he visited nightly in his dreams. The jingling of the nursery rhymes and the rushing of the river echo with the pure music of words and sounds that bubble from fountains of never-ending joy. Thus "nonsense" in MacDonald's story means neither mindlessness nor stupidity, neither absurdity nor contradiction. Nonsense is the magic spell that opens the door to the playfulness that is an earthly hint of heaven. Diamond links such holy nonsense to a creature he calls a "silly," which

---

4   George Macdonald, *At the Back of the North Wind* (Mahwah, New Jersey: Watermill Press, 1985), 127, 125, 109.

Diamond defines as "a kind of angel—a very little one." Nonsense is the musical language of mirthful fairies and joyful angels.

But the poet and storyteller in the novel, Mr. Raymond, enriches "silly" by recalling its older meaning—blessed, innocent, and simple. A silly, then, is an ancient term for an angel or a fairy—a pure spirit from a heavenly realm whose speech overflows with childlike joy. In the novel, nonsense assumes the form of nursery rhymes, fairy tales, and dreams—each of which functions as a window into a higher world whose light spills down into ours. These types of stories are imaginative, playful, and wild—outside the realm of realistic fiction or ordinary prose. Babies, angels, and fairies revel in nonsense, and Diamond, who has been transported to their world in his dreams, returns with the music of the bubbling river that goes on forever—echoes that inspire him to compose the nursery rhymes without end. Nonsense, then, is sheer fun, the love of play for its own sake, and the highest form of enjoyment. In Diamond's words, "I make songs myself. They're awfully silly, but they please baby, and that's all they're meant for" (174). Nonsense—play—is an end in itself. As Chesterton writes in *Orthodoxy*, "Happy the man who does the useless things."[5]

Diamond asks his mother if nonsense is "a very good thing," comparing it to the "pepper and salt that goes into the soup." Hence humor is what gives the savor to humdrum existence and the drab routine of work. Nonsense is the poetry of ordinary life that saves it from being prosaic.

5　G.K. Chesterton, *Orthodoxy* (New York: Doubleday, 1990), 19.

It is nonsense, as any time-management consultant would surely tell us, to look away for long from our anxieties over money and work. As the dour proverb warns us, "Time is money." Comic authors like these would agree, but they would turn things on their head. Indeed, it requires a dose of nonsense to set us free from our preoccupations, to lift the yokes from our necks so we may look up to see the stars, or down at the children waiting for us to join them in a game. Without nonsense man lacks imagination and never learns to play with children, and he lacks the wit to play with words, ideas, or his mind. Nonsense is evidence of liveliness and of a youthful spirit. As Chesterton remarks in *Orthodoxy*, "Angels can fly because they can take themselves lightly," and "a characteristic of great saints is their power of levity" (120). Although nonsense does not have a literal meaning, present historical fact, or represent scientific truth, it provokes us to gain poetic knowledge—to make original metaphors, see fresh comparisons, and form striking analogies in new ways. Diamond illustrates the wisdom of nonsense when he illuminates the reality of Divine Providence to his mother. The anxious mother worries about money, is troubled that her husband is unemployed, and laments "we shall have nothing to eat by and by." But her child's playful, imaginative mind responds with nonsense that makes perfect sense:

There's a piece of gingerbread in the basket, I know.
But the birds get through the winter, don't they?
I think there must be a big cupboard somewhere, out of which the little cupboards are filled, you know, mother? (107)

Comparing humans to birds and cupboards to barns, Diamond's playful mind and poetic imagination somehow relieve his mother's burden of worry. While she rightly concerns herself with making sure they all have food, it is Diamond who adds "the pepper and salt that goes into the soup." He lightens his mother's gravity by invoking a fairy's levity and restores their world to balance. Inspired by his simpleness, she remembers to trust in the providence of God.

Nonsense is healthy medicine and counteracts the disease of seriousness. In Chesterton's words from *Orthodoxy*:

> Pride is the downward drag of all things into an easy solemnity. One "settles down" into a sort of selfish seriousness; but one has to rise to a gay forgetfulness. A man "falls" into a brown study; he reaches up at a blue sky. Seriousness is not a virtue. . . . Satan fell by the force of gravity (121).

As MacDonald demonstrates in *At the Back of the North Wind*, children—and all the things that delight children (nursery rhymes, fairy tales, imaginative stories, and nonsense)—are the antidote to moroseness, even despair. Recognizing the same truths about nonsense that MacDonald captures in his novel, Chesterton writes, "Imagination does not breed insanity," and "Everywhere we see that men do not go mad by dreaming." It is the absence of fun, the lack of playfulness, and the loss of the imagination that lead to madness. Chesterton explains:

Exactly what does breed insanity is reason. Poets do not go mad; but chess players do. Mathematicians go mad, and cashiers; but creative spirits very seldom. . . . Poetry is sane because it floats easily in an infinite sea; reason seeks to cross the infinite sea, and so make it finite (121).

It is contact with the world "at the back of the North Wind," the divine world, that heals the mind and preserves sanity, and it is only by way of dreams, fairy tales, nursery rhymes, and poetry—non-rational modes of knowing—that one glimpses the heavenly realm. All through the novel, Diamond communicates with the North Wind only when he is asleep, recalling his travels as dreams, not revelations. After reciting his rhymes and songs, Diamond explains the source of his poetry as a mystery: "Sometimes he would say, 'I made that one'; but generally he would say, 'I don't know; I found it somewhere'; or 'I got it at the back of the North Wind.'" Diamond's explanation corresponds with Chesterton's recognition that the dreams and visions of imaginative literature represent windows into a holy, heavenly kingdom:

The poet only desires exaltation and expansion, a world to stretch himself in. The poet only asks to get his head into the heavens. It is the logician who seeks to get the heavens into his head. And it is his head that splits (121).

Modern man badly needs to transcend the workaday world of money, routine, schedules, and repetition to acquire the balance and sanity that counteract the morbidity of seriousness. Nonsense is medicine for the spirit.

In *A Midsummer Night's Dream*, Shakespeare also depicts the healing medicine of playfulness and associates nonsense with wisdom. The play contrasts the deadly earnestness of the daytime business world with the lighthearted mirth of the fairies reveling in the night. The grim Aegeus insists that his daughter Hermia marry the husband he chose or find herself locked up in a nunnery. The realm of the forest where Puck and the fairies frolic offers this real problem a magical solution. Oberon, the king of the fairies, prescribes play as a cure for the love-madness that afflicts all these Athenians. Through the potion he sends Puck to squeeze on the eyelids of foolish lovers, play and revelry ensue that will cure their confusion and quarrels. Comedy abounds in the play as Puck puts the love juice in the wrong lovers' eyes: Lysander and Demetrius were both in love with Hermia, but as a result of Puck's mistake, they now both love Helena. Before the night has ended, however, the king of the fairies cures the minds and eyes of the foolish lovers, matching Jack with Jill. The lighthearted fairies with their playfulness heal the heavy hearts of the lovers and reflect a higher wisdom than the letter of the law enforced in Athens. In other words, the forest, the realm of imaginative play, embodies a higher form of knowledge than the city of coldly rational philosophers. All the healing, humanizing activities in *A Midsummer Night's Dream* result from the medicine of laughter and the playfulness that the lighthearted fairies provide.

A Midsummer Night's Dream depicts simple, ordinary workingmen—"the rude mechanicals"— engaged in harmless fun as they rehearse a play entitled "The most lamentable comedy and most cruel death of Pyramus and Thisby." In their rehearsal and performance, one of the players, Flute, insists that he must refuse the woman's part of Thisby: "I have a beard coming." Bottom promises not to frighten the ladies if he plays the lion's part: "I'll speak in a monstrous little voice, 'Thisne, Thisne.'" To avoid the shock of Pyramus killing himself with a sword on stage, the mechanicals agree to compose a prologue that informs the audience that "Pyramus is not kill'd indeed" and that Pyramus is not Pyramus but Bottom the weaver. So as not to terrify the women, the actors request another prologue that announces, 'If you think I am come hither as a lion, it were pity of my life. . . . I am a man as other men are." Since the play requires a wall that separates the two lovers, the actors improvise: "Some man or other must present Wall . . . and let him hold his fingers thus, and through that cranny shall Pyramus and Thisby whisper" (1.2; 3.1).

More nonsense ensues. The queen of the fairies, also anointed with the love juice that will compel her to fall in love with the first creature she sees, stumbles into the rehearsal and beholds Bottom wearing an ass's head. When the ethereal queen from the pure world of fairies casts her eyes upon the lowly, ass-headed dolt, her farcical love song begins, "What angel wakes me from my flow'ry bed?" On the day of the actual performance, the play's bill of fare reads, "A tedious brief scene of young Pyramus and his love Thisby; very tragical mirth," and the ridiculous prologue begins, "If we offend, it is with our good will. / That you should think, we come not to offend, / But with good will." Finally, the master of the revels forewarns the king of the silliness that awaits him if he selects the play about Pyramus and Thisbe as part of the nuptial festivities: "For in all the play / There is not one word apt, one player fitted." All this delightful nonsense of weavers and joiners playing at acting transforms these common men from "rude mechanicals" into good-natured, lovable characters who have not lost the playfulness of childhood. Playfulness humanizes and gentles their roughness, reawakens their love of fun, makes them more affable, warms their hearts, and lifts them into a world of pure joy that transcends business, work, and routine (3.1; 5.1)

Without the salt and pepper of playfulness, the humbling medicine of humor, and the liberating poetry of nonsense, man lives in a world devoid of levity, laughter, and mystery. We see this depicted starkly in Orwell's *1984*, where inventiveness is reserved for useful lies, and creativity for new methods of torture and domination. As Orwell writes, "It struck him [Winston] that the truly characteristic thing about modern life was not its cruelty or insecurity but simply its bareness, its dinginess, its listlessness."[6] One of the radical changes that is the result of Big Brother's socialist regime is the prohibition of church bells tolling a popular nursery rhyme: "Oranges and lemons say the bells of St. Clement's, / You owe me three farthings, say the bells of St. Martin's." To maintain sanity in the mad, inhuman world of totalitarian collectivism, Winston vows to assert certain timeless truths to uphold his dignity: "The obvious, the *silly*, and

---

6   George Orwell, *1984* (New York: New American Library, 1981), 130, 7, 206.

the true had to be defended" (emphasis added). Without the church bells tolling the nonsense of children's songs, "Oranges and lemons say the bells of St. Clemens," humans lose their grip on reality because man cannot live by reason alone. As long as playfulness has a place in human life, we can keep our grip on reality: "stones are hard, water is wet, objects unsupported fall toward the earth's center"—and nonsense is good.

In *1984* the poetry of nursery rhymes no longer evokes innocent laughter, because nothing is innocent anymore. Language itself is devoid of wordplay and puns, and bubbling verses give way to sterile words and euphemisms: "unperson" for a dead man, "joycamp" for forced-labor camp, "ungood" for evil, "Minipax" for Ministry of War. The liveliness of lyrics gives way to the deadness of lies: "WAR IS PEACE," "FREEDOM IS SLAVERY," TWO PLUS TWO EQUAL FIVE," and "IGNORANCE IS STRENGTH." Although these supposed maxims defy common sense, they do not constitute nonsense. Each of these slogans has a deadly serious purpose: to dull the mind and numb the heart.

The grisly seriousness of Big Brother and the fanaticism of the Party manifest themselves in the Draconian punishments for Thoughtcrime. Winston is humiliated, starved, tortured, and undergoes psychological conditioning for behavior modification until he confesses, "I love Big Brother." Chesterton uses the term "maniac" to describe ideologues who would resort to means like this. He describes the intellectual monomaniac, sunk in his seriousness and narrowness: "He is in the clean and well-lit prison of one idea: he is sharpened to one painful point" (22). Whereas the mystical imagination of the child who travels to the back of the North Wind inhabits a large universe that acknowledges both heaven and earth, the lunatic's theory suffers from "the suffocation of a single argument" that cannot breathe or expand. Therefore, ideology must ban nonsense, just as it strives to erase every vestige of mystery and the supernatural world.

In a world that welcomes children and all that delights them, the life of the imagination flourishes, and playfulness is a normal part of life. Children link heaven and earth. The nonsense they enjoy as sheer fun hints at the pure joys of heaven, just as a "silly" is merely a name for a very small angel. MacDonald depicts the child as a messenger from Heaven, a mediator who brings a vision of God to man and lifts man's mind to contemplate God:

> Where did you come from, baby dear?
> Out of the everywhere into here
>
> Where did you get your eyes so blue?
> Out of the sky as I came through.
> What makes the light in them sparkle and spin?
> Some of the starry spikes left in.
> But how did you come to us, you dear?
> God thought about you, and so I am here (270–271).

The fairy tales, nursery rhymes, and books of wonder children enjoy also evoke intimations of immortality. Like the window in Diamond's room where the North Wind enters ("windows are holes to see out of," she tells the boy), these stories connect the human world to a higher realm. No wonder that the sociopaths who govern Orwell's world do their best to abolish sex and deprive Party members of children.

Absent the child, playfulness disappears with all the wholesome benefits it provides. The fairies and angels do not exist. The world is left bereft of imaginative fun, the comic spirit, and the spice of life. We lose the candor of the child who proclaims, "The Emperor has no clothes!"

How sad that so many modern men and women are choosing to postpone or even sacrifice parenthood, that married couples are taught by the culture to regard possible pregnancies as a medical side effect of intercourse, to be managed by any means necessary. In this void created by the absence of children, we take ourselves, our work, our politics, and our portfolios too seriously, losing balance and perspective. When we do "regress" in the absence of playful children, we tend to slip back into adolescence, a time of self-absorption without innocence, self-assertion without wisdom. We regard our selves and our whims with murderous seriousness. Everything offends, everything is a source of harassment, and every small irritation is cause for legal action.

The virtue of playfulness, then, consists in the skill of remembering and preserving the essence of childhood: lightheartedness, imagination, and humor. To have a sense of humor is to learn humility and lowliness, the ability to laugh at oneself and see the human comedy. And to be humble is simply to tell the truth, to remember man's beginning and his earthly end: "ashes to ashes, and dust to dust."

VI. Piety: The *Aeneid*, *1984*, and *Brave New World*

One of the best-kept secrets to living a rich, happy life is a virtue the Romans called *pietas*, which comes down to us as piety. When we moderns hear this word, we picture (perhaps) an old peasant woman venerating an icon in Moscow or Guadalupe. While we might envy her simple certainties, we do not see what we could possibly learn from such a person. She has superstitions, while we have certain knowledge; she clings to the dead past, whereas we claw our way into the future. Her life is narrow and sterile, but our vistas expand with every scientific discovery. So we tell ourselves. So young Soviets must have thought, secure in their paradigms that predicted the future infallibly as they scoffed at the old people creeping out of Russia's crumbling churches.

But what if the virtue we associate with the elderly and with peasants turned out to be something much stronger than it seems? What if it proved to be the force of gravity that holds society together and cements one generation to the next? What if it, in fact, were the last and strongest bulwark of freedom, without which the hapless individual had no hope of standing up against the social engineering practiced by ideologues with power? We have good reason, in the stories of men like Lech Walesa and Aleksandr Solzhenitsyn, to suspect that this might be so. Two of the most influential novels of the twentieth century, *1984* and *Brave New World*, with the truth-telling power of great works of art, depict the long culture war between piety and tyranny—and offer strategic insights about where the battle lines lie today.

First, a little historical background. The Roman virtue of *pietas* was seen not as a sentimental, nostalgic attachment but rather as a form of rendering strict justice, giving back the respect we owe to the gods, our ancestors, our parents, and the traditions that shaped our identity. We cannot directly repay such benefactors, so we offer them reverence, respect, gratitude, and praise. The best way to honor such blessings we have received is to pass them along ourselves, to "pay the debt forward." In Virgil's *Aeneid*, the Roman hero Aeneas exemplifies *pietas* throughout the epic in his profound sense of devotion to the gods and to his family:

> I am Aeneas, duty-bound, and known
> Above high air of heaven by my fame,
> Carrying with me in my ships our gods
> Of hearth and home, saved from the enemy.[1]
> (1.519–22)

Escaping the burning city of Troy, Aeneas tries to save all that he holds dear, lifting his aged father on his shoulders, leading his young son Iulus by the hand, worrying about the safety of his wife Creusa, who follows them in their flight, and carrying with him the "household gods" that blessed each family's hearth. As Aeneas explains to his

---

1   Virgil, *The Aeneid*, tr. Robert Fitzgerald (New York: Random House, Inc., 1990),17.

hostess, Queen Dido, the story of his escape, he shows how such *pietas* can inspire self-sacrifice:

> Then come, dear father. Arms around my neck:
> I'll take you on my shoulders, no great weight.
> Whatever happens, both will face one danger,
> Find one safety. Iulus will come with me,
> My wife at a good interval behind. (2.921–25)

In powerful contrast, Orwell's *1984* (1949) and Huxley's *Brave New World* (1932) depict the triumph of ideology against the wisdom of the ages and the perennial truths of the Judeo-Christian tradition. The revolution in thought depicted in each of these novels has parallels both in the Western past and in our present: in the radical ideas that sparked the French Revolution and in those that launched the culture wars of the late twentieth century. In *1984* and *Brave New World*, ideology supplants the moral wisdom of Western civilization by altering the past, changing the structure of the family, and eliminating religion as a cultural force in society. In *Reflections on the Revolution in France*, Edmund Burke acted like an eighteenth-century Aeneas, trying piously to save what he held sacred from invaders who sought to destroy it. Burke considered the revolution the wholesale destruction of an ancient, enduring Christian civilization that embodied chivalry, reverence, and honor—venerable customs, traditions, and moral sentiments that were jettisoned in the name of false notions of "*liberte, egalite,* and *fraternite.*" In our own culture wars, assorted ideologies attack the traditional moral norms and established civilized ideals that have formed the basis of Christian civilization. We have been taught by cultural elites that the only way to honor the rights of women and of sexual minorities is to slough off the moral patrimony of the past, overturn the traditional ideals of family and marriage, and relegate religion to the private sphere. Our own culture wars seem on the surface more bloodless than the French Reign of Terror until one factors in the lives of the unborn.

In *1984* the main character, Winston Smith, has a vague recollection of his family from his childhood years and remembers his wife, Katharine, a woman who mysteriously disappeared from his life during the purges after the revolution. Winston is a man without a wife and family, his entire past erased along with the history of England. In his official position at the Ministry of Truth, Winston is engaged in the ultimate form of revisionist history: he alters its facts to fit the current Party line, deleting information and records that do not conform to ideological theory. As O'Brien, a powerful member of the Inner Party, argues, "We, the Party, control all records, and we control all memories." Winston's only contact with the truth of the past is his own memory, not the official records of the Ministry of Truth. As he explains to his lover Julia, "Every record has been destroyed or falsified, every book has been rewritten, every picture has been repainted, every statue and street and building has been renamed, every date has been altered." [2]

Winston realizes the richness of the fading past when he visits an antique shop and marvels at the beauty of

---

2   George Orwell, *1984* (New York: New American Library, Signet Book, 1981), 203, 128.

a hand-made mahogany bed, the craftsmanship of an old-fashioned glass clock, and a rare sculptured glass paperweight shaped in the form of a rose—all works of art that evoke in Winston "a sort of nostalgia, a sort of ancestral memory." These masterpieces are banned from Oceania because the Party rightly sees beauty as a threat: it elevates the mind to a contemplation of eternal realities that transcend Big Brother, the Party, and the Revolution.

In *Brave New World*, Mustapha Mond, the Controller of this utopian society, explains that censorship is required to purge the influence of the past upon the present and to prevent a critical comparison between the ways things are and the way things ought to be: "We haven't any use for old things here. . . . Particularly when they're beautiful. Beauty's attractive, and we don't want people to be attracted by old things. We want them to like the new ones."[3] Thus the great art, literature, and wisdom of earlier cultures are banished from *Brave New World*: Shakespeare's plays, the Holy Bible, *The Imitation of Christ*, and the works of Cardinal Newman are all notably absent from schools, libraries, and homes. (It just so happens that the same books are missing from college curricula today.) Old age is not associated with wisdom but with ugliness: missing teeth, wrinkles, and flabbiness. Mandatory euthanasia at age sixty keeps health and sex appeal the supreme values in *Brave New World* and accents the cult of the new, the young, and the modern: "Youth almost unimpaired until sixty, and

---

3   Alduous Huxley, *Brave New World* (New York: Harper & Row, 1989), 225.

then, crack! the end." The ideological revolution in *Brave New World*, the Controller explains, has been "to shift the emphasis from truth and beauty to comfort and happiness." Whereas in past ages "knowledge was the highest good, truth the supreme value," today utility, efficiency, ease, and instant gratification fill the bill. And no one notices what has been lost. (111, 234)

In *Reflections on the Revolution in France*, Burke explains how the revolutionaries have disowned a great moral legacy in their irreverence toward France's noble traditions, which had cultivated that land of saints and knights. In attacking monarchy, priesthood, and hierarchy as the basis for French civilization, the Jacobins have terminated "the great primaeval contract of eternal society," the partnership between the generations that links those who are living, those who are dead, and those who are to be born—a relationship between a society and its past that Burke compares to that between children and their father: "[W]e are taught to look with horror on those children of their country who are prompt rashly to hack that aged parent in pieces." To Burke, the moral traditions and civilized norms of a society deserve the same kind of "reverence" and "awe" that Aeneas showed his parents and ancestors. Burke views the moral "reforms" of the French Revolution as a reversion to barbarism and a violation of "all natural sense of wrong and right"—a radical "revolution in sentiments, manners, and moral opinions" that subverts "antient institutions" and "antient principles."[4]

---

4   Edmund Burke, *Reflections on the Revolution in France* (New York: Penguin, 1982), 194–195, 177, 175, 172.

We need only compare the sexual mores of modern life with those of our grandparents to see that a similar revolution, of equal extremity and perhaps more profound importance, has occurred in our own society. Likewise in universities, departments that once devoted themselves to passing on "the best that has been written and thought" in Western civilization now chase after ideological grievances or focus on teaching crowd-pleasing ephemera, replacing required courses in Shakespeare or Chaucer with electives that study graphic novels and video games. In the legal field, judges discard both the sanctity of precedent and the principles of natural law, and render decisions that fit the agenda of our governing revolutionary class.

Ours is not the first revolution to attack the family and marriage. Nazi and Soviet antifamily policies were designed to liquidate loyalty to any authority but the Party. By their very antiquity and presumptive power, such institutions serve as roadblocks on the road to utopia. Likewise in these novels: in *1984*, Big Brother does not allow members of the Party the natural right to marry and found a family. Winston Smith is forbidden to court a woman, to fall in love, or to satisfy the natural desire for fatherhood. The Party cultivates sexlessness among its female members, who deliberately avoid beautifying themselves or accenting their femininity: "He had never before seen or imagined a woman of the Party with cosmetics on her face" (118). Notorious for its sexual puritanism, the Party promotes its agenda of the supremacy of the state and demotes the primacy of the family—for instance, through the Junior Anti-Sex League, which discourages romance. On the other hand, in the Prole district, where the common people are allowed to marry and have children, sexual permissiveness is the rule: "Promiscuity went unpunished; divorce was permitted" (62).

Thus Winston suffers the fate of a man living in a sexless society denied the normal pleasures of courtship, romance, love, and marriage. The natural attraction between the sexes is a forbidden pleasure for Winston because it would commit his life to his wife and children instead of to the state. A Manichaean contempt for marriage and procreation combines with sexual liberation to blast the foundations of marriage and the family in *1984*.

In *Brave New World*, the family is obsolete because children are conceived in test tubes via assembly-line production in the Central London Hatchery and Conditioning Centre. They are reared in government-controlled nurseries where they are conditioned for their social destiny as determined by the Controllers of the state. Neo-Pavlovian behavior modification involving electric shock, loud noises, and hypnopaedia (sleep-teaching) indoctrinate the child's mind with mechanical responses and mindless slogans, "till at last the child's mind is these suggestions, and the sum of these suggestions is the child's mind." Love and life are separated, and sexuality and procreation are divorced. The motto of the day is "civilization is sterilization," and words like *mother* and *father* are stigmatized: "To say one was a mother— that was past a joke: it was an obscenity." Natural childbirth carries with it social disgrace, dismissed as "gross viviparous reproduction," and fatherhood is equally disgusting: the word "for 'father' was not so much obscene as . . . merely gross, a scatological rather than pornographic impropriety." While incubators and test tubes replace mothers and fathers, and nurseries assume the role of families, men and women pursue the cult of pleasure through the euphoric drug "soma," the pornographic feelies, and recreational promiscuity ("Everyone belongs to everyone else") (28, 115, 153).

Pandering to the carnal nature of man and exploiting his propensity for sloth, the Controllers of *Brave New World* offer their subjects boundless comfort and pleasure, which they are willing to take in return for dropping such obsolete abstractions as freedom and self-respect.

In such worlds as Orwell and Huxley depict, the story of Aeneas would seem to ordinary readers a bizarre work of science fiction, whose hero's motivations were simply incomprehensible. It was just such a radical break with the past that the French revolutionaries sought. They achieved it, in part, by indulging in a series of atrocities that broke down social taboos and numbed the public until it was incapable of outrage. Burke denounced the hardheartedness that countenanced the slaughter of monks and nuns, unarmed nobles, the king, the queen, and even their children. He found it morally repulsive that young children were, "with the tender age of royal infants, insensible only through infancy and innocence of the cruel outrages to which their parents were exposed" 168). Recoiling in horror, Burke writes,

> As things now stand, with every thing respectable destroyed without us, and an attempt to destroy every principle of respect, one is almost forced to apologize for harbouring the common feelings of mankind (175).

To Burke, the most venerable moral ideals and most civilized manners enshrined in Western civilization—chivalry, honor, knighthood, and "the spirit of a gentleman"—had been abandoned in the name of political innovation, as good became evil and evil good:

> All the decent drapery of life is to be rudely torn off. All the super-added ideas, furnished from the wardrobe of a moral imagination, which the heart owns and the understanding ratifies, as necessary to cover the defects of our naked shivering nature, and to raise it to dignity in our own estimation, are to be exploded as a ridiculous, absurd, and antiquated fashion (171).

In short, the ideological attack on morals, manners, and "the common feelings of mankind" undoes centuries of education, refinement, and civilization. Common decency, respect for women and children, and the sense of the sacredness of human life are all dismissed as absurd or antiquated. Man is reduced to the level of an animal, so that he may be governed like one.

A similar revolution in moral sentiments has been at the heart of the culture wars, and the ethos that has seemed to emerge triumphant is something that Bl. Pope John Paul II called a "culture of death." As he wrote in *Evangelium Vitae*:

> On a more general level, there exists in contemporary culture a certain Promethean attitude which leads people to think that they can control life and death by taking the decisions about them into their own hands. (#15)

This Promethean attitude—manifested in the technological control and manipulation of unborn life, in abortion, in physician-assisted suicide, and in attempts to reshape or abolish marriage—is eerily reminiscent of the dystopia Huxley warned against. In Huxley's novel, people organize their lives around the availability of contraception and abortion. Typical of all the women in her society, Lenina "wore a silver mounted green morocco-surrogate cartridge belt, bulging . . . with the regulation supply of contraceptives" (50). The physician-assisted suicide she must undergo at age sixty comes in the form of extra dosages of soma, with the promise that she will enjoy "an eternal soma holiday." She is told that her life has meaning in purely ecological terms, since "we can go on being socially useful even after we're dead. Making plants grow" (73).

Both in *1984* and in *Brave New World*, religion is removed from the lives of people, and Christianity becomes a relic of the past. When Winston discovers a picture of a church in the antique shop in the Prole district, fond memories of the past awaken as he remembers the rhyme "Oranges and lemons say the bells of St. Clement's." The church had been converted into a museum with various propaganda displays, and every vestige of the sacred had been destroyed after the political revolution had replaced God with Big Brother: "Everything faded into the mist. The past was erased, the erasure was forgotten, the lie became truth" (64). Without religion as a cultural force, modern life in *1984* lacks a supernatural, transcendent dimension and acquires an insufferable blandness and dullness: "It struck him that the truly characteristic thing about modern life was not its cruelty and insecurity, but simply its bareness, its dinginess, its listlessness" (63), In *Brave New World*, God has been replaced with science and technology that conjure utopian visions of efficiency, comfort, and pleasure. Mustapha Mond the Controller explains, "God isn't compatible with machinery and scientific medicine and universal happiness" (64). This kind of non sequitur is precisely the sort of argument nowadays deployed with widespread success by the apostles of the New Atheism.

The ideologues in *1984* and *Brave New World* portray religion as a form of ignorance and superstition that harks back to the Dark Ages, an impediment to freedom and progress and a new world order where man determines truth, law, and morality. In *1984*, propaganda contrasts the enlightened modern world, the product of the socialist revolution, with the benighted ages of faith. Big Brother manipulates the objective order of reality, even calling into question that "stones are hard" and "water is wet." Winston's greatest fear is that Big Brother will dictate that "two and two made five, and you would have to believe it." Big Brother replaces God, the state becomes an intolerant church, and "doublethink" displaces reason.

In *Brave New World*, the Controller argues that Christianity is obsolete and superfluous: humans no longer need the comforts and consolations of religion because the brave new world has eliminated pain, suffering, tragedy, and grief. Instead of learning as Christians do that suffering can prove redemptive, modern men believe in "[g]etting rid of everything unpleasant instead of learning to put up with it." As the Controller teaches, "There isn't any need for a civilized man to bear anything that's seriously unpleasant" (245, 243). Self-denial, faithful love, heroism, and nobility are archaic virtues in a society whose idea of happiness consists of "seven and a half hours of mild, unexhausting labour, and then the soma ration and games and unrestricted copulation and the feelies." The Controllers in *Brave New World* assume the role of Divine Providence and act as the arbiters of life and death from the test tubes in the Fertilizing Room to the death conditioning that culminates in the Slough Crematorium.

The French Revolution also attacked the Christian foundations of the social order. Inspired by skeptical, atheistic freethinkers who mocked religion, the Jacobins conceived of the state as a purely human institution governed by the light of abstract reason and emancipated from the superstitions of religion. In contrast, the pious Burke argues that "[a]ll other nations have begun the fabric of a new government, or the reformation of an old . . . by some rites or other of religion." Burke reflects outrage at the blasphemy and sacrilege of the Reign of Terror that issued in the murder of bishops and the seizure of church property and savaged two of mankind's noblest institutions, monarchy and religion. In Burke's view, "man is by his constitution a religious animal," and "religion is the basis of civil society, and the source of all good and all comfort." Unlike the Enlightenment thinkers, who viewed religion as an oppressive burden interfering with progress, Burke equates Christianity with culture: the "Christian religion . . . has been our boast and comfort, and one great source of civilization amongst us" (186–188). Cherishing tradition rather than innovation and esteeming the accumulated experience of the entire human race ("the general bank and capital of nations, and of ages") rather than the abstract theory of rationalist philosophers with their small "private stock of reason," Burke defends the timeless moral wisdom of the world perpetuated by religion:

> We know that we have made no new discoveries; and we think that no discoveries are to be made in morality; nor many in the great principles of government, nor in the ideas of liberty, which were understood long before we were born (182).

Our modern secular culture accepts a similar presumption that man has discovered a new morality independent of the Bible, two thousand years of Christian tradition, and the natural law—what Burke calls "the collected reason of ages."

The ideological attack upon the past, the family and marriage, and religion are all brazen attempts to reinvent society, deny the nature of things, invert the hierarchy of being, and escape the obligations of the moral law. The changes initiated by such revolutions deify man and exalt man's power and sense of control. Such ideologies deprive man of his dignity and human freedom to choose what is true. Because their goals cut against the very grain of reality, the servants of these ideas must resort to deception, coercion, and violence. Since the voice of the past is the single most potent dissent against the reformers' agenda, it must be silenced.

Thus the pious old woman praying before an icon, with whom we began this essay, becomes a profoundly powerful figure. It is she who will whisper the truths about God and man in a still, small voice—and she will be heard, by men like Lech Walesa, Aleksandr Solzhenitsyn, and Karol Wojtyla. What these men learn from such babushkas conforms with common sense and "the moral sentiments" of the human heart. It is reaffirmed by the great art and poetry of the past, the venerable institutions of society, and the timeless truths of the Christian faith. Thus piety becomes a force of liberation from the tyrants of today.

As Winston writes in his diary, "Freedom is the freedom to say that two plus two make four. If that is granted, all else follows" (69). As John the Savage insists in *Brave New World*, "I don't want comfort. I want God, I want poetry, I want real danger, I want freedom, I want goodness" (246). As Burke states, "We have real hearts of flesh and blood beating in our bosoms" (182). So Pope John Paul II writes in *Evangelium Vitae*:

> Human life and death are thus in the hands of God, in his power: "In his hand is the life of every living thing and the breath of all mankind," exclaims Job (12:10). (#39)

> Truly great must be the value of human life if the Son of God has taken it up and made it the instrument of the salvation of all humanity! (#33)

These sobering truths do not enslave man to God; they defend him from other men who are playing God. While ideologues view their fellow men as objects to manipulate, pious men regard them as members of one great family, part of a partnership "between those who are living, those who are dead, and those who are yet to be born." The weight of history, the perennial nature of the family, and the authority of religion remind us of the unchanging nature of things, the absolute nature of good and evil, and the fallen condition of mankind in desperate need of the wisdom of the past, the love of a family, and the truth about God.

VII. Moderation: *Don Quixote*

Cervantes's *Don Quixote* depicts the famous friendship of the knight-errant Don Quixote de la Mancha and his beloved squire, Sancho Panza. As they travel in search of adventures to restore the ideals of knighthood—chivalry, courtesy, honor, truth, justice, and magnanimity—and to revive the golden age, these immortal characters form a complementary pair whose relationship reflects the integrity of human nature and the unity between the body and the soul. In the unique bond between the knight and his squire, Cervantes presents a catholic vision of the world that encompasses all reality. He paints both the physical and the spiritual; the real (the way things are) and the ideal (the way things ought to be); the virtue of innocence and the virtue of prudence (the gentleness of the dove and the wisdom of the serpent); the reality of mystery and the truth of reason; the romance of adventure and the contentment of ordinary life; and both the goodness of the natural world and the happiness of supernatural life. Even though the knight and the squire often argue about whether windmills are giants or a barber's basin is Mambrino's helmet, the friendship of Don Quixote and Sancho Panza does not oppose but instead reconciles these different perceptions, virtues, and points of view to achieve an ideal balance that does justice to all of human nature and all of reality.

Heresies exaggerate one aspect of the truth but disregard other parts (for example, Arianism, which acknowledges the humanity of Christ but rejects his divinity), and ideologies twist the truth to fit abstract unfounded theories (such as newfangled notions of marriage that reject its normative meaning as the union of two sexes open to new life). But the fullness of truth neither exaggerates nor minimizes any part of the whole spectrum of knowledge.

While Platonists, Gnostics, and Manicheans see only enmity between the soul and the body, the orthodox Christian view of man's spiritual and corporal nature neither glamorizes the physical nor etherealizes the spiritual. For Plato, the body is a prison from which the soul strives to escape, and for the Manichean the soul is too pure and spiritual to inhabit a corruptible physical body. In the Christian vision, however, the physical and the corporeal are good not only because everything God created was good but also because the Incarnation (the Word made flesh) sanctifies the human and natural world. The body is the temple of the Holy Spirit, and the soul informs and ennobles the body with the image of God. Don Quixote and Sancho Panza's friendship depicts this union of the body and soul as complements that enrich and integrate human nature. While Sancho thinks constantly of his bodily needs of food, sleep, comfort, and safety, Don Quixote inspires Sancho to fast, to sleep outdoors, to make sacrifices, to endure hardships in the Sierra Morena Mountains, and to seek heroic adventures. While Don Quixote aspires to the lofty ideals of the true, the good, and the beautiful, Sancho tempers the knight-errant's idealism with the sobriety of proverbial wisdom and common sense. Don Quixote chastises Sancho's low standards, and Sancho ridicules Quixote's impossible ideals. For example, when Sancho assumes the governorship of an island, his master instructs him to rise to the dignity of his office: "Do not wear your clothes baggy and unbuttoned, Sancho, for a slovenly dress is proof of a careless mind"; "Do not eat garlic or onions, lest the stench of your breath betray your humble birth"; "Drink with moderation, for drunkenness neither keeps a secret nor observes a promise"; "Be careful, Sancho, not to chew on both sides of your mouth, and do not on any account eruct in company."[1] The knight-errant is exhorting his squire to transcend his animal nature and conduct himself like a gentleman with a sense of propriety and delicacy. On the other hand, when Quixote's ideals or imagination lose contact with reality, Sancho mocks his master. When the knight-errant insists that his Lady Dulcinea's disenchantment depends on Sancho's whipping his own flesh with 3,300 lashes, the squire makes fun of the preposterous idea: "Faith and skin! . . . three thousand lashes indeed! I'd as soon give myself three stabs in the belly with a dagger as these stripes: devil take this method of disenchantment" (336). Thus Cervantes makes both knight and squire endearing and lovable. As Sancho says of Quixote, "On the contrary, he has a soul as simple as a pitcher: he could do no harm to anyone, but good to all, nor has he any malice in him; why, a child would convince him 'tis night at noon-day, and 'tis on account of this simplicity that I love him as the cockles of my heart." And as Don Antonio says of Sancho, the squire's drollery "is enough to transform

---

1   Miguel de Cervantes Saavedra, *Don Quixote*, ed. Walter Starkie (New York: New American Library, 1957), 346–347.

melancholy itself into mirth." The grave "Knight of the Rueful Countenance" is counterbalanced by the jovial, jesting squire with his hilarious proverbs and mother wit. Sancho's earthy, robust laughter cures Quixote of abstraction and fantasy, and Quixote's noble idealism curbs Sancho's self-indulgence. In these two characters, Cervantes depicts the goodness of both the soul and the body, neither exaggerating the immateriality of the human soul as pure spirit nor caricaturing the lowliness of the body as animalistic buffoonery.

Likewise, the teaching authority of the Church never loses sight of the highest Christian ideals and never compromises its standards to accommodate the world. Christians who cleave to its historic teachings will cherish the virtue of purity and chastity, uphold the sanctity of marriage, honor the fruitfulness of marriage and the gift of children, and defend the sanctity of human life from birth to natural death. The Church always sets its sights on the way things ought to be, but it never ignores the way things are in a fallen, imperfect world. Coupled with the sublime idealism of Christian moral teachings that exhort every person to aspire to sainthood—"Be ye perfect, even as my Father in Heaven is perfect"—is the cardinal virtue of prudence, the wise moral judgment to determine the best course of action in practical affairs in the ordinary business of life. While the Christian contemplates the noblest ideals, he also values the art of the possible. When Don Quixote encounters the goatherds who welcome the knight and his squire with warm hospitality, Quixote ponders the way things *ought to be* and reflects on the golden age when "all things were in common," when "all then was peace, all friendship, all concord," when "neither fraud, nor deceit,

nor malice had yet interfered with truth and plain dealing,"
and when "modest maidens went about . . . without fear
of danger from the unbridled freedom and lustful desires
of others" (55). Don Quixote is adamant and unwavering
in honoring the code of a knight-errant: he never battles
opponents who have not been dubbed knights; he remains
always faithful to his Lady Dulcinea del Toboso; he always
honors his promises and never reneges on his word. On
the other hand, when Sancho assumes the governorship
of an island, he demonstrates the wisdom of Solomon
in the practical matters of daily life. When two plaintiffs
present their case to Sancho—a customer bringing a tailor
a small piece of cloth and slyly requesting five caps from
the scanty material, and the tailor cunningly fashioning
five small useless caps that fit no human head—Sancho
punishes them both as knaves: "I give judgment that the
tailor lose the making and the countryman the stuff, and
that the caps be given to the prisoners in jail, so there's an
end of that" (356). However, when Don Quixote's lofty
idealism loses contact with reality, Sancho laughs at his
master. For example, hearing loud, terrifying sounds at
night that the knight associates with the movements and
weapons of giants, Quixote arms himself for a glorious
adventure of battle only to discover that the mysterious
sounds amount to no more than the alternating thuds of
the fulling hammers—not the heroic exploit he imagined.
This anticlimax provokes Sancho's irrepressible, hearty
burst of laughter at the folly of his master: Sancho "burst
out loud and long with such force that he had to put his
hands to his sides to prevent them from splitting" (90). On
the other hand, when Sancho's prudence degenerates into
the cunning of the fox, Quixote exposes the deceit. When

Sancho lies about delivering Quixote's love letter to his beloved Dulcinea to spare himself a tedious journey, the knight catches the squire in his guile. After Sancho claims that he lost the letter but remembered it by heart and had it copied, the knight reveals that he is not hoodwinked: "Do you know, Sancho, what amazes me? The swiftness of your return: why it seems to me as if you went and came back in the air, for you have been away only a little more than three days, although El Toboso is more than thirty leagues hence" (155). Thus the orthodox ideal of balance tempers sublime ideals with common sense and complements the art of the perfect with the art of the possible. It values both the contemplative and the active life.

This Christian balance also includes the harmony of mystery and reason. The Church acknowledges both the mysterious, invisible realm of angels and saints and the ordinary sensory world of common experience. Lucifer and the fallen angels, St. Michael and the archangels, and the Seraphim and Cherubim testify to a hidden spiritual realm inaccessible to the five senses. The mystery of the Trinity and the miracles of Jesus transcend human understanding, but at the same time the Church prizes the power of human reason and the gift of wisdom, as the Old Testament books of wisdom—Proverbs, Ecclesiastes, Sirach—and the parables of Jesus illustrate: "If riches are a desirable possession in life, what is richer than wisdom who effects all things. . . . And if anyone longs for wide experience, she knows the things of old, and infers the things to come" (Wisdom of Solomon 8: 5; 8). In the parable of the dishonest steward, Jesus commended his shrewdness:

Then he said to another, "And how much do you owe?" He said, "A hundred measures." He said to him, "Take your bill, and write eighty." The master commended the dishonest steward for his prudence; for the sons of this world are wiser in their own generation than the sons of light. (Luke 15: 7–9)

In Cervantes's novel, Don Quixote constantly alludes to the darkness of the diabolical world with his references to "enchantment," such as the magic of Freston the wizard who opposes all the noble works of knights-errantry. When a practical joke is played on Quixote—a bag of cats with jingling bells unleashed in the middle of the night on his bed—Quixote reacts with fury: "Avaunt, ye malicious enchanters. Avaunt, ye wizard scum! I am Don Quixote of La Mancha, against whom your vile intentions are of no avail" (370). To the knight, evil always disguises itself as the appearance of the good, malicious magicians "making the beautiful ugly and ugly beautiful." While Quixote uses the vocabulary of magic and necromancy to identify the mystery and insidiousness of evil, Sancho speaks in the common language of proverbs: "An ass will carry his load but not a double load"; "God's help is better than rising at dawn"; "'Tis the belly carries the feet, not the feet the belly." While the spiritual realm of magic is sheer nonsense to Sancho, the squire thrives upon the sound judgment of practical wisdom that his proverbs reflect. Again, his canniness is born out in his gubernatorial judgments—for instance, when an old man hands a staff to his creditor and swears in court that he has paid his debt—testimony the creditor calls a lie. Noticing the old man's wily gesture of giving his cane to the plaintiff while taking an oath and swearing he paid his debt, Sancho suspiciously breaks open the staff and discovers the ten crowns of gold. Thus Quixote's understanding of the origin of evil as diabolical and Sancho's recognition of the cunning lies of scoundrels complement one another. Quixote never excludes the supernatural explanation, and Sancho never overlooks the natural reasons. Orthodox Christianity has always valued both the speculative intellects of the philosopher and the mystic and the practical intellects of the prudent and the political.

The Catholic vision of life views the human drama as "the wildest of adventures," to cite Chesterton's expression. The miracles of the Old and New Testaments and the Incarnation depict the Lord as the God of surprises whose Divine Providence shapes history with unforeseen and unimagined events. As St. Augustine wrote in *The City of God*, God died for man but once but will die for man no more—an event in history that overturns the pagan cyclical view of history that Augustine calls "the unreal and futile cycles of the godless."[2] It was an unprecedented, unrepeatable event in the drama of salvation. St. Augustine in the *Confessions* describes the "divine romance" of God's infinite love for each individual soul in famous words: "O omnipotent Good, you who care for each one of us as though he was your only care and who cares for all of us as though we

---

2 St. Augustine, *The City of God*, tr. Marcus Dodds (New York: The Modern Library, 1993), 404.

were all just one person."[3] In the life of adventure or romance, one does not count the cost or calculate losses but gives and sacrifices with unlimited generosity and risks all for the sake of a sublime ideal or noble love. While the Church honors the glorious deeds of saints and the daring adventures of martyrs inspired by the greatness of love, she also praises the humility of simple lives consecrated to the love of neighbor and the service of God. The vocation of fatherhood and motherhood in ordinary family life furthers God's kingdom on earth as much as heroic deeds.

The friendship of Don Quixote and Sancho Panza celebrates both the excitements of the adventurous life and the joys of the simple life. Always "in search of adventures"—as a true knight-errant who aspires to assist widows and orphans, to rescue damsels in distress, and to redress wrongs by combating evil—Quixote rejects the advice of his closest friends and relatives. They counsel him to remain at home in comfortable security as Alonso Quixano rather than venture abroad and abandon himself to Divine Providence. In desperation, the housekeeper says to Quixote, "Truly, master, if you do not stay still and quiet at home, and cease rambling over hill, over dale, like a restless spirit, looking for what they call adventures, but which I call misfortunes, I shall have to call upon God and the king to send some remedy." Quixote's adventures, however, do not prove to be rash misfortunes but resplendent deeds that transform a drab iron age into a golden era exalted with pageantry, ritual,

---

3   *The Confessions of St. Augustine,* tr. Rex Warner (New York: New American Library, 1963), 66–67.

poetry, and romance. The knight addresses the plain wenches as lovely ladies, regards a country lass as the Lady Dulcinea del Toboso, calls a utilitarian barber's basin the precious Mambrino's helmet, refers to common inns as grand castles, calls ordinary events glorious adventures, and turns prosaic language into poetic elegance. For example, when Quixote addresses the landlady of an inn as "beautiful lady" and compliments its servants with gracious courtesy ("I shall keep engraved for all time in my memory the service you have done me, and I shall be grateful to you as long as I live"), the women are surprised at his gallantry: "Not being accustomed to such language, they gazed at him wonderingly and thought he must be a far different kind of man from those now in fashion" (61). Quixote aims to transform a crass, self-centered, materialistic epoch into an honorable, beautiful, chivalrous time in which liberality supplants avarice, romantic love overcomes selfish lust, and self-sacrifice overrules self-interest. Adventure to Quixote inspires not only lofty ideals in manners and morals but also venturesome boldness. Whether Quixote confronts the arrogance of a troupe of actors, challenges the offensive performance of a puppet show, or intervenes in the forced marriage of young lovers, he risks defeat, ridicule, and injury. Adventure to Quixote means taking sides, living according to ideals, and being unafraid of losses: "But, good Sancho, get up on your ass and follow me, for God, Who provides for all, will not desert us; especially, being engaged, as we are, in his service."

However, the knight and the squire also relish the ordinary, unspectacular life and the grace in each day's blessings. When they receive the gracious hospitality of the goat herders and share their potluck supper, the knight recalls the humble, unspoiled life of the golden age devoid of the false sophistication and pomp of the court, a time when innocent, modest maidens "outshone our court ladies of today arrayed in the rare, outlandish inventions which idle luxury has taught them" (55). After Sancho's brief rule as governor of an island, he prefers the humble, uncomplicated life of a squire to the burdens and responsibilities of a ruler. As Sancho admits after his experiment of governing an island, "I got . . . experience enough to know that I'm no hand at governing ought else but a herd of cattle, and that the wealth a fellow earns by such governorships has got to be paid in hard labour, loss of sleep, and in hunger too . . ." (390). While the knight and his squire win fame for their adventurous and comical exploits and earn kudos for their surprising victories, they never lose their appreciation for the goodness of food, friendship, conversation, hospitality, and love. Quixote reminds Sancho that "God exalteth the humble," and Sancho insists that "what I eat in my own corner without fuss and frills tastes far better, though it's not but bread and onion, than turkey at tables where I have to chew slowly, drink but a sup . . . nor do other things which a man is free to do when he's alone." Thus the knight and the squire live both the daring romance of the Christian life of self-giving in the pursuit of the highest ideals and practice the ordinary humility of service to others in the role of Good Samaritan.

In the mutual bond of their friendship, Quixote and Sancho recognize both the goodness of the natural world and the happiness of heaven. Sancho's keen relish for cheese, bread, onions, and wine; his fond affection for his wife, Teresa, and his daughter, Sanchica; his sheer delight in Quixote's company and conversation; the knight's appreciation for the beauty of his peerless Dulcinea and the goodness of romantic love; the comedy, mirth, and laughter of Sancho's proverbs and Quixote's foolish mistakes; and the good fortune and providential events in their adventures all depict a natural world replete with simple joys and abundant pleasures. Whether they are in the company of simple goatherds or grand dukes and duchesses, Quixote and Sancho savor the blessings before them, whether acorns and cheese or sumptuous banquets. Whether they sleep outdoors in the Sierra Morena Mountains or in the inns Quixote calls castles, the two friends encounter good company and much cheer and broaden their experience with the knowledge of men and manners. As Sancho says, "He who would see much must live long," and knight and squire participate in all of life as they descend into caves, ascend mountains, travel vast plains, and enter villages. They live a full, rich life as they embrace all of reality and partake of many of life's deepest sources of pleasure. As Sancho explains to his wife, "[T]here's naught in this world so pleasant as for an honest, decent man to be squire to a knight-errant on the prowl for adventures. . . . I know by experience, but when all's said and done, it's a fine thing to be gadding about spying for chances, crossing mountains, exploring woods, climbing rocks, visiting castles, lodging in inns at our own sweet will, with the devil a farthing to pay" (205). The knight and squire's love of life, however, does not blind them to the reality of heaven and the supernatural joys of eternal life. On his deathbed, Quixote asks for a priest to make his final confession, exercises "true Christian resignation" in accepting God's will, and dies a happy death: the notary remarks that "he had never read of any knight who ever died in his bed so peacefully and like a good Christian as Don Quixote" (432). The knight's final words praise God: "Infinite are His mercies, and undiminished even by the sins of men" (429)—a final testimony that verifies Quixote's constant trust in Divine Providence, which always inspired his vocation of knight-errantry: "But, good Sancho, get up on your ass and follow me, for God, Who provides for all, will not desert us." *Don Quixote* gives glory to God for the goodness of creation and for the gift of heaven. The Christian faith integrates an earthy realism with an otherworldly outlook.

The restoration of Western culture depends on recovering such an integrated, holistic view of human nature and reality as that captured by Cervantes's great classic—a view of the world that George Weigel in his recent *Letters to a Young Catholic* describes as "an optic, a way of seeing things, a distinctive perception of reality," "a sacramental imagination," the "Catholic both / and; nature *and* grace, faith *and* works, Jerusalem *and* Athens, charismatic *and* institutional, visible *and* invisible."[4]

---

4   George Weigel, *Letters to a Young Catholic* (New York: Basic Books, 2004), 10.

VIII Courtesy: *The Idea of a University* **and** *A Midsummer Night's Dream*

St. Thomas Aquinas described the beautiful as "the attractive aspect of the good," the part that reminds us that virtue in itself is never drab, but finally charming, winning, and irresistible. Good morals express themselves in gracious manners, and beautiful manners reflect a noble mind, a kindly heart, and the thoughtfulness that leads us to please and honor others. When goodness becomes pompous, priggish, or censorious, it loses its beauty and repels when it should allure. The disciples who answered Christ's call to "Come, follow me" were attracted not only to his moral teaching but also to the beauty of his goodness: "Immediately they left their nets and followed him" (Matthew 5:20). The early Christian community also radiated the attractiveness of goodness, inspiring the famous remark, "See how they love one another." Goodness, then, transcends keeping the letter of the law, fulfilling obligations, and paying debts. While these duties reveal a sense of responsibility and a respect for justice, they fail to evoke wonder or inspire the heart. The splendor of virtue performs the maximum, not the minimum, as Christ's miracles and sacrifice illustrate. True goodness is poetic, even when it works through the prosaic.

While the Pharisees honored the Sabbath, fulfilled the law, and prayed in the synagogues, they did not have the large heart of the Prodigal Son's forgiving father or the charity of the Good Samaritan. While Malvolio in Shakespeare's *Twelfth Night* was an orderly, punctilious steward who obeyed orders with scrupulous diligence, he behaved with pompous gravity and lacked all sense of mirth, provoking Sir Toby's famous remark: "Dost think, because thou art virtuous, there shall be no more cakes and ale?"[1] Malvolio's censorious faultfinding ("Have you no wit, manners, nor honesty, but to gabble like tinkers at this time of night?" [2.3.93–94]) spoils innocent revelry and cultivates no friendships. While Pamela, a simple maidservant and the heroine of Samuel Richardson's epistolary novel *Pamela* (1740), defended her chastity and boasted of her virtue, she resisted the seduction of the aristocratic lord for mercenary rather than moral reasons: so that she would receive his offer of marriage and gain the status of a lady. "Virtue Rewarded," the subtitle of the novel, insinuates that Pamela submitted only when the stakes were lucrative enough. In another unflattering image of "goodness," Isabella in Shakespeare's *Measure for Measure* depicts the frigidity of virtue. While she appears noble in rejecting the lustful Lord Angelo's proposition to release her brother from a death sentence at the price of her virginity, she betrays her coldness in showing no compassion for her brother's cruel punishment and in passively resigning herself to his fate: "'Tis best that thou diest quickly" (3.1.151). Neither the

---

1   *The Major Plays of Shakespeare,* ed. G.B. Harrison (New York: Harcourt Brace Jovanovich, Publishers, 1968), 859.

self-righteousness of the Pharisees, the pompous pride of Malvolio, the smugness of Pamela, nor the frigidity of Isabella will win anyone's heart or inspire emulation. Although these characters uphold the law and avoid serious evil, they have no appeal. Their self-regarding virtue remains restricted and limited, and even their good deeds do not reveal the great love that evokes the wonder of the beautiful.

Virtue loses its radiance when it appears petty, niggardly, or economical at the cost of charity or magnanimity. Christ's love knew no limits and abounded in the generosity of miracles—for example, the miracle of the five loaves and the two fish, which resulted in "twelve baskets full of the broken pieces that were left over" (Matthew 14: 20). Mary Magdalene's lavish anointing of the feet of Christ with rare perfumes earned her the praise of God: "She hath loved much." The virtue of knightly liberality gives and serves with unstinting generosity and sacrifice, as Chaucer's noble knights from "The Knight's Tale" illustrate. Theseus, the knight who hosts the tournament, "spared no cost in preparing the temples and the theater" to decide the contest between two rival knights both vying for the hand of the beautiful noblewoman Emily in marriage. Arcite, the victor who accidentally falls from his horse and suffers a fatal injury, magnanimously encourages his beloved Emily to marry his rival: "If ever you decide to marry, do not forget Palamon, that noble man."[2] The greatness of virtue, then, leaps over the narrow gates of minimalist morality, aiming at the highest ideals.

---

2   Geoffrey Chaucer, *The Canterbury Tales*, tr. R,M. Lumiansky (New York: Modern Library, 1954), 52.

The beauty of goodness appears in a giving heart that abounds in inexhaustible generosity—an abundance that the hospitable hearts of Baucis and Philemon epitomize in Hawthorne's "The Miraculous Pitcher," as their home always welcomes travelers with profuse kindness. Their goodness is so beautiful and touching that the Greek gods, traveling in the disguise of beggars, call their food nectar and ambrosia and present them with the gift of the miraculous pitcher that always refills after it is emptied—a gift that corresponds to the generous hearts of the elderly couple who give without ceasing. Without such openness as theirs, virtue—which should be glorious—is merely bland and colorless.

The beauty of goodness manifests itself not only in charity, magnanimity, and hospitality but also in manners, "the poetry of conduct," as C.S. Lewis referred to the virtue of civility. As Henry Fielding writes in *Tom Jones*, one must not only *be* good but also *appear* to be good so that manners complement morals. Gracious civility, courteous words, and refined conduct give morality a "poetic" quality that adorns virtue with beautiful apparel that is immediately striking and powerfully appealing. For example, the chivalrous Don Quixote was not only a courageous knight in battle but also a true gentleman in speech and action, always honoring women with decorous speech: "I beseech your ladyships, do not flee, nor fear the least offense. The order of chivalry which I profess, doth not permit me to do injury to any one, and least of all to such noble maidens as your presences denote you to be."[3] In contrast, in Austen's *Pride*

---

3   Miguel de Cervantes Saavedra, *Don Quixote*, ed. Walter Starkie (New American Library, 1957), 21.

and Prejudice, Elizabeth Bennet, the epitome of courtesy, at first rejects the aristocratic and dashing Darcy because he offended her with his boorish conduct and deplorable manners, refusing to dance with her or exchange civil conversation. (The bad first impressions he had created made him appear ill bred, even though he later proves his noble character.) Thus gracious manners correspond to beautiful clothing, the outward appearance or first impression that adorns, attracts, and invites. Without affability or manners, the beauty of goodness resembles the lamp hidden under a bushel.

In *The Idea of a University,* Cardinal Newman identifies the special marks of a gentleman who exemplifies the poetry of conduct. First, "he is one who never inflicts pain," a person who measures his words to avoid "whatever may cause a jar or a jolt in the minds of those with whom he is cast." Acting always with tact and respect for the feelings of others, the gentleman seeks to create a hospitable atmosphere: "his great concern being to make every one at their ease and at home." He takes a personal interest in everyone: "he is tender toward the bashful, gentle toward the distant, and merciful to the absurd." At the same time he is not officious or intrusive as he lets the social flow of the occasion assume its own spontaneous direction: "he is mainly occupied in removing the obstacles which hinder the free and unembarrassed action of those around him." The gentleman possesses the art of conversation, the knowledge of when to speak and when to be silent, the ability to introduce general topics of conversation and to avoid personal matters and unpleasant subjects. He never dominates the conversation, resorts to gossip, or speaks incessantly about himself: "he guards against unseasonable allusions, or topics which may irritate; he is seldom prominent in conversation, and never wearisome." The civility of a gentleman shuns aloofness, gloom, resentment, or arrogance in his relationships. He remains always the magnanimous man who "interprets everything for the best" and seeks to make friends even of his enemies, observing the proverb that "we should ever conduct ourselves toward our enemy as if he were one day to be our friend." In the company of discourteous or unpleasant people, he always maintains his composure. Always patient and forbearing, "He has too much good sense to be affronted at insults, he is too well employed to remember injuries, and too indolent to bear malice." In a word, the gentleman puts others first and places himself last; he honors persons with special marks of thoughtfulness and subordinates his own preferences, pleasures, opinions, and convenience for the sake of the happiness of others. He brooks no pettiness, narrow-mindedness, vindictiveness, or meanness, for his sense of what Newman calls "fastidiousness" or good taste "becomes the enemy of extravagances of any kind" and "shrinks from what are called scenes."[4] Newman's ideal of the gentleman, then, illustrates the importance of both *being good* (morals) and of *appearing* so (manners), in order that beauty reflect goodness and goodness reveal beauty.

St. Francis de Sales (1567–1622), the bishop of Geneva who devoted himself to the conversion of Calvinists,

---

4   John Henry Newman, *The Uses of Knowledge* (Harlan Davidson, Inc.: Wheeling, Illinois, 1948), 103–104.

impressed everyone by his civility, graciousness, amiability, and charm. His exquisite manners illustrated that a drop of honey does more wonders for human relationships than a gallon of gall: "Nothing is ever gained by harshness," he writes in *Introduction to the Devout Life.*[5] Cheerful and gregarious by nature, St. Francis enjoyed the company and conversation of kings, nobles, cardinals, and ordinary people who all felt the beauty of his goodness— what one biographer calls his "never failing cheerfulness," "tremendous charm," "strong gentleness," and "social sensitivity and delicacy."[6] This French saint, a master of *savoir faire*, was able to obey St. Paul and "become all things to all people," adapting to the different temperaments and individual natures of each person. In fact, as a university student , he vowed to engage in civil conversation with all people at social functions. In his imaginary letter to St. Francis de Sales, Pope John Paul I praises "the gentlest of saints" for his exquisite graciousness: "Already as a student in Padua, you made a rule for yourself never to avoid or curtail a conversation with anyone, no matter how unlikable or boring; to be modest and without insolence, free without austerity, pliant and without dissent."[7] In one of his writings de Sales writes, "I shall never despise anyone, nor altogether avoid him, the more so in that it would give the impression of being proud, haughty, severe, arrogant,

---

5   St. Francis de Sales, *Introduction to the Devout Life* (Garden City, New York: Doubleday, 1972), 207.

6   Michael de la Bedoyere, *SaintMaker* (Manchester, New Hampshire: Sophia Press, 1998), 13: 5.

7   Pope John Paul I, *Illustrissimi* (Boston: Little, Brown and Company, 1978), 103.

critical."[8] Thus the art of pleasing conversation is one of the beautiful attributes of goodness. In *The Devout Life*, the saint of courtesy gives much practical advice about the importance of civil conversation and teaches that goodness is attractive because of its attention to little things. Loving one's neighbor as one's self demands that persons not ignore the company of others or avoid conversations: "To be too reserved and to refuse to take part in conversation looks like lack of confidence in the others or some sort of disdain." It is a person's duty to pay social obligations and not be accused of ill-breeding: "If people visit you or if you are called out into society for some just reason, go as one sent by God and visit your neighbor with a benevolent heart and a good intention" (189). All these amenities give virtue an inviting appearance, natural appeal, and irresistible charm.

Because dress and language especially manifest the beauty of goodness, St. Francis does not overlook the importance of clothing or the propriety of words. Because improper dress shows a lack of respect to others and insults their dignity, humans are obligated to present themselves in company in a tasteful and elegant manner: "It is a sort of contempt of those you associate with to frequent their company in unbecoming attire." Beautiful dress is perfectly compatible with modesty, and elegance complements simplicity: "I would have devout people, whether men or women, always the best dressed in a group but the least pompous and affected." Modesty of speech, which reflects purity of heart and sensitivity

---

8   Quoted in *SaintMaker*, 37.

to the feelings of others and avoids giving offense, must accompany modesty of dress: "be careful never to let an indecent word leave your lips." This tactfulness of speech and tastefulness in dress forms the foundation of all social life, cultivates true friendships, and develops affectionate hearts. Goodness is beautiful when it communicates kindness and love and spreads happiness: "How good it is to love here on earth as they love in heaven and to learn to cherish one another in this world as we shall do eternally in the next!" (193, 194, 174).

In order for goodness to be beautiful, it must convey generosity, magnanimity, and courtesy, and *also* possess another quality, one that Shakespeare's fairies in *A Midsummer Night's Dream* epitomize—a *love of goodness for its own sake.* In Shakespeare's comedy the fairies play for the sheer love of it and revel like children who relish fun as an end in itself. When they leave their frolics of the night at the appearance of dawn, the fairies adorn the world with the jewelry of dewdrops: "And I serve the Fairy Queen, / To dew her orbs upon the green" (2.1.8–9). This playful, spontaneous lightheartedness of the fairies captures the essence of goodness as an act of joy and love that also leaves something beautiful in its wake. In the play, the fairies heal all complications of human relationships with gentleness and delicacy. Because Hermia will not marry the man chosen by her father, Aegeus, he threatens her by invoking the law of the land. Theseus, the Duke of Athens, threatens Hermia with two draconian measures:

Upon that day prepare to die
For disobedience to your father's will,

Or else to wed Demetrius, as he would,
Or on Diana's altar to protest
For aye austerity and single life. (1.1. 86–90)

When Oberon, the King of the Fairies, overhears the problems of the lovers as they flee into the forest at night to evade the rigid severity of the law of Athens, he commands Puck, "that merry wanderer of the night," to anoint the eyelids of the sleeping lovers with the love juice of the wild pansy. With lighthearted mirth and the gentle touch of a few drops of a magical potion quietly placed on the eyes in the silence of sleep, Oberon cures the rift between father and daughter with the playful spontaneity of creative fun—in place of lethal threats and punishments. The fairies' painless healing touch alleviates the lovers' problems with the soothing medicine of laughter, a more powerful remedy than the mortal measures proposed by the father and the duke. When Theseus discovers the reconciliation that has occurred, he marvels, "How comes this gentle concord in the world . . . ?" (4.1.147). Unlike the oppressive letter of the law that threatened Hermia with the ultimatum "Either to die the death, or to abjure / Forever the society of men," the comic spirit of Oberon and Puck in their fairylike mirth and graceful movements—they "[h]op as light as bird from brier"—brings the enchantment that dispels gravity and gloom from the atmosphere. Doing good in the darkness of the forest while the lovers are asleep and hiding in the secrecy of night, the invisible fairies *play* as they heal and do good; their virtue is silent, not obtrusive or officious; it is lively, not perfunctory. When playfulness accompanies goodness, it charms and enchants. This magic of the fairies beautifies the world and adorns it with the dewdrops, pearls, rubies, and "fairy favors" they leave behind as they do good mysteriously and anonymously—giving without expecting to receive, giving without being seen, noticed, or rewarded. This pure, mirthful spirit of goodness produces the beauty symbolized by the radiant atmosphere of the fairies that dwell "[b]y fountain clear or spangled starlight sheen."

In order for goodness to be attractive, then, it must be beautiful and evoke wonder and admiration. Generosity in all its forms, proper manners toward all people and on all occasions, and the pure enjoyment of doing good for its own sake give virtue a luster that the mere performance of duty does not radiate. As Cardinal Newman writes in his commentary on Aristotle's *Poetics*, "With Christians, a poetical view of things is a duty—we are bid to color all things with hues of faith, to see a Divine meaning in every event, and a superhuman tendency." He explains that Christianity itself is poetical: "Revealed religion should be especially poetical—and it is so in fact. While its disclosures have an originality in them to engage the intellect, they have a beauty to satisfy the moral nature." Likewise, the miracle of the loaves and fish, the banquet thrown for the Prodigal Son, the liberality of the dying knight, the hospitality of Baucis and Philemon, and the hard-won thoughtfulness of the learned bishop Francis, all possess this poetical quality. When goodness is beautiful and poetical, Newman explains, "it presents us with those ideal forms of excellence in which a poetical mind delights, and with which all grace and harmony are associated."[9] The poetry of conduct, then, involves adornment and refinement, dressing up in words, deeds, manners, and clothing that show virtue in all the beauty that by nature it possesses. Thus goodness never falsely appears prosaic but shines forth and reveals its true self, which is Glory.

---

9   John Henry Newman, *Poetry with Reference to Aristotle's Poetics*, ed. Albert S. Cook (Cornell University Library: Ithaca, New York, 2009), 1 ff.

IX Humility: The Tales of the Brother Grimm and of Hans Christian Andersen

Money is a serious subject. We all care about the state of the economy, and some of us scrutinize interest rates, stock markets, and unemployment rates. Government spending, exorbitant taxes, college tuitions, and the cost of oil and health insurance are no laughing matters. Avarice (in the form of greed or miserliness) is one of the seven deadly sins. Bankruptcy, credit card indebtedness, and poverty also evoke grave concern. But money can also be funny. When professional athletes pout, sulk, argue, and demand to be traded because an $8 million salary does not suffice, the comic spirit enters. When humans lack self-knowledge, lose their grasp of reality, and develop obsessions about money (like King Midas's) that make them one-sided "humor" characters, then the medicine of laughter needs to prescribe a cure for the madness of Mammon worship that consumes fools.

The subject of wealth—winning kingdoms, marrying the king's daughter, using magical wishes to generate gold—informs many of the fairy tales of the Grimm brothers and Hans Christian Andersen. These stories portray a myriad of characters whose grim preoccupation with money does not produce an increase in luxury and affluence but instead humiliation and embarrassment. On the other hand, many lighthearted, unworldly characters that do not pursue the goal of riches with covetousness or possessiveness experience good fortune and prosperity. Fools and simpletons thrive more than the greedy and the miserly. The innocent and the carefree who possess no eye for profit acquire kingdoms and win the hands of princesses. In folktales the most foolish thing is to take money too seriously, and the wisest thing is to treat it lightly.

For example, in the Grimm tale "The Fisherman's Wife," the wife feels cheated that her husband, who had caught a great talking fish only to throw it back in the water because it was an enchanted prince, did not request some reward: "Did you not ask for anything? [W]e live very wretchedly here in this nasty stinking ditch; do go back, and tell the fish we want a little cottage."[1] After the fisherman returns to the sea, he requests a cottage that the fish grants immediately. The fisherman's wife then sends her husband to request more favors and greater sources of wealth: the luxury of a castle, the grandeur of a king, the treasure of an emperor, the splendor of a pope—and each wish is granted. Finally, the insatiable woman demands the glory of the sun. She is shocked at the fish's reply: " 'Go home,' said the fish, 'to your ditch again!' and there they live to this very day" (28). Rising to greater and greater heights of magnificence, the fisherman's wife falls precipitously into a ditch—the sudden comic fall from high to low that the avaricious provoke by their immoderate desire for possessions.

---

1 *Grimms' Fairy Tales* (New York: Penguin Books, 1971), 23.

In the Grimm story "The Turnip," a poor soldier who seeks to improve his fortune chooses the life of a gardener and sows turnips. One of the plants produces "the prince of turnips," a tuber so enormous that it fills a two-ox cart. Unprofitable for selling and tasteless for eating, the turnip appears a useless commodity until the gardener decides to offer it as a gift to the king. " 'What a wonderful thing!' said the king; 'I have seen many strange things, but such a monster as this I never saw' " (89). Moved by gratitude and touched by pity for the gardener's poverty, the king bestows wealth upon the poor man: "You shall be poor no longer. I will give you so much that you shall be even richer than your brother" (89). The rich brother, learning of the king's reward of gold, flocks, and lands to the gardener, decides he will surpass his brother in the competition for wealth. Envious, the rich brother gets "together a rich present of gold and fine horses for the king; and [thinks] he must have a much larger gift in return" (89). Appreciative of these munificent gifts, the gracious king will not be outdone in generosity, so he thinks of his most unique and hence precious possession: the giant turnip. And that is what the greedy older brother gets. The innocent gardener, who gave without expecting to receive and hoped for nothing, is blessed by the king's liberality. The cunning rich brother, who gave in a calculating spirit, wins a vast, inedible turnip. The comic spirit plays and jokes with money to keep it from becoming an object of idolatry as simpletons win the stakes and the crafty lose a fortune.

In Hans Andersen's tale "Little Claus and Big Claus," the rich Big Claus, who owns four horses, in a fit of anger strikes poor Little Claus's one horse and leaves him destitute. After flaying his horse so at least he can sell its hide, Little Claus approaches a farmhouse, where he discovers the wife hiding the parish clerk in a chest as her husband arrives.

When the farmer asks Little Claus about the contents of his sack, he replies, "Oh, that's a wizard!" and specifies its powers, which include conjuring up fish, wine, and roast beef—the food the wife had hid in the oven when her husband arrived. When the amazed farmer asks if the wizard can also conjure up the devil, Little Claus directs him to the chest and describes the devil as "the spitting image of a parish-clerk." Dazzled, the farmer pays a bushel of money to purchase "the wizard" (the horsehide). When Big Claus learns that his friend with a bushel of money acquired his fortune from selling his horsehide, Big Claus slaughters all four of his horses and travels to town to sell them for a bushel of money, only to be ridiculed as a madman. Infuriated at the trickery of Little Claus and vowing revenge, Big Claus ties him in a sack to drown him in the river. When Big Claus takes a rest stop in a church, Little Claus shouts from the sack, "I'm so young, and I'm on the way to heaven already!" A cattle driver who overhears him replies, "I'm so old, and I can't get there yet!"[2] Gladly exchanging places, the old man releases Little Claus from the sack and offers him all his cattle in the hope of reaching heaven. When Big Claus travels home and discovers Little Claus driving a herd of cattle, he exclaims, "What on earth! Haven't I just drowned you? . . . But where did you get all those

---

2   *The Fairy Tales of Hans Christian Andersen*, (New York: Oxford University Press, 2009), 24.

fine cattle from?" (25). Little Claus explains that he descended into the river where he was welcomed by a lovely lady who offered him herds of cattle. Of course, the humorless, literal-minded Big Claus, who cannot spot a joke, decides to copy his friend and jumps into the river in a sack and drowns. Thus, the fun-loving, joking, impish Little Claus gathers bushels of money and herds of horses by using his playful imagination and lighthearted sense of humor, whereas the ponderous, somber, dull Big Claus gives away his valuables and plunges to his death—all because he overvalued money.

The Grimm story "The Miser in the Bush" contrasts both sane and mad views of money. A miserly farmer has not paid his simpleminded servant any wages for three years, at which point the laborer threatens to leave. The farmer dupes his hired hand by offering him a penny for each year's labor—a meager sum that nevertheless lifts the poor man's spirits: "I can now travel into the wide world, and make myself merry" (100). Poor in pocket but rich in happiness, the servant, dancing and singing, pities a penniless dwarf and parts with all his earnings. In return for his kind deed, the dwarf gratefully offers the servant three wishes, but the hired hand does not request gold or silver; instead, he asks for a bow, a fiddle, and "that everyone should grant what I request" because "I like many things better than money" (101). The more lighthearted and carefree the simpleton's attitude toward money, the more robust his sense of humor grows. With his bow he shoots a thrush that the miser is eager to purchase: "I would give a great deal of money to purchase such a one" (101). As the miser climbs a bush to retrieve the thrush, the poor man plays his fiddle—and "the miser began to dance and spring about, capering higher and higher in the air" (101). As the miser's clothes are shredded to rags by the thorns, he learns that the music of the fiddle that tosses him in the brambles epitomizes his comical punishment for "shaving" many poor souls too closely—a punishment that the fiddler will not terminate until the miser empties his purse of the one hundred florins he had fleeced from a poor man. Enraged at losing his fortune, the miser pleads robbery before a judge, claiming the thief carried a bow and a fiddle. When the judge condemns the fiddler to the gallows, the poor man exercises his third wish—that no one should deny his request. Thus he implores the judge, "I do not ask my life; only let me play upon my fiddle for the last time" (103)—a simple request that produces the hilarious result of judge, clerks, jailor, and miser all in perpetual motion dancing and capering with no end in sight until the judge promises to release the fiddler and guarantee the return of his one hundred florins. The music stops when the miser confesses to stealing the money and takes the place of the fiddler at the gallows. Prosperity and good fortune redound to the poor servant who was content with three pennies, donated all his coins to a hapless dwarf, and requested a worthless fiddle instead of precious gold. Poverty and humiliation accompany the grasping miser who cheated the poor, hoarded his wealth, and lied to keep his possessions. The merry fiddle that causes all the jumping and bouncing separates the miser from his fortune and releases the riches from his grasping hands. The topsy-turvy whirl of playing and dancing in the story mocks the pomposity of money as the merriment of life makes light of the gravity of money.

The same insistence that money is not the highest good provides the laughter in "Hans in Luck," the Grimm tale about an apprentice who begins his journey homeward with a heavy piece of silver "as big as his head." Trudging along with the burden of carrying the weighty silver over his shoulder, Hans watches with longing as a horseman speeds along the road. Quick to make a profit, the shrewd rider dupes the simpleton into exchanging his silver for a horse. When the horse stumbles and Hans falls into a ditch, the apprentice decides to trade the animal for a cow. Eyeing his gain, a sharp shepherd who bargains with Hans exchanges a common cow for an expensive horse. These transactions continue through the story as Hans takes a loss each time, paying dearly for goods that prove useless. The cow kicks him in the head and leaves him unconscious. The pig that Hans gets for his cow gives him a guilty conscience when a cunning farmer tells the naive apprentice, "[Y]our pig may get you into a scrape . . . the squire has had a pig stolen out of his stye" (9). When Hans barters his pig for a goose, he is tricked again by a crafty tradesman. Finally, Hans arrives in a village where a grinder envies the goose and convinces him he will always have money in his pocket if he purchases a grindstone and practices the trade. Thus, in his final business deal Hans acquires "a common rough stone" when he had begun his ventures with a great lump of silver. Cheated, duped, and used by all the artful tradesmen, Hans returns home with nothing of monetary value. After he loses even his grindstone in a pond, he completes his journey with no money, no possessions, and no animals—a condition that does not beget the sadness of loss but produces a sense of mirth and good fortune. "'How happy am I!' cried he. 'no mortal man was ever so lucky as I am'" (11).

All these tales satirize the foolishness of the greedy and the miserly whose love of money robs them of mirth, lightheartedness, and a sense of humor. In their worship of wealth they will stoop to the basest levels of cunning, lose every trace of common sense, and act with the dullest of minds. Covetousness robs these fools of self-control (the fisherman's wife constantly demands more and greater possessions), good judgment (Big Claus will jump into a river to find his flock of sheep), laughter (the rich brother sees no irony in the king's gift of an overgrown turnip), and compassion (all the traders are pitiless in exploiting poor Hans). The sin of avarice dehumanizes and distorts the greedy as they equate happiness with material possessions instead of simple joys. Like the sinners guilty of avarice in Dante's *Purgatorio* whose penance consists of lying prostrate and gazing on the dirt, the worshipers of money grovel and cast their glances downward. For example, the miser in "The Miser in the Bush" creeps into the bushes, and Big Claus crawls into a sack to be thrown into the bottom of a river.

In these folktales the poor, the simple, and the fools who do not dig in the dirt or crawl on their bellies to find wealth turn up material success in imaginative and creative ways. On the one hand, the rich brother in "The Turnip" cunningly and greedily seeks to win the wealth of the poor brother. On the other hand, the poor brother with no thought of gain offers a simple gift only to receive a fortune. While Big Claus—slaughtering all four of his horses in imitation of Little Claus's sale of one horsehide—fails in his financial venture, Little Claus jokes about the wizard in his sack to produce a bushel of money. While Little Claus laughs and plays his way to good fortune, Big Claus groans and labors on the road to frustration and humiliation. " 'Out of the town with him!' they cried, and Big Claus, thrashed as he had never been before, had to take to his heels for all he was worth" (20). Whereas the miserly farmer who hoards every penny to accumulate riches loses every cent, his diligent servant who gives his few coins to a poor dwarf receives three magical wishes and one hundred florins. Blessed are the poor in spirit in these folktales because they harbor no envy or jealousy for the goods and money of others. Because they are happy-go-lucky and carefree like Hans, their treasure lies not in gold but in innocence. Childlike in their simplicity and playful in their intelligence, these simple and poor characters lack guile and worldly wisdom. What they lack in shrewdness, they possess in mirth and gain in luck. Rather than scheme, cheat, lie, and die for money, the simpletons and fools laugh at gold and make light of wealth. "I like many things better than money" (101), says the poor servant of the miserly farmer. Relieved to be unburdened of his lump of silver, Hans values a simple life above all his worldly goods. Little Claus cannot take riches too seriously because of all his jests about his bushels of money. In deadly seriousness Big Claus asks, "My, where did you get all this money from?" Little Claus jokingly replies that he sold his grandmother: "I've just sold her and got a bushel of money for her!" (22). In short, the only folk who are blessed with luck are those who can make sport of money by giving it away or being moral and playful as they gain it.

The plodding (Big Claus), the crafty (the rich brother), and the grave (the miser), those who lack a sense of humor, fail to see a joke, or cannot part with their gold, think that might makes right, assume that the strength of the lion and the cunning of the fox explain success, and hold that money is "the one thing necessary." Having no lighthearted, comic spirit about riches, they disregard the mystique of Lady Luck and do not comprehend the paradox of the lucky fool or the strangeness of beginner's luck. Like King Midas, the greedy in folktales lose all. To be deadly serious and humorless about money is to lose touch with reality and the myriad of simple pleasures that define true happiness. Those who fail to appreciate the comedy of money—its relative unimportance in the scale of human values—suffer the tragedy of money, the madness of losing everything for nothing.

Despite the serious role of the economy in everyone's life, and the God-given duty to exercise prudent stewardship, money is not the *summum bonum* or even the be-all and end-all. The comedy of money in folktales provides a perennial wisdom that resists the exaggeration of riches as the primary source of human happiness and satirizes fortune hunters for their insatiable desires, petty stinginess, and artful deceits. In contrast to the fisherman's wife's cupidity that demands more and more, "Hans in Luck" exemplifies poverty of spirit that needs less and less. In contrast to Big Claus's pursuit of wealth by the crudest and coarsest of means (slaughtering his four horses and killing his grandmother), Little Claus gains his bushels of money by the use of his native wit and nimble mind. In contrast to the rich brother in "The Turnip," who invests something to gain more but acquires nothing, the poor gardener gives without expecting to receive but acquires wealth. The comedy of money in these stories provides the medicine to restore sanity, cure flights of fancy, and bring fools back down to earth. Modern man also needs to curb his restless acquisitiveness of material things, to free himself of consumerism—the urge to gain more and more money, even by devious and dishonest means, the better to purchase more and more needless things. While these folktales honor honest toil, industrious work, and frugal living, they satirize the anxiety about money that proceeds from a disregard for Divine Providence, a failure that Christ addressed in the Sermon on the Mount: "Therefore, do not be anxious, saying, 'What shall we eat?' or 'What shall we drink?' or 'What shall we wear?' For the Gentiles seek all these things; and your heavenly Father knows that you need them all. But seek first his kingdom, and all these things shall be yours as well" (Matthew 6:31–33).

In George MacDonald's *At the Back of the North Wind*, a child illuminates the simple truth about money that escapes the worldly wise and the acquisitive: an obsession with money robs a person of happiness, entangles and complicates a person's life, and destroys the purity of innocence. When the mother complains to her son Diamond that their neighbor Mr. Coleman has lost his money, that his father's injury prevents him from earning an income, that the provisions in the house are dwindling, and that "we shall have nothing to eat by and by,"[3] she feels the burden of the world's complex economic realities. The

---

3   George MacDonald, *At the Back of the North Wind* (Mahwah, New Jersey: Watermill Press, 1985), 106.

child—lacking the fretfulness of his mother—responds in utter simplicity, "Are you sure, mother?" (106). He notices a piece of gingerbread in the basket, observes that the birds find food in the winter, and mentions the stocked cupboard of his aunt. When Diamond's mother attempts to cure the silliness of her impractical son by comparing him to a sparrow that never thinks of the snow and frost, Diamond simplifies the problem. He calls the berries on the trees the "birds' barns" that sustain them all winter. Unconvinced by his mother's picture of their complicated financial situation ("But there are no such barns for you and me, Diamond), the boy says the obvious: "Ain't there, mother?" (106). He decides to call the basket a "barn" and remembers that his aunt's copious cupboard also resembles a barn. The child then concludes that a big cupboard (barn) somewhere must be supplying his aunt's pantry and the basket in his home because "I haven't got even a cupboard, and I've always had plenty to eat" (107)—a self-evident truth that unknots all the worries of his mother. The poor and the humble in folktales discover this truth that an innocent child explains to a prudent mother: "Somewhere" there is a great barn of inexhaustible supplies that stocks the trees in winter for birds and cupboards and baskets in homes. Whereas the avaricious and the miserly (and the overly fretful) see the problem of money as a grave matter, the lowly and the simple treat the subject of money comically and lightly—as a matter of luck, not shrewdness; as a matter of play more than work; and as an occasion for hope and trust rather than scheming and plotting. If a simple person is willing to work honestly, to wait patiently, to hope steadfastly, to give generously, and to use his imagination creatively, he will seek first the kingdom of God and discover that money has been added unto him.

X. Generosity: *The Merry Adventures of Robin Hood*

A person may do many things with money: spend it, save it, invest it, hoard it, waste it, bequeath it, or hide it. Everyone purchases groceries and pays bills; the prudent save from their earnings; the daring speculate and watch money reproduce money; the misers gloat upon the treasures they have accumulated; the foolish squander their money on unnecessary luxuries or burden themselves with debt; and old-timers hide their money under the bed or bury it in the yard. However, there is another use of money that is distinctly Christian, the epitome of the Christmas spirit: the joy of releasing it and giving it away, forgetting about being acknowledged or rewarded, and remembering that money is only paper or metal, not something precious. The Christmas season restores this sane view that money is a means to an end, not an end in itself. Although, as St. Paul stated, "If any will not work, let him not eat," Christ also reminded the world that "man does not live by bread alone." The Christmas season is the ideal time to cure the mind of its adult obsessions and fantasies about money and to conquer the habit of buying only necessities. As O. Henry's beloved story "The Gift of the Magi" illustrates, spending money for gifts of love is one of the highest arts of civilization. In the story a young married couple struggling to make ends meet save pennies to buy one another a treasured gift. Della can purchase only a chain for Jim's prized watch if she cuts off her luxurious hair and sells it for a wig; Jim can only afford to buy the expensive jeweled combs for Della's gorgeous hair if he sells his valuable watch. On Christmas day, Della presents Jim with the chain for the watch he sold, and Jim offers Della the golden combs for the hair she cut short—a comic, awkward moment that makes both gifts impractical. However, despite the uselessness of the gifts O. Henry compares their presents to the gifts of the Magi, for they too "sacrificed for each other the greatest treasures of their house." While Jim and Della appear foolish because their gifts serve no immediate use, the chain and the combs make perfect sense as Christmas presents: "Of all who give and receive gifts, such as they are the wisest,"[1] O. Henry writes, because the gift from the heart that does not count pennies is the surest token of pure love.

While all men and women who live responsible lives must balance their budgets and use prudence and frugality in their spending habits through the course of the year and throughout the many years of a lifetime, Christians are also obligated to practice the virtue of liberality. Just as it is wise to save, it is healthy to spend. Weddings, graduations, birthdays, anniversaries, and many special occasions like Christmas require this virtue of openhanded generosity that reflects the joy of giving when the event and the person justify this kind of munificence. If human beings only save money or use it exclusively for utilitarian purposes or necessary expenses, they never learn the

---

1 *41 Stories by O. Henry* (New York: New American Library, Signet Classic, 2007), 70.

lesson that money periodically *needs to be given away*—by way of charity or gifts—lest the habit of economy breed an excessive attachment to wealth or a loss of trust in Providence. Ultimately, as Dante demonstrated vividly in the *Purgatorio*, gold and silver come from the dirt, and the avaricious who worship Mammon as the god of gold deserve the punishment of lying prostrate on the ground groveling for the metals in the earth that ruled their lives and constituted their only treasure. Without holidays and celebrations where gifts enhance the festive spirit of the atmosphere, economic man would never learn the art of detachment from money or gain an appreciation for the inestimable worth of spiritual joys. The Christmas season is the time to remember this most Christian discipline of the art of self-forgetfulness that detachment from money cultivates.

In this most Christian of festivals, a season without parallel in other festivals or holidays—secular or religious—a form of joy and giving known as the Christmas spirit with roots in "merry old England" and the stories of Saint Nicholas teaches the invaluable lesson that it is more blessed to give than to receive. Saint Nicholas threw three bags of gold into the chimney or window of a poor family whose daughter could not marry because of a lack of dowry. Saint Nicholas carried his bag of gold in the middle of the night and rode quickly away to escape attention and recognition—a deed that illustrates an old proverb that says "Do good by stealth and blush to find it fame." No one is supposed to see Santa Claus and tooth fairies. The Christmas spirit, then, not only motivates the virtue of liberality and the joy of giving but also the quality of anonymity that seeks no formal acknowledgement or public honor for the good deed born of a pure heart. The stories of Robin Hood, set in the days of "merry old England," especially capture this ineffable magic of Christian generosity that both rich and poor can practice. In Howard Pyle's *The Merry Adventures of Robin Hood*, the author introduces his hero and his companions as "living the merriest of merry lives" because "these jocund fellows" relish robust laughter and revel in friendship that thinks nothing of the parting of money for the sake of the happiness and relief of others. When Sir Richard of the Lea attempts to repay his debt to Robin Hood, who rescued him from poverty and the loss of his land, Robin and his band refuse the offer: "Sir Richard . . . thou wilt pleasure us all if thou wilt keep that money as a gift from us at Sherwood. Is it not so my lads?"[2] Without reservations, all the men shout "Ay!" with a resounding voice. Like St. Nicholas, Robin Hood and his men release their money with no reservations or conditions as they tender gifts with glad hearts that easily dispense with their fortunes for the cause of relieving the sorrows or adding to the happiness of others.

A genuine, spiritually centered Christmas reminds the world about the relative unimportance of money in the larger scheme of things. Without such occasions to restore our hierarchy of values, the impulse of avarice develops in the form of greed, stinginess, selfishness, and hardheartedness. Nathaniel Hawthorne's "The Golden Touch" retells the myth of King Midas, who wished

---

2   Howard Pyle, *The Merry Adventures of Robin Hood* (New York: Dover Publications, Inc.,1968), vii, 182.

for the power to make gold willy-nilly, even though he already possessed a fortune. (As a Greek god in disguise observes, "You are a wealthy man, friend Midas! . . . I doubt whether any other four walls, on earth, contain so much gold as you have contrived to pile up in this room.")[3] Despite his wealth, the king's unhinged desire for increase leads him to gain a magical power that robs his world of all the pleasure, beauty, and wonder that filled his life. After his wish comes true of possessing the golden touch, he transforms the roses in his garden, the food at the breakfast table, and eventually his daughter, Marygold, into lifeless, metallic objects.

Without the Christmas spirit to check the golden touch, man easily becomes enslaved to money as Midas's obsession with gold illustrates. After the shock of touching his daughter and changing her into a statue, Midas comes to value the worth of flowers, food, and children more than all the gold in the world. Once flowers have lost their sweet fragrance, once food lacks its delicious flavors, and once Marygold turns into metal and no longer greets her father in the morning with a rose in her hand and a dimple in her cheek, Midas learns of precious gifts whose value cannot be measured in gold. He remarks, "A piece of bread . . . is worth all the gold on earth" (89). The Christmas spirit offers this unworldly perspective on money and curbs man's acquisitive instinct. It safeguards a person's humanity from the worship of gold to appreciate simple pleasures

---

3 Nathaniel Hawthorne, *A Wonder-Book* (New York: Alfred A. Knopf, 1994, Everyman's Library Children's Classics), 73.

filled with wonder that homes, children, and gifts bring in this holy season.

Such cheerful giving without counting the cost or craving any return lifts man from the realm of business transactions to a spiritual world that does not keep accounts. It ennobles man to do things gratis, and to do things gratis distinguishes a knight or a gentleman. In Cervantes's *Don Quixote*, the knight-errant and his squire are welcomed into the hospitable company of goatherds who offer them potluck and provide generously for their guests—a kind deed that reminds Quixote of the golden age. Indeed, the quixotic spirit of chivalry is inspired by the sense of service to widows, orphans, and the defenseless that performs knightly deeds freely and exemplifies these selfless magnanimous acts. As Quixote explains to Sancho, according to venerable tradition, "I cannot break the rule of the Order of Knights-errant, of whom I know for certain that they never paid for lodging or anything else in the inns where they stayed" (89). The Christmas season cultivates this habit of doing things and giving things for "free." As Quixote remembers, the golden age was not acquisitive or possessive but a time of innocence when a higher ideal lifted man beyond the exchange of money as the primary relationship among men. Charity, friendship, hospitality, and magnanimity all possess this sense of gratuitousness that gives the Christmas season—residually, in its modern commercialized form—its mysterious spiritual power.

Shakespeare also captures this lightheartedness and mirth in *A Midsummer Night's Dream,* as King Oberon, Puck, and the fairies perform the kind favors and generous deeds of a St. Nicholas and a Robin Hood in the middle of the night, in the atmosphere of absolute silence and perfect secrecy. Demetrius, who courted Helena and pledged his love with the promise of marriage, abruptly jilts her to pursue Hermia—a love suit that her father approves even though Hermia is betrothed to Lysander. As these lovers travel through the forest, King Oberon overhears the quarrel of Demetrius and Helena and commiserates with the heartbroken woman who cries to Demetrius, "The wildest hath not such a heart as you" (2.1.229).[4] Determined to intervene and heal this breach, the king of the fairies sends the mirthful Puck to find a medicinal flower whose love juice works magic: "Anoint his eyes; / But do it when the next thing he espies / May be the lady" (2.1.261–263). The playful Oberon and the fun-loving Puck bring to this sad affair the frolicsome mirth of the fairy spirit that performs its hidden good deeds while the lovers are asleep and unaware of any beneficent spirits. Puck identifies himself as a reveling mischief maker who relishes surprises and thrives on good cheer: "I am that merry wanderer of the night. / I jest to Oberon, and make him smile" (2.1.43–44). While the lovers are lulled into a deep slumber, Oberon and Puck perform their work of relieving melancholy, healing broken hearts, and reconciling the alienated lovers as they perform their "fairy favors" in the course of the evening's darkness. They do good by stealth. They bring gifts in the night and escape detection. They appear and disappear in the mystery of the dark forest. They love goodness for its own sake and do good deeds with a

4   *The Major Plays of Shakespeare* ed. G. B. Harrison (New York: Harcourt Brace Jovanovich, Publishers, 1968), 523.

pure heart—a purity that the dewdrops they place on the flowers symbolize as they are called "rubies" and jewels: "I must go seek some dewdrops here, / And hang a pearl in every cowslip's ear" (2.1.14–15).

Without the sacrificing hearts of Jim and Della, the charitable heart of St. Nicholas, the bountiful heart of Robin Hood, the noble heart of Don Quixote, and the pure hearts of Oberon and Puck, the enchantment of Christmas would not exert its magic during the yuletide season, and the Christmas spirit would not transform a culture. The season of Christmas awakens the human sentiments that recall the simplicity of childhood and the innocence of fun as the highest of ideals, and it puts to rest the calculating, reckoning mind that is always adding and subtracting. Human beings work *in order to play*. The purpose of earning money is to spend money for loved ones and the poor. There is a time to save and a time to spend. There is a time to put money in the bank and a time to empty the pockets. Without the forgetting of money—the throwing of the bags of gold down the chimney when the occasion or person justifies it—man's identity becomes equated to *homo economicus* and his human life resembles the busy, industrious ant who lives in order to work. Without the sacrifices of Jim and Della, love never becomes real or incarnate. Without the liberality of Robin Hood, man is soon riddled with the anxiety of never having enough and always feels the need for *more*, until he might even wish for "the golden touch." Without the noble heart of Don Quixote, man imagines that all human relationships are based on exchanges of money or on quid pro quo. Without the puckish, lighthearted spirit of the merry wanderers of the night, man descends into ponderous gravity and takes himself, his work, and his money all too seriously. Thus the Christmas spirit cures a multitude of ills and offers elfin medicine that operates like the gentle anointing of the eyelids that purges excesses and restores sanity in *A Midsummer Night's Dream.*

Excessive preoccupation with money in the form of wasteful spending, miserly saving, acquisitive gaining, uncontrollable consuming, and obsessive worrying about security is the mad way of the world, but Christmas is not of this world. Christmas originates in the miracle and sacrifice of divine love that the Magi honor. It intimates a heavenly world of total giving that St. Nicholas demonstrated with the bag of gold he offered as a special blessing. It hearkens to the tales of merry old England in which Robin Hood and other magnanimous men scorned the worship of money and distributed it with abandon, always trusting in Divine Providence. It evokes the golden age that Don Quixote momentarily experiences in the hospitality of the goatherds that recalls a past age of innocence that valued truth, goodness, beauty, courtesy, kindness, and nobility more than possessions. And the generosity of the Christmas spirit restores the fairy realm of childhood to a jaded world overburdened with work, preoccupied with money, and worried about the future. All men, regardless of age, need to feel young again, recall their childhood, and use their imagination to see the lighthearted merry wanderers of the night who rejoice in bringing fairy favors, kind deeds, and bountiful gifts in the stillness of the night to people who need to leave behind the busy city, enter the mysterious forest, and close their eyes in rest in order to receive the miraculous surprises prepared for them by a heavenly world of angelic beings who never check their savings accounts.

XI. Simplicity: *The Wonder Clock*

Howard Pyle's *The Wonder Clock* (1887), a collection of folktales and fairy tales with illustrations that depict the various scenes of a twenty-four-hour period in a typical home of the time, organizes the stories according to the hours of the day, beginning at one a.m.

> One O'Clock
> One of the Clock, and silence deep
> Then up the Stairway, black and steep
> The old House-Cat comes creepy-creep
> With soft feet goes from room to room
> Her green eyes shining through the gloom
> And finds all fast asleep.[1]

The setting of the stories is a household that provides domestic comforts, simple pleasures, and a variety of sources of contentment, all on a modest scale. Even the hour of one o'clock in the morning is not devoid of its exquisite moments and special sense of peacefulness. The gleaming green eyes of the cat and its sly movements punctuate the darkness with a beautiful light and a natural movement that is reassuring of a familiar, human world that always feels like home. Two o'clock in the morning is not marked by dreary darkness or lifeless immobility, for a black bird crows and a red cock answers

---

1   Howard Pyle, *The Wonder Clock* (New York: Harper & Brothers, 1915), 1.

as the moon shines brightly. The universe is not a cold, impersonal place. Inside the home, Gretchen "Turned in bed, / And tossed her arms / Above her head" as the dog stretches: "And, breathing deep, / He settled down / Again to sleep" (15). So Gretchen and the hound, turning and stretching, settle into their favorite positions and enjoy the sweetness of sleep in the cozy snugness of home. In the dead of night, at three a.m., the rooms are feeling cold as the ashes in the fireplace die, but life goes on even in darkness and sleep: "The Board-Floor creaked, / The Grey-Mouse squeaked, / And the Kobold dreamed its ear he tweaked" (27).

There is never a lack of activity, a sound of life, a touch of humor, or something happening in this world of the home, even though the busyness of the day has passed and the time of rest has arrived. Floors creaking, creatures stirring, sleepers dreaming, fires glowing—the nighttime realm stirs with its own round of normal business and brims with its own unique sounds, sights, and movements. Every hour has its pleasure, and both night and day offer appetizing, welcoming delights. This is the poetry of the home, the song of daily life in its ordinary rounds around the clock.

In *The Wonder Clock* each of these simple pleasures is savored as something delicious to enjoy, something inviting to anticipate with delight, or something comical to relish for a joke. At five o'clock in the morning, the maid Gretchen stumbles down the stairs freezing, "[a]nd pokes the fire with a frown," complaining, "Plague on the fire!" In the meantime the master of the household abruptly jumps out of bed: "Wife, Wife, it's five o'clock!" (49). Every day brings its humor and its share of mischievousness. The character of the Kobold (goblin), who plays the part of an impish child blowing ashes in the maid's eyes at five o'clock and later at seven o'clock, "Peeped in every pot and pail, / And grinned, and pulled the Pussy's tail" (77). These normal interruptions and antics and the everyday accidents (Gretchen breaks a cup while washing dishes) are the diversions that prohibit life from assuming a rigid, inhuman order that has no room for laughter and lightheartedness. The beginning of a new day at six o'clock brings cheer and hope: "The Door is open, / The Dew is bright; / Forgotten now is the lonesome Night, / And the Starling whistles, 'All is right' " (63, 68). The welcome sight of breakfast—bread, honey, eggs, and cream—whets the appetite, as the taste of wholesome food testifies to the goodness of God's creation that abounds in the variety of pleasures each day brings. By seven and eight o'clock in the morning, the revelry of children's play fills the house ("Around, / Around and about, / The Kobold played in and out"), and children frolic on their way to school "With hop and jump, / By hedge and stump" (77, 89). Laughing, playing, eating, learning: no hour of the day is without its accompanying pleasure, and the course of the day— the clock of wonder—is an invitation to partake of the abundance of God's plenty. The poetry of the home is never without a pleasure, laugh, or song, day or night.

While the children learn deportment and obedience at school, where the schoolmaster disciplines them to "walk by Rule, / And bow before they leave the School" (104), the heartwarming, civilizing amenities of domestic life prepare the riches of hospitality for the homecoming at noon and at the end of the day: "They're baking Pies at

Home," and at ten o'clock Gretchen the maid prepares a special treat as she takes "Some dough, and makes, / For little John, a Saucer Pie." Now the beds are made, and the dishes and pots are washed and placed "[o]ut in the pleasant Sun to dry" (121). Working in one's own home, performing the domestic chores for the beloved persons in one's life, cooking nutritious meals as an act of love, and appreciating the beautiful weather all lend a magical aura to the day. There is not only the excitement of the beginning of a new morning but also the expectation of special refreshments during the course of the day. By eleven o'clock the pies have been taken out of the oven, and the irresistible, tantalizing smells of home cooking and sweet pies linger in the air, transforming the kitchen into a paradise. The Kobold licks his lips as his "glistening eyes" yearn for the feast that noontime brings when "The Bread is cut, the Soup is hot, / The cabbage simmers in the pot" as Gretchen fills the beer mugs from the cellar, "cool and brown" (135, 149). The menial tasks and ordinary, humble work of life do not have to be tedious, drab, or humdrum. A pie in the oven, a homemade brew, a joking spirit, a sunny day, and a hospitable home lift the quality of everyday existence from the prosaic to the poetic.

The afternoon and evening hours continue this theme of looking forward to each and every hour of the day for the satisfaction of completing some duty, for the gratification of some pleasure, for the diversions provided by animals, children, and imps, and for the variety of the gifts and blessings a day brings. Whether it is helping Johnnie play ball, seeing the cat sleeping in the sun, watching the kitten find a mouse hole at five p.m., celebrating the end of work with tea at six, hearing the children shout and play at seven, or snuggling the children in bed by eight and looking forward to the sweetness of a good night's rest at nine—this ordinary, unspectacular day abounds in the quiet, natural, universal joys of domestic life that are invested with riches and wonders. Deep peacefulness, a rhythmic pace of life, the balance of work and play, and a natural innocence govern this way of life. All throughout the day there is the steady reminder that "all is right." At one o'clock in the morning, the cat finds "all fast asleep"; at two, the old hound stretched and "settled down again to sleep"; at three o'clock the Kobold dreams and smiles in his sleep, and at four he awakes, sighs, "[a] nd turn[s] upon his other side" (1, 15, 27, 39). No one is restless or troubled at night. All during the day there is the joy of meaningful, rewarding work. A ten o'clock the beds are made; at five a.m. the milking is done. At eight o'clock "The plays are done, / And the prayers are said, / And the Children are snugly / Tucked in bed" (253). One completes the day with a clean conscience about fulfilling the day's obligations. Hearing the sighing of the wind and the clock saying "tick-a-tock" gives further reassurance of the tranquility of a life lived in tune with nature and God, which inspires the poetry of the home and hearth.

When all are wrapped in Slumbers sleep,
About the house, with stealthy Tread,
With flowered Gown, and night-capped Head,
Dame Margery goes, in Stocking Feet.
She stops and listens at the Doors;
She sees that everything is right,

And safe, and quiet for the Night,
Then goes to Bed, and sleeps, and snores. (267)

Although it depicts an agricultural society in the late nineteenth century, *The Wonder Clock* illuminates important universal truths about the human condition: human happiness is the sum of little things or ordinary pleasures from a hearty home-cooked meal to an honest day's work to a refreshing night of sleep; the art of living entails always looking forward to some simple, innocent pleasure of each day to enrich and renew the spirit; contentment follows from living in tune with nature and God, in accordance with nature's rhythms—the "wonder clock" of the universe. The domestic life in a family is the most comical of places, a world of play, mirth, laughter, and lightheartedness epitomized by the bright eyes of the Kobold, who chases the goose, blows ashes in the maid's eyes, peeps in every pot and pail, pulls the cat's tail, pries into the cupboard, and hops across the floor; culture begins in the home, where one learns to appreciate the wealth of blessings each day provides, which each hour of the clock announces. *The Wonder Clock* teaches that every day is a gift and each hour of the day a glimpse into the goodness and beauty of creation in both its homespun simplicity and surprising variety and rich goodness. The world of the home in its wonder clock of varied delights and joys provides inexhaustible sources for the poetry of the home that contemplates God's infinite goodness. In Emily Dickinson's words, "Eden is that old-fashioned House we dwell in every day."

What has happened to this wonder clock today—to the insight that each hour, each day, and each season affords its special delectations and that wisdom orders the day so that the fullness of these joys is tasted again and again? In his sophistication and cosmopolitanism, modern man has lost his taste for these simplest but most rewarding of life's pleasures. In *The Napoleon of Notting Hill*, Chesterton writes, "It is of the new things that men tire—of fashions and proposals and improvements and change. It is the old things that startle and intoxicate. It is the old things that are young. . . . But we who do the old things are fed by nature with a perpetual infancy."[2] The wonder clock involves this cyclical, recurring experience of the old, familiar things, day in and day out, from the preparation of breakfast to the tucking of children into bed—a repetition of daily activities that never results in boredom, jadedness, or world-weariness. The pleasure is never exhausted, and each day one looks forward again to the smell of home-baked pies and the laughter of children playing. These old things that intoxicate and nourish are the permanent, lasting sources of joy and wonder that inhere in work and play and that honor nature's laws and God's design. Cooking breakfast, building a fire, tending the chickens, milking the cows, watching the children play, coming home to tea, going to church, saying prayers, and going to bed and hearing the wind sigh at night are all part of a normal day's activity in *The Wonder Clock*, but they also require direct contact with nature and God—the fire and wind, chickens and cows, children and bedtimes, prayers and pews. No one attempts to escape reality or lives in

---

2   G.K. Chesterton, *The Napoleon of Notting Hill* (New York: Dover Publications, 1991), 157.

an imaginary world; nature and God are ever-present; children and animals appear everywhere. Everyone hears and obeys the clock—the natural and divine order.

Modern man has been rendered mostly deaf to the chimes of the clock of wonder. Instead of the hearty breakfast of pancakes and eggs at home, commuters rush to Dunkin' Donuts for a morning snack. Instead of beds being made and dishes being set out to dry in the sun and pies baking in the oven, mothers and wives hasten to their jobs outside the home. Instead of children coming home from school and playing outdoors ("Run, Johnie, / And play with your Ball"), they retire to babysitters, day-care centers, and after-school supervised activities. Forgetting that there is a time to work and a time to rest ("[t]he Work is over for the Day"), corporate America demands a sixty-hour week for the ambitious to get ahead. Instead of being "wrapped in Slumbers sweet" and knowing that "everything is right, / And safe, and quiet for the night," many require sleeping pills, Prozac, and other tranquilizers to calm the spirit. Instead of the pranks and amusements provided by impish spirits or the comedy of kittens, various media outlets invade the home in the name of entertainment. These modern habits offer no special refreshment or delightful boon to lighten or rejuvenate the weary spirit in the course of the day. How does one look forward to going to the day-care center or working after hours? The modern pace of the day lacks all the poetry of the home and the hearth in *The Wonder Clock*, where some pleasure or satisfaction belongs to each hour and the repetition of life's quintessential joys never dulls.

Instead of acknowledging the wonder clock that corresponds to nature's seasons and rhythms and God's higher laws, too many of us ignore it. Statistics bear out how many of us forget to follow nature, marry, have children, found a home, play, relax, have leisure, or come to know God. Modern-day life allows little time or room for the poetry of life and the home, for the pure and simple appreciation of life's greatest joys, and for the contemplation of the gift of life. The home, family, and children have lost their association with fun and enjoyment and have ceased to become the primary sources of contentment, fulfillment, and happiness. If I might turn to the very modern device of citing sociological trends, a well-informed expert will bear me out here. In *Conjugal America*, Alan Carlson delineates the low esteem in which family life is held in American culture:

For nearly 40 years, Americans have engaged in a broad retreat from marriage and marital child bearing. The marriage rate has fallen from 148 (per 1,000 unmarried women, ages 15–44) in 1960 to 82 in 1996, a decline of 45%.The remarriage rate has fallen even faster. The divorce rate doubled over the same period, while the number of cohabiting heterosexual couples climbed from 250,000 to 4,200,000 in 1998.

Meanwhile, births within marriage have also fallen from 4.03 million in 1960 to 2.6 million in 1997, an absolute decline of 36%. If one looks to the marital birthrate, the decline is 45%, and still continuing, toward levels portending depopulation.

Overall, the number of "nonfamily households" (dwellings without marriage or children) has soared from 7.9 million in 1960 to an estimated 31.5 million in 2000. In short, all is not well with heterosexual marriage and fertility; marryin' and breedin' may be disappearing.[3]

Why have the home and family lost their romance, poetry, and charm that radiate from the wonder clock?

If the family is not instituted by God but engineered by man, if marriage is not sacramental and indissoluble but temporary and tentative, if the home is not the center of civilization but just an arbitrary arrangement, and if children are not gifts and blessings but burdens and inconveniences, then the home, family, and children lose their inestimable worth and immeasurable prestige. They are not worth working for, living for, sacrificing for, dying for, and singing about. They are devoid of poetry and idealism. Inspired song and romance finally depend upon the existence of absolute truths and enduring, transcendent, unchanging ideals. The greatest works of our culture were crafted to celebrate (even in the face of difficult questions) the heroic virtues, nobility, courage, and the sublimity of love. The *Aeneid* ("Of arms and the man I sing") portrays the magnanimity of "pious Aeneas," who will sacrifice for his family and country. *The Song of Roland* glorifies the nobility of knighthood and its unwavering sense of honor. *Henry V* praises the patriotism of the English ("We few, we happy few, we band of brothers") at the Battle of Agincourt. *Romeo and Juliet* ("O she doth teach the torches to burn bright!") exalts the sublimity of the miracle of human love. And—going backward in

---

3   Alan Carlson, *Conjugal America* (Piscataway, NJ: Transaction Publishers, 2008), 113–14.

time, but returning to our subject—the *Odyssey* honors a man and a woman who love their home and family above all else, the intelligent and daring Odysseus and the patient Penelope, "a wife in whom all virtues meet, flawless Penelope, who has proved herself so good and wise, so faithful in her wedded love!" In addition to these epic poems of praise for heroic excellence, there is the poetry of the home in *The Wonder Clock*, which elevates humble work and domestic life, transforming the honest toil and simple, innocent pleasures of the home into glimpses of heavenly peace and reminders of Eden. Just as beautiful clothing adorns and dignifies human beings so that their divine image shines and the body reveals the soul, so too literature elevates and decorates both the simplest and noblest of virtues and the most human and heavenly ideals so that their divine origin illumines. The poetry of the home captures the sacred nature of humble dwelling places where a fullness of continual joy overflows into each hour, each activity, and each room of the household. The modern world, however, has substituted an ideology of the individual for the poetry of the home.

How does ideology differ from poetry? Like education, poetry educes or brings forth what is there, and gives and lends shape, form, and adornment to that which is praiseworthy or admirable. The poet sees the wonder and glory that dwell in natural and human things, as Gerard Manley Hopkins does in his famous "Pied Beauty":

Glory be to God for dappled things—
For skies of couple-color as a brinded cow;
For rose moles all in stipple upon trout that swim;

143

Fresh firecoal chestnut-falls; finches' wings;
Landscape plotted and pieced—fold, fallow, and plough
And all trades, their gear and tackle and trim.

On the other hand, ideology twists, tortures, and truncates. Like Procrustes, who either stretched or chopped off the legs of his victims to fit his notorious bed, ideology does violence to reality and distorts truth to accommodate its arbitrary theories. Poetry, however, captures the splendor of the form (*splendor formae*) that dwells in matter and lets it speak for itself—as Hopkins does in marveling at the many examples of pied beauty that appear throughout creation in the variegated tones of the sky, in the mixed colors of brindled cows, in the rainbow streaks of trout, in the motley of the landscape, and in the multiplicity of human talents and gifts that constitute "all trades, their gear and tackle and trim." Poetry sees the truth shouting from the housetops everywhere: the glory of God shines in the sky above, in the water below, and on the landscape surrounding the earth, and it manifests itself in the vast heavens and in the small bird, in the animal kingdom and in human nature.

Ideology, in contrast, does not see the splendor of the form in matter or acknowledge a natural purpose or God-given design in creation. It resists recognizing the inherent structure of reality—the givenness of things—presuming always to *improve on* nature, to redefine established universal meanings, and to substitute human willfulness for divine wisdom. Hence, all the attacks on the poetry of the home involve a denial of the universal truths that the poets sing about: "All is well" or "Glory be to God for dappled things" or "Home is the definition of God" (Emily Dickinson). Instead, ideology resorts to legal sophistry and verbal gymnastics to strip away the romance of the family. Propaganda emanating from the putatively highest authority on earth—the United Nations—shatters the understanding of "family" with the (seemingly harmless) claim that families come in a "plurality of forms," and asserts that there are not in fact two sexes, but five separate and distinct "genders." Several U.S. states and an American president have revised the traditional, normative meaning of marriage so it may include two men or two women. Academics routinely deny the existential reality of maleness and femaleness and regard these universal norms as mere social "constructs." As a logical implication, they shutter all-male student clubs or all-female dorms.

Can one still write of *The Privilege of Being a Woman* as Alice von Hildebrand has or praise the beauty of families as Louisa May Alcott did in *Little Women* ("I think families are the most beautiful things in all the world!") after such disillusionment has become nearly universal? We must consider what options are left to us once, in Edmund Burke's famous words, "all the decent drapery of life is . . . rudely torn off. All the superadded ideas, furnished from the wardrobe of a moral imagination, which the heart owns, and the understanding ratifies, as necessary to cover the defects of our shivering nature, and to raise it to dignity in our own estimation, are . . . exploded as a ridiculous,

absurd, and antiquated fashion."[4] Without the poetry
of the home, life degenerates to the survival of the fittest
and the most barbaric.

Truth can survive the assault of ideology because it has
weathered the centuries. G. K. Chesterton notes:

> The Pagans actually had Household Gods. They
> worshipped the house; they treated it as a temple;
> not metaphorically but literally. They sacrificed to
> gods who were conceived as present in that place, as
> distinct from other places.[5]

Ideology does not recognize the household gods and
does not see sacredness or beauty in homes, families, or
marriages—only outdated, arbitrary human conventions.
But "pied beauty" really exists, and the poetry of the home
is as realistic and concrete as couple-colored skies and
brindled cows. Jane Austen writes, "Ah! There's nothing
like staying home for real comfort," and she describes
in *Mansfield Park* the poetry of the home in almost the
same spirit as *The Wonder Book*—as a constant series
of fulfilling tasks, heartwarming comforts, and awaited
pleasures. Fanny Price, the heroine of simple tastes, moral
integrity, and pure heart, finds her home a healing refuge
and a haven of contentment because "after anything
unpleasant," there she "can find immediate consolation

---

4 Edmund Burke, *Reflections on the Revolution in France*, in *The Works of the Right Honourable Edmund Burke*, vol. 2 (London: Henry G. Bohn, 1864), 515–16.

5 G. K. Chesterton, "The Private Lives of the Moderns," in *The Collected Works of G. K. Chesterton*, vol. 21 (San Francisco, Ignatius Press, 1990), 511.

in some pursuit, or some train of thought. Her plants, her books . . . her writing desk, and her works of charity and ingenuity, were all within her reach . . . she could scarcely see an object in the room which had not an interesting remembrance connected with it."[6] In the same vein, Water Rat in *The Wind in the Willows* also acknowledges the poetry of the home when he revels in his life on the river as a "world":

> It's brother and sister to me, and aunts, and company, and food and drink, and (naturally) washing. It's my world, and I don't want any other. What it hasn't got is not worth having, and what it doesn't know is not worth knowing. Lord! What times we've had together! Whether in summer or winter, spring or autumn, it's always got its fun and its excitements.[7]

One can ignore the home and fail to appreciate its goodness, as the Prodigal Son did, but the alternative is destitution and rags. When as a penitent he returns to his father's home, he is once again vested in beautiful clothing and rediscovers the poetry of the home he had rejected: "Bring forth the best robe and put it on him; and put a ring on his hand, and shoes on his feet" (Luke 15: 22). One can dismantle the home as an ideologue and substitute convenient theories for accumulated

---

6   Jane Austen, *Mansfield Park* (New York: Penguin Books, 1975), 173.
7   Kenneth Grahame, *The Wind in the Willows* (New York: The Penguin Group: Puffin Books, 1987), 13.

wisdom, but Mother Nature and the poets always have the last word because, in Chesterton's phrase, "it is the old things that are young" and "of the new things that men tire." One can mock the romance of the home and supplant it with the iconoclasm of the individualist, but the difference will be as real as that which distinguishes surviving from living *well*.

XII. Hope:
Shakespeare's Miracle Plays

In a wedding ceremony, the couple acknowledges the reality of change in the world, as bride and bridegroom vow to cleave together "for better, for worse; for richer, for poorer; in sickness and in health; till death do us part." The world's sorrow consists in such mutability, as human beings suffer the loss of happiness, health, fortune, and life. In Shakespeare's *King Lear*, the king's faithful servant, in witnessing Lear's dying moments, cries out, "World, world, O world! / But that thy strange mutations make us hate thee, / Life would not yield to age" (4.1.10–12). These "strange mutations" or heartbreaking losses lend to human life its tragic dimension. The classical definition of tragedy is "a sudden fall from high to low" as the wheel of fortune turns and the man standing at the top asserting, "I rule," finds himself lying prostrate at the bottom of the wheel admitting, "I am without rule." The Christian vision of the world, however, transcends the tragic view because it acknowledges the mysterious power of God's Divine Providence to bring good out of evil, light out of darkness, and life out of death, as Christ's death and resurrection testify. This miracle evokes wonder and causes a transcendent joy that hints at the sheer scope of heavenly beatitude that Dante describes in the *Paradiso*: "And so my mind, bedazzled and amazed, / Stood fixed in wonder, motionless, intent, / And still my wonder kindled as I gazed" (canto 33, 97–99, tr. Dorothy Sayers).

Shakespeare's miracle plays—*The Tempest, The Winter's Tale,* and *Cymbeline*— begin tragically and end comically, hence the term "tragi-comedies" to define the genre. The tragedy in these plays involves profound, irreparable losses—the sudden fall from high to low that marks the human condition in a contingent, erratic world in which shocking changes destroy happiness. In *The Tempest,* Prospero, the Duke of Milan, is betrayed by his usurping brother; Prospero loses his power as governor and is sent to sea with his baby daughter, Miranda, to drown. However, he is miraculously saved from disaster "by Providence divine" and marooned on a lonely island. There Prospero and Miranda find new life. Fifteen years later a ship approaching the island en route to a wedding faces a storm that imperils all on board. The opening scene of the play is destructive and deadly, as thunder and lightning wreak havoc, and mariners desperately jump into the sea to save their lives: "Farewell, my wife and children!" one of the mariners cries. As members of this shipwreck arrive on Prospero's island in isolated groups, each concludes that the other passengers have drowned. King Alonso believes his son Ferdinand has died. Ferdinand thinks he is the sole survivor. The two fools Stephano and Trinculo imagine that they alone have escaped (1.2; 2.1; 2.2).

However, no one has drowned and none have been lost at sea. While the characters all suffer loss—some unjustly, others justly, still others merely foolishly—no one's fate is tragic. "Not a hair perished, / On their sustaining garments not a blemish, / But fresher than before," as Ariel remarks at the conclusion of the storm (1.2.217–19). All the separated members of the ship are eventually reunited, brothers are finally reconciled, everyone presumed lost or dead is found alive, and everything valuable and precious is returned. However, life does not merely return to the status quo or resume its former course. Everything is "fresher than before," not merely the clothing. Everything lost that is returned brings a heightened joy and instills a more profound appreciation and gratitude. Nothing is ever taken for granted again.

Prospero, the bookish Duke of Milan, had delegated his brother Antonio to rule in his place so that he might cultivate the liberal arts and immerse himself in learning—an imprudent decision that tempted Antonio to seize power and plot Prospero's death at sea. Prospero's carelessness caused his profound loss. King Alonso's loss of his son Ferdinand during the tempest was not a random accident but Prospero's act of retribution for Alonso's conspiracy with Antonio to overthrow him. Alonso and Antonio's tyranny and duplicity caused their loss at sea. Ferdinand's shipwreck does not result from either his folly or vice but follows from a crime his father committed in the past. Thus these sudden losses and erratic changes happen for a number of reasons, ranging from imprudence to pride, but some suffer as the innocent victims of the sins of others. These losses come as a shock that awakens guilt, causes soul searching and examination of conscience, and clears the mind. In other words, what Hamlet calls "the slings and arrows of outrageous fortune" are not wanton acts of cruelty without rhyme or reason but parts of a wise design and providential order governed by moral law. The lost will be found and returned when justice is satisfied, when contrition is experienced, and when the truth is acknowledged.

When Prospero's daughter Miranda wonders at the story of her escape from death on the sea and asks, "How came we ashore?," her father answers, "By providence divine"—a miracle (1.2.159). When Antonio and Alonso discover their safety on the island and find themselves alive rather than drowned, their servant Gonzalo also marvels at the miracle of their escape: "But for the miracle, / I mean our preservation, few in millions / Can speak like us" (2.1.6–8). He is astonished at the beauty and lushness of the island and in awe at the transfigured radiance of their clothing: "That our garments, being, as they were, drenched in the sea, hold, notwithstanding, their freshness and gloss, being rather new-dyed than stained with salt water" (1.2.61–64). When Ferdinand recovers from the tempest and finds himself a lone survivor on land, he too beholds a miracle, the incomparable beauty of Miranda: "Admired Miranda! / Indeed the top of admiration, worth / What's dearest to the world!" (3.1.37–38). While the tempest is raging and the mariners are yelling, "We split, we split, we split!" tragedy looms. No one is thinking of the hand of Divine Providence or imagining that Prospero through his power and wisdom controls the storm and intends justice, forgiveness, and reconciliation. Prospero allows the shipwreck to bring good out of evil, restore the rightful rule of Milan, punish the grasping despots, and temper justice with mercy. All that is lost is found, all the natural bonds that have been severed are joined again, and no one dies or suffers harm. As Prospero says:

Though with their high wrongs I am struck to th'
quick,
Yet with my nobler reason 'gainst my fury

Do I take part. The rarer action is
In virtue than in vengeance. They being penitent,
The sole drift of my purpose doth extend
Not a frown further. (5.1.25–28)

In a world where God's Divine Providence rules, the tragic appearance of the tempests and the sudden losses belie the comic happy ending that Prospero intends. He takes away to give back. He deprives the passengers on the ship of the temporary or false happiness they enjoy to replenish them with a more complete and abundant happiness without guilt or shame. His tempest cures them of fantasies and delusions and restores them to the moral truths about good and evil. Although none of the characters perfectly fathoms the design of his great wisdom and masterful art, he orders all things for the happiness of each person and for the common good of all.

While still a baby, Miranda lost her home in Milan and her privileged status as the daughter of the Duke of Milan—she an innocent victim of the machinations of Antonio and Alonso. As Duke of Milan, Prospero loses his political power as governor because he devoted more time to the contemplative life than to the active life of ruling his people. A passenger on a drowning ship, Ferdinand nearly perishes, a hapless victim of his father's treacherous treatment of Prospero. As a witness of the terrifying storm that devastates the ship, Alonso concludes he will lose his life and see his son drown—his punishment for conspiring with Antonio. Recalling all the deaths on the ocean from accidents of weather, Gonzalo laments, "Our hint of woe / Is common; every day some sailor's wife, /

The master of some merchant, and the merchant, / Have just our theme of woe (2.1.4–6). The sea is notorious for its perils. However, all these characters lose something smaller to gain something greater. While Miranda loses the culture and luxury of Milan, she finds on the foreign island the joy of love and marriage to Ferdinand: "I would not wish / Any companion in the world but you; / Nor can imagination form a shape, / Besides yourself, to like of" (3.1.54–57). While Prospero loses his governorship of Milan, he gains the greater happiness of witnessing his daughter's blessed marriage and hearing the repentance of all those who wronged him. While Ferdinand imagines all is lost and he alone is alive, he discovers the most beautiful and purest wife in Miranda: "But you, oh, you / So perfect and so peerless, are created / Of every creature's best" (3.1.46–48). Alonso never expects to see his son alive again, let alone happily in love with the "admired Miranda," but his joy is doubled when he beholds his married son and the beautiful bride. While Gonzalo laments the destruction wrought by the storm and the loss of many lives, he is in wonder at the miracles he has witnessed—the whitewashed garments "being rather new-dyed than stained with water" and the appearance of paradise on the island: "Here is everything advantageous to life. . . .How lush and lusty the grass looks!" (2.1.68, 49, 52). This profound joy of recovery and reunion transcends ordinary pleasure and hints of supernatural bliss. All who experience the finding of the lost exclaim in wonder at the reality of a miracle and feel a fullness of joy that reaches perfection.

As a miracle play, then, *The Tempest* presents a Christian vision of the world that portrays God in His justice, mercy, and wisdom returning to man in the ripeness of time all the precious things he has lost to folly, imprudence, or injustice. Although it appears that the wheel of fickle fortune turns in erratic ways to rob man of his temporal happiness, Fortune does not reign supreme. In the play, Prospero's ethereal servant, Ariel—whimsical, flighty, and impulsive—personifies the mutability of events, but Ariel, obedient to Prospero's orders, performs a subordinate role similar to the duty of an apprentice to a master. Fortune means change, from high to low, from joy to sorrow, from riches to poverty. In the first part of the play, Ariel creates the tempest, alters the weather in other ways, and separates the travelers into three different groups who all appear lost. The joy of attending a wedding turns into the sorrow of watching a funeral. Willful and reckless, Fortune appears to govern the world. However, everything that Ariel does as the servant of Prospero corresponds to Fortune's role as the handmaiden of Divine Providence. Reassuring Prospero that no one is injured or drowned ("Not a hair perished"), Ariel not only causes the storm but also performs a miracle: the garments of the survivors appear "fresher than before." While Ariel drove Ferdinand from the security of the ship into the furor of the waves, he also led him to Miranda, whose name means "miraculous" and whom Ferdinand calls a "goddess." While Ariel terrifies Antonio and Sebastian with thunder and lightning and the claws of a Harpy, threatening these "men of sin" with "perdition worse than any death / Can be at once,", he is stirring their conscience and awakening their guilt—effecting a miraculous conversion: "These are not natural events; they strengthen / From strange to stranger," Alonso confesses after his repentance (5.1.227–28).

Divine Providence with its miracles governs the world, not fickle Fortune. All these miracles signify the newness of what Ferdinand calls his "second life" after he falls in love with Miranda and the newness of the transfigured garments with their "freshness and glosses, being new-dyed than stained with salt water." When the lost is found, a new life begins, a new joy fills the heart, and a new vision of the world exalts the mind. In Miranda's famous words, "How beauteous mankind is! O brave new world / That has such people in't" (5.1.184–85).

The Christian vision of *The Tempest*—that of comedy after tragedy—prefigures the mystery of eternal life and supernatural beatitude. The resurrection from the dead and all it implies—the glorified body, reunion with loved ones, and the beatific vision—undoes loss and death. They promise a greater happiness and a more ecstatic joy than natural pleasures in the human world. They excite the sense of wonder and awe that accompany all miracles from the hand of Divine Providence. The conclusion of *The Tempest*—the happy marriage of Ferdinand and Miranda, forgiveness and reconciliation between brothers and enemies, the deliverance of all the passengers from death to life, and the accomplishment of perfect justice—hints at a heavenly paradise that St. Paul described in a famous passage: "Eye hath not seen, nor ear heard, neither have entered into the heart of man, the things which God hath prepared for them that love him" (1 Corinthians 2:9).

This happiness, however, needs to be earned in the same way that Ferdinand won the hand of Miranda. Prospero did not grant him the hand of his daughter until he had proved himself worthy of this prize by carrying logs.

As Prospero explains, "But this swift business / I must uneasy make, lest too light winning / Make the prize light" (1.2.450–52). Offering the hand of his daughter to Ferdinand as a "rich gift," Prospero explains his higher purpose to Ferdinand: "All thy vexations / Were but my trials of love, and thou / Hast strangely stood the test" (4.1.5–7). The reward always outweighs the work, for to serve Prospero is to be in amazement at his generosity. Prospero desires to give new life to the wedded couple by blessing their marriage as he invokes spirits to bestow upon their marriage "Long continuance, and increasing, / . . . Earth's increase, foison [abundance] plenty, / Barns and garners never empty" (4.1.106–111). Prospero's gifts to Ariel also surpass his labors. For his faithful service to his master, Ariel receives his freedom—a freedom he had lost when the witch Sycorax implanted him in the tree from which Prospero rescued him. Thus Prospero restores the lost, doubles the joys, makes all things new, and performs miracles that multiply the happiness. The ending of *The Tempest* does not return to the old past but promises a more glorious future that heals wounds, deepens love, strengthens human relationships, and evokes contemplative wonder at the extravagant goodness of life's purest joys.

In the storm that begins *The Tempest*, the tragedy of life runs its course in a fallen world filled with injustice, death, and each of the seven deadly sins. In such a world, everyone suffers. Everyone loses some priceless possession, either a beloved person, a great source of honor, or a prized gift. The world in its strange mutations robs Prospero of his happiness as the Duke of Milan, subjects Ariel to the slavery of the witch Sycorax, and endangers the lives of the members of the ship. Everything is subject to chance and loss. The world breaks peoples' hearts, spoils their happiness, afflicts their bodies, and ultimately destroys them. This tragic vision of life portrays the human condition as a cruel experience that finally conquers everyone. The tragic vision, however, only views the tempest as it occurs in act 1 and only records the cries of the seamen as they jump into the water thinking of death. It does not detect the mysterious, invisible presence of Prospero, who intervenes in the storm and prepares to save all from drowning. The tragic vision misses the whole story of the tempest, especially the miracle of good coming out of evil, joy out of sorrow, and life after death.

The Tempest, like each of Shakespeare's miracle plays or tragic-comedies, dwells on this theme of the lost being found and life arising out of death. For example, in *The Winter's Tale*, a child called a "bastard" by her father Leontes is abandoned by him "[t]o some remote and desert place" (2.3.176) to perish—a lost daughter who is found in the desert country by a shepherd who calls his discovery "fairy gold" and comments to his son, "Thou mettest with things dying, I with things newborn" (3.3.116–17). Having falsely accused his wife, Hermione, of adultery, Leontes imprisoned her, and after sixteen years believes her dead. After confessing his sin and admitting guilt for his false charges ("a saintlike sorrow"), Leontes beholds the statue of his (presumably) late wife—only to see Hermione breathe and move, no statue of stone but his living wife. Lost and found, life out of death, good out of evil—these providential events produce the most exquisite form of happiness as tears of joy flow in the wonder of experiencing a miracle. A witness to these events observes,

> Then have you lost a sight which was to be seen, cannot be spoken of. There might you have beheld one joy crown another, so and in such manner that it seemed sorrow wept to take leave of them, for their joy waded in tears. There was casting up of eyes, holding-up of hands, with countenance of such distraction that they were to be known by garment, not by favor. Our King, being ready to leap out of himself for joy of his found daughter, as if that joy were now become a loss, cries, 'Oh thy mother, thy mother!' then asks Bohemia forgiveness, then embraces his son-in-law. . . .
> . . . now he thanks the old shepherd. (5.2.46–59)

Leontes's cup of joy is overflowing, as he cannot sufficiently thank or appreciate his daughter, wife, son-in-law, and the shepherd. The fullness of his happiness cannot contain itself as the depths and heights of his elation express themselves in tears. This heavenly bliss transcends all human pleasures. It encompasses the joy of the heart, as father and daughter, husband and wife, reunite in the intimate bond of love. It touches the depths of the soul because Leontes's repentance and sorrow for sin have redeemed him. As one of the lords remarks, "At the last, / Do as the Heavens have done, forget your evil, / With them forgive yourself" (5.1.4–6). It delights his senses as he sees, hears, and embraces both his daughter and his wife in the body, for Hermione is not a mere statue but flesh and blood ("The very life seems

159

warm upon her lip"). It illuminates his mind with the sublime truth of the hand of Divine Providence, whose abundant goodness, mercy, love, and care have no limit. Leontes's complete joy and total happiness of heart, soul, body, and mind is the foretaste of the heavenly joy that Francis Thomas described in *The Hound of Heaven*:

> All which I took from thee I did but take,
> Not for thy harms,
> But just that thou might'st seek it in My arms.
> All which thy child's mistake
> Fancies as lost, I have stored for thee at home:
> Rise, clasp my hand, and come.[1]

Why does Prospero lose his governorship of Milan? Why must tempests occur? To lose or nearly lose something precious—one's life, child, or authority—is to value it more appreciatively and to cherish it more dearly as a divine gift. When blind, gullible, weak human beings—tempted by avarice, distracted by pleasure, and divorced from reality— neglect their primary duties and sacrifice the bonds of loving relationships for the sake of worldly things, God temporarily withdraws his gifts to return them later when they are esteemed with gratitude and embraced as the priceless treasures of divine love. Heaven and eternal joy consist in finding the treasure saved, collected, and preserved, never to be lost or wasted again.

---

1 Reprinted in *Flowers of Heaven: One Thousand Years of Christian Verse*, Ed., Joseph Pearce (San Francisco: Ignatius Press, 2005), p. 224.

XIII. Obedience:
The Gospel Account of the
Wedding at Cana

The miracles in the Bible portray God's profound generosity as evidence of his infinite love, which gives beyond limit and measure. Whether it is providing daily manna in the wilderness to the Israelites or instructing the disciples "to put out into the deep and cast your nets" (Luke 5:4, Revised Standard Version, Catholic Edition), God gives in copious amounts. Peter and the fishermen are astounded. Their boat is sinking because of the weight of their great catch, and the nets are bursting with 153 fish! "For he was astonished, and all that were with him, at the catch of fish which they had taken" (Luke 5:9). At the marriage feast in Cana, the Lord again provides with an abundance that amazes the guests, who marvel at both the profusion and the goodness of the wine: "Every man serves the good wine first; and when men have drunk freely, then the poor wine; but you have kept the good wine until now" (John 2:10). Jesus's mother intercedes for the wedding guests and petitions her son, "They have no wine," and then instructs the servants, "Do whatever He tells you" (John 2:3, 5). And she leaves the matter entirely in His hands. Christ, however, does not single-handedly perform the miracle without human participation and willing collaboration. Instead, he commands the servants, "Fill the jars with water" (John

2:7). He gives others a small part to play in this drama while He performs the great work of changing the water into the wine. Christ takes the ordinary matter of the water and transforms it into the extraordinary miracle of the wine. He uses the small deed of the servants, who fill six jars with water, and performs the mighty work of a miracle. In other words, Christ multiplies the goodness and blesses the actions of the servants, who behold their good intentions and honest efforts producing great wonder. As Christ promised in another setting, anyone who makes a great sacrifice—leaving families, houses, and lands for His sake and for the gospel—"receives one hundredfold now . . . and in the age to come eternal life" (Mark 10:31). God's generosity knows no bounds but requires the involvement of man in some minimal way.

Christ waited until his mother appealed to his power, and he depended upon the willingness of the servants to do their humble part in cooperating with his request. Christ's role, Mary's part, and the servants' efforts all unite to change the occasion from one of dearth to one of plenty. God gives abundantly, but He requires obedience ("Do whatever he tells you"), faith, and humility. Christ's miracle here is not creation ex nihilo but a miracle that requires matter—the intercession of Mary, the carrying of the water, and the willingness to obey and believe. Man must do his part and contribute a portion, some ingredient that God can use to spread goodness, produce abundance, and multiply the joy. Even though man performs a minor role and does a small service, his part is essential in this great drama of God's miracle. God's way is to have man share in his glorious work, whether it is Mary assenting to be the handmaid of the Lord, servants obeying their master, or disciples baptizing all nations in his name. God's great divine love for man responds to man's simple love for God.

This story summarizes the role of God's providence in human life. So often man has no wine and finds himself deficient. So often man is in dire need and lacks something essential in his life or for his complete happiness. The marriage at Cana teaches that Christ provides the missing element, the fullness of joy and the abundance of life that changes the plain to the beautiful, the ordinary water to "good wine," the meagerness of life to the joy of the feast. Two things move the heart of Christ to supply the extra wine—the request of his beloved mother whom he cannot refuse and the readiness of the servants to carry out his commands. The intercessor for the wedding guests makes all the difference because of the purity of her heart, and the docility of the servants offers no resistance to God's will. Christ asks little but does much. However, he does not do everything. Before man receives, he must ask; before man finds, he must seek; before God enters, man must open the door. God's nature is to increase the amount that man brings to him—as evidenced by the multiplication of the five loaves and two fish to feed the five thousand.

Man cannot come empty-handed. He must bring Christ something: a mite, a few fish, a loaf of bread, a jar of water; or a clean conscience, a pure heart, a good intention, a fervent prayer, contrite tears. The virtue of religion is to give God his due, whether it is praise, honor, worship, or sacrifice. Christ, then, receives these simple offerings and modest gifts and converts them into wonders. It is the nature of God to receive our sacrifices and then change them into blessings. In Augustine's *Confessions*, a priest reassured Monica that her passionate cries for the soul of her decadent son could not go unheard: "As you live, it is impossible that the son of these tears should perish."[1] Just as the sacraments require matter—water, bread, wine, oil—as the substance out of which are created "the masterworks of God," which bestow grace, so too Christ's miracles incorporate the acts, words, and tears that man brings to be touched and transformed by God's power. In a certain sense, nothing can come from nothing if man brings no offer of gifts or acts of love to God for his miraculous power to increase, beautify, and purify.

God's miracles also depend upon man's obedience and humility, his willingness to "[d]o whatever He tells you." If man does not uphold his marital vows, refuses to be fruitful and multiply, dishonors innocent life, neglects the Sabbath, the Commandments, or the Beatitudes, then God lacks the simple human ingredients needed for miracles. Although God, who created the world ex nihilo and for whom nothing is impossible, does not absolutely require man's offerings to produce miracles, he chooses to make man fulfill some obligations as proof of his faith and as acknowledgment of his dependence. Without God, man can do nothing. Yet, out of man's small gifts does Christ make something great. In the *Confessions*, Augustine, referring to Scripture, acknowledges God as one "Who art able to do above that which we ask or think" (183). With the daily prayers of Monica petitioning God for the soul of her son, the miracle of Augustine's conversion happened. According to Augustine, "But to you, fountain

---

1   *The Confessions of St. Augustine*, tr. Rex Warner (NAL Penguin: New York, 1963), 68.

of mercies, she poured out her prayers and her tears more copiously than before, begging you to hasten your help and lighten my darkness" (112). God answered Monica's daily prayers beyond her wildest dreams ("above that which we ask or think"), in recognition of which she utters her profound gratitude shortly before her death: "Now God has granted me this beyond my hopes" (202). Monica's deep love of God moves the Divine Heart to reward her prayers in extraordinary measure. As Augustine explains, "And so you changed her mourning into joy, a joy much richer than she had desired and purer than that which she looked for by having grandchildren of my flesh" (183).

God always asks man for some evidence of his love, some proof of his trust in Divine Providence, some movement in his direction. Mary's *fiat*, "let it be to me according to thy word" (Luke 1:38), gave proof of her love for the Lord. When Christ invited Peter and Andrew to "[f]ollow me, and I will make you fishers of men," they too embraced the invitation (Matthew 4:19). Christ healed the centurion's paralyzed servant because of the soldier's great faith: "Go; be it done for you as you have believed" (Matthew 8:13). When two blind men approached Jesus and pleaded, "Have mercy on us, Son of David," he answered their prayer only after he saw their profound belief: "Do you believe I am able to do this?" Their eyes were opened only after they said "Yes, Lord" (Matthew 9:28). When the prodigal son abandoned his wasteful life and returned to his father sorrowful and contrite, the welcome he received surpassed all his expectations. His remorseful words, "Father, I have sinned against heaven and before you; I am no longer worthy to be called your son; treat me as one of your hired servants," touched the father's merciful, kind heart, and he overwhelmed his son with his boundless generosity: "Bring quickly the best robe, and put it on him; and put a ring on his hand, and shoes on his feet; and bring the fatted calf and kill it, and let us eat and make merry" (Luke 15:22–23). Christ gladly proffers his boundless love and performs extraordinary wonders but only on the condition of man's participation in the good work.

Likewise, before feeding the crowds, Jesus asked the disciples for some indication of the food available: "How many loaves have you?" When they brought the seven loaves and few fish, Christ's generosity not only multiplied the meager portions to provide for the large number but also produced an overabundance: "And they all ate and were satisfied; and they took up seven baskets full of the broken pieces left over" (Matthew 14:20). In another situation when the disciples are worried ("We have no bread"), Christ recalls the two miracles of feeding that they already had witnessed: He multiplied five loaves for the five thousand with twelve baskets remaining and used seven loaves to feed the four thousand with seven baskets remaining (Mark 8: 14–21). The God of increase and plenty asks, "Do you not yet perceive or understand?" Christ offers the best wine, the most plentiful food, the greatest miracles, and priceless rewards at the cost of a loaf of bread, a jug of water, a simple deed, an act of faith, a contrite heart. He is willing to give all, the best, the most precious at the cost of a "yes" or a tear or a touch: "For she said, 'If I touch even the hem of his garment, I shall be made well' " (Mark 5:28). To inherit eternal life, the rich young man is advised to keep the Commandments, part with his wealth, give to the poor, "come, follow me," and then "have treasure in heaven" (Matthew 19:21). For a small price, Christ again offers eternal life to those who gave him food, drink, and clothing, welcoming them into "the kingdom prepared for you from the foundation of the world" (Matthew 25:34). They receive this great inheritance of a king for performing simple acts of charity to ordinary people: "Truly, I say to you, as you did it to one of the least of these my brethren, you did it to me" (Matthew 25:40).

The miracle at the wedding at Cana and the other miracles of Christ illustrate the nature of divine love that will not be outdone in generosity. Man gives a pittance but inherits a fortune. He invests a small sum or does honest work but earns riches beyond compare. He asks, believes, follows, and obeys only to receive a hundredfold. Like the multiplying of the wine at the wedding and the multiplying of the bread and the fish to feed the thousands, the Last Supper once more communicates the infinite treasury of divine love that changes the bread and wine into the Body and Blood of Christ in the greatest of miracles. In following Christ, in keeping his commandments, in believing him to be the messiah, the disciples—like the servants who brought the six pitchers of water—provide the bread and wine and receive the heavenly food of eternal life: "This is the bread which comes from heaven, that a man may eat of it and never die" (John 6:50). In this ultimate act of God's boundless generosity, He gives man the miracle of divine life and eternal joy.

While God works miracles to heal, to feed, and to resurrect the dead, He does not perform wonders to amaze the crowds, to satisfy the curious, or to impress Satan. When asked for a sign, Christ did not comply:

"An evil and adulterous generation seeks for a sign, but no sign shall be given to it except the sign of Jonah" (Matthew 16:4). Christ did not jump from the pinnacle of the Temple to prove He was the Son of God attended by the angels or change stones into bread to demonstrate his divine power. These temptations to resort to magic to astonish skeptics or to pander to the mob amount to sensationalism and trickery. They do not serve as spiritual or corporal works of mercy and hence would not teach anything about divine love, confidence in God, or faith in Christ's words. The signs that please the crowds represent spectacular displays and vainglory, but as Caryll Houselander writes in *The Passion of the Infant Christ*, God is not a public broadcaster:

> We imagine that God must show all that there is, flaunt it before our eyes like a banner to compel our conversion to Him. . . . But God does not approach us as a propagandist; He approaches us as a lover.[2]

Explaining further, Houselander notices how God does good in stealth and silence:

> He is as silent, as secret, and hidden, in the Host as He was in Advent or in the tomb.

> It has always been Christ's way to come first in secret, to come in a hidden way, to be secret even in those in whom He abides, whose life He is, to be known first by His love. . . .

---

2 *The Passion of the Infant Christ* (New York: Sheed & Ward, 1949), 32.

God approaches gently, often secretly, always in love, never through violence and fear. (27, 27, 46)

God's miracles, then, the proofs of God's mysterious love, come as revelations that evoke wonder. They approach without fanfare, advanced publicity, announcements, or advertising. They occur in the humble circumstances of ordinary life, whether people are fishing, eating, or at a wedding. In quiet awe these miracles speak powerfully and clearly a simple message: God reserves the riches of his miraculous powers for those who ask him, approach him, follow him, and believe in him. Christ is waiting to change the water into wine, but someone must intercede and say, "They have no wine." Christ is ready to feed the thousands, but someone must bring a few loaves and a handful of fish. Christ is willing to reward his followers a hundredfold, but they must first feed and clothe the least of their brethren. Christ desires the disciples to fill their nets, but they must first cast them in the place he chooses. Christ yearns to grant the rich young man eternal life, but the wealthy man must first detach himself from his wealth. God, like the father of the prodigal son, wants to regale his son with a sumptuous banquet, but the son must first seek forgiveness. Christ always heals the blind, the lame, the deaf, and the possessed, but they must first demonstrate "great faith." Christ offers sanctifying grace and divine life through the sacraments, but man must thirst for these heavenly gifts, as the woman at the well yearned for the living water (John 4:15; 7:37). In other words, miracles are the fruit of the mutual giving and receiving of love.

The signs and wonders that the crowds craved, however, lacked this reciprocity of love. The crowds wanted only to receive, not to give; they were disposed for diversion, not for gratitude. Like propaganda, the magic that Satan tempted Christ to perform in the wilderness appealed to fame and vainglory, not the humble desire to know the goodness of God's love. Christ did not change stones into bread when Satan proposed it, but converted water into wine when His Blessed Mother intervened. In the wilderness, there was no urgent need (Jesus was intentionally fasting) and no human desires, but at Cana the guests were thirsty, and the reciprocal love of mother and son inspired the miracle. Satan's intention was temptation, but the Blessed Mother's motive was love.

Thus, when God in his compassion sees hunger, thirst, need, or suffering, he reciprocates through miracles that manifest his infinite generosity, and out of an inexhaustible abundance gives increase to man's portion. When men heed the Virgin's words and "[d]o whatever he tells you," when they keep the Commandments, imitate Christ, pray, and have faith, there is no conceivable limit to God's love and its power of multiplication. "Do whatever he tells you" can mean any number of things; we may be called to fill jars with water, to cast nets in another part of the sea, to bring him five loaves, or to go and sin no more. It can also mean to keep holy the Sabbath, to confess sins, to forgive one another, to love one another as Christ loved us, to be fruitful and multiply, or to keep together what God has joined. This is the small price man pays for the miracles of God's fatherly love in all its fruitfulness: "What no eye has seen, nor ear heard, nor the heart of man conceived, what God has prepared for those who love him" (1 Corinthians 2:6).

XIV. Justice: *Macbeth*

Being human means, in part, being barraged with information. Each of us is inundated from childhood with words and voices, advice and purported wisdom, truth claims and claims to authority. To be human is to listen, sift through this multiplicity of views, and discern what is real. Some voices speak the words of truth that give light to the mind, while others spin illusions like the music of the Sirens, which leads men to their destruction in the *Odyssey*. Sometimes we hear the simple truth in all its eloquence, while at others we are subject to flattery, pandering, and equivocation. To live well is to know the truth and to surrender to it, rather than to fudge the facts to serve some selfish purpose. But that is the very moral struggle that determines the outcome of each human life—the conflict between hard truth and comforting falsehoods. It is this clash that sets in motion the drama of one our greatest plays in English, Shakespeare's *Macbeth*.

The protagonist, Macbeth, is torn between the voice of his conscience and the lurid promises of the "weird sisters," or witches. What they offer is magic, a shortcut to one's ambitions that spurns honest effort, violates nature, and flouts the moral law. In other words, they offer the very modern, utilitarian argument that the end justifies the means.

As the three witches enter in the first scene, they utter the famous words that inform the whole moral conflict of the play: "Fair is foul, and foul is fair" (1.1.11). They recall the famous words of Satan in *Paradise Lost:* "Evil, be thou my good." That is, right is wrong and wrong is right; man is woman and woman is man; human beings are animals and animals are human beings. Reality, moral law, and human nature do not possess a fixed, determined, God-given nature. The witches do not acknowledge the nature of things and hence do not respect the nature of any thing in particular—be it man, woman, the soul, or the natural law. They pretend that they can reverse the normal meanings of words, eliminate the natural distinctions that form the basis of truth and reality, and invent a new morality. As the devils and witches speak in riddles and obfuscate moral truth by blurring the natural categories that distinguish right and wrong, they create the moral chaos that damns the souls of both Macbeth and Lady Macbeth. As the witches use words in an equivocal sense and redefine the meanings of things, they lead Macbeth into fantasy as he imagines that fate has decreed "Hail, king that shalt be" (1.5.10). As the witches speak in half-truths—"none of woman born / Shall harm Macbeth" (4.1.80–81)—they confound the human mind with hidden knowledge ("Seek to know no more"). In *Macbeth* the witches—like the Father of Lies—embody the voices of temptations that seduce, deceive, and confuse with the most artful manipulation of language.

Whether it is the magic of alchemy, astrology, or witchcraft, the psychology of temptation remains the same. The devilish arts make flattering promises or grandiose predictions that belie the truth. The witches offer instant gratification, something for nothing, gain without work—raping fortune to gain kingship or usurping power instead of earning it or humbly submitting to it. The voices of temptation tell Macbeth what he will gain if he murders Duncan but never hint at what he will lose ("Methought I heard a voice cry 'Sleep no more' " (2.2.34). Thus, while alchemy promises immediate wealth through the magic of the elixir, and astrology offers godlike knowledge of the future, the witches seduce Macbeth with the riddles and half-truths that delude him with the greatness of kingly power and an infallible knowledge of his fate. Evil speaks a certain tongue and expresses itself in the gibberish of the witches that circumvents the truth, twists the structure of reality, and darkens the mind. As Macbeth discovers too late, the witches' words have tortured his mind and ruined his life: "And be these juggling fiends no more believ'd, / That palter with us in a double sense, / That keep the word of promise to our ear, / And break it to our hope" (5.8.19–22). Shakespeare illustrates in *Macbeth* the cunning of evil in the use of flattery and charming words to pander to a person's base desires and validate his sins. Without the words of the witches' greeting to Macbeth on the heath, their repeated prophecies of his greatness, and their constant reminders of his charmed fate, Macbeth would have escaped his tragic fall from high to low.

The witches not only fill Macbeth's ear with suggestions but also devise opportunities for thoughts to become actions. As the witches reassure him that fate decrees him King of Scotland, he and Lady Macbeth soon find the ideal situation to execute their plans and arguments to rationalize their sins. Fate in the form of the weird sisters has decreed their destiny of greatness. King Duncan's visit has presented the perfect moment for the fulfillment of their ambitions of power—a moment that may never recur. Greatness befalls those who seize the moment and rape fortune, as Machiavelli advised in *The Prince*; glory rewards those who "catch the nearest way," as Lady Macbeth remarks. However, in the drama of good and evil at the moment of temptation, other voices speak to the mind. Macbeth hears the voice of conscience written on his heart and in his mind. As he considers murdering Duncan during his visit to Macbeth's castle, the natural moral law speaks the simple truth: Duncan is a king who deserves the service of his subjects, a guest in Macbeth's castle entitled to the hospitality of a visitor and a kinsman to be honored by the obligations of family. Macbeth changes his mind: "We will proceed no further in this business" (1.7.31). Macbeth struggles to resist the voices of temptation: "Let not light see my black and deep desires" (1.4.51). He ponders the effects of the deed and fears the punishment for murder: "If the assassination / Could trammel up the consequence, and catch / With his surcease success, that but this blow /Might be the be-all and end-all here" (1.7.1–5). However, even though the witches whisper evil thoughts and arrange attractive opportunities, Macbeth's consent or refusal determines the outcome.

While Macbeth deliberates, Lady Macbeth overcomes Macbeth's scruples of conscience by insulting his manliness: "Art thou afeard / To be the same in thine own act and valor / As thou art in desire?" (1.7.39–41). While the weird sisters flatter Macbeth's ambition for greatness, Lady Macbeth ridicules his lack of boldness:

"When you durst do it, then you were a man" (1.7.49). She asserts her own fierce audacity in her renunciation of femininity and motherhood to achieve her lust for power, boasting "unsex me here, / And fill me from the crown to the toe top-full / Of direst cruelty" (1.5.42–44). Thus as Macbeth and Lady Macbeth consider the prophecy of the witches, the commission of murder, and their own aspirations for greatness, they allow the outside voices to dictate their actions. Macbeth's inner voice of conscience is shouted down by the seductive allurements of the witches and the insistent urgings of his wife, who never questions the morality of her deeds, or their consequences: "We fail? / But screw your courage to the sticking place, / And we'll not fail" (1.7.59–61). The suggestions of the weird sisters, the fortuitous occasion of Duncan's visit to Macbeth's castle, and now the consent of Macbeth and Lady Macbeth to the murder illustrate the psychology of temptation in all its subtlety—as the multiple voices of the three witches and Lady Macbeth reiterate their message and wear down Macbeth's resistance.

Black magic, another name for the lure of temptation, promises Macbeth instant gratification: the crown of Scotland awaits the great soldier at the cost of one bloody deed. The weird sisters, like other devils such as Mephistopheles in Christopher Marlowe's *Dr. Faustus*, offer something for nothing, reward without toil. Macbeth at last accedes and wantonly seizes the kingship. What is worse, the witches equivocate— foretelling only what Macbeth will *gain* by way of worldly power but never hinting what he will lose in terms of sleep, peace, sanity, happiness, and at last his soul. This is the dark, hidden knowledge of the witches that escapes man's mind.

The witches' riddle that *fair is foul and foul is fair* denies the nature of things; Macbeth acts as if he does not own a moral nature with a conscience; Lady Macbeth pretends that she can violate her maternal, womanly nature. But the tragedy of *Macbeth* exposes all the lies of the witches and all the self-deception of the usurpers. Foul is not fair, as both husband and wife quickly discover— Macbeth recoiling in shock after committing the murder and looking at his bloody hands ("This is a sorry sight") and troubled by his conscience ("But wherefore could I not say 'Amen'?"). Just as every cut or wound produces blood, every evil deed bleeds guilt. Man's moral nature obeys natural and divine law just as his body follows physical laws. Man's nature is mortal and fallible. He is not an omniscient, omnipotent god, as Macbeth learns when the forest "moves" despite the prophecy that "Macbeth shall never vanquish'd be until / Great Birnam wood to high Dunsinane hill / Shall come against him" (4.1.92–94). Despite the witches' promise that "none of woman born" can defeat Macbeth, he learns too late that Macduff was "untimely ripped" from his mother's womb by Caesarean section. Although the weird sisters deny the nature of things, Macbeth's tragedy illustrates the hard facts that form the basis of reality. Man is weak and fallible, not almighty or omniscient. Man by nature is moral and human, not a cruel beast who can kill without feeling guilt. A woman is not a man, and she cannot eradicate her nature by pretending that acts of violence do not affect her mind, body, and soul, or by boasting, as does Lady Macbeth, that she could tear an infant from her breast and kill him: "And dashed the brains out, had I sworn as you / Have done to this" (1.7.58).

Because Macbeth and Lady Macbeth ignore their human and moral nature and believe the lie that morality is malleable, they suffer all the consequences of violating the moral law. Nature will out, and guilt always follows sin. Macbeth suffers shock and trauma at the horrific nature of his act and cannot return the daggers to the chamber or blame the groomsmen: "I am afraid to think what I have done; / Look on't again I dare not" (2.2.51–52). The horrific crime Macbeth has committed tortures his mind with images of blood that symbolize the weight of his guilt: "Will all great Neptune's ocean wash this blood / Clean from my hand?" (2.2.60–61). After he murders Banquo to protect his kingship and avert the prophecy of Banquo's sons dethroning him, Macbeth suffers nightmares and is haunted by Banquo's ghost. Lady Macbeth also feels the consequences of her crimes as she begins sleepwalking in the night, a symptom the doctor calls a "great perturbation in nature, to receive at once the benefit of sleep, and do the effects of watching!" (5.1.10–11). She compulsively washes her hands, crying, "Out, damned spot!" and "What, will these hands ne'er be clean?" (5.1.39; 48). The images of blood, the nightmares of ghosts, and the obsession with the washing of hands all reveal the effects of guilt and the need for contrition, confession, and absolution. Macbeth's nature cannot be changed from that of a moral human being to that of a savage beast. Lady Macbeth's feminine nature cannot be reforged as masculine. Two persons with consciences cannot be denatured and acquire the qualities of wild animals. The violation of one's human, moral, or sexual nature, then, cries out for vengeance and produces tragic suffering, reducing human life to "a tale / Told by an idiot, full of sound and fury, signifying nothing" (5.5.26–28).

Thanks to the artful lies of the weird sisters, Macbeth and Lady Macbeth imagine that the soul does not inform the body or control the passions with the power of reason. Husband and wife try to act as if man were a creature of instincts and urges ruled by an uncontrollable will, a state of mind and body for which the Renaissance English developed a term: "madness." In its original meaning, it referred to the infinite, insatiable desire that knows no bounds or any sense of temperance. Whether it is Dr. Faustus's unlimited desire for knowledge in Marlowe's play, Volpone's unbridled avarice for inexhaustible wealth in Ben Jonson's play of that name, Satan's excessive love of glory in Milton's *Paradise Lost*, or Macbeth's vaulting ambition, the uncontrollable will subordinates reason and disobeys conscience. "Reason panders will," as Shakespeare wrote in *Hamlet*, reason functioning only as the slave of the will and justifying all its choices by making the weaker argument the stronger. Where madness rules, the soul disappears. Neither right reason, the voice of conscience, nor the cardinal virtue of prudence controls this voracious appetite—which rages as if man were merely a body without a soul, not a rational animal capable of moderation, self-control, and the conquest of temptations. It is, in Banquo's words, "the insane root / That takes the reason prisoner" (1.2.84–85).

Another dangerous delusion is to conflate the body with the soul, or to pretend that one or the other does not exist. To their pain, Macbeth and Lady Macbeth learn that the soul has a separate spiritual nature that distinguishes it from the body. No matter how much the Macbeths in their willfulness scorn or twist the truth of the moral law, the soul discerns the truth with irrefutable clarity. When Macbeth utters, "Naught's had, all's spent" (3.2.4), he learns the honest truth about the witches' sophistry. His murders have gained him nothing but guilt and self-loathing. When Macbeth summarizes all life as "a tale told by an idiot, full of sound and fury, signifying nothing," he is really just describing his own existence and what he has made of it. Evil is not as glamorous or as adventurous as he and his wife imagined, but rather is as loathsome as its advocates, the weird sisters. The soul sees that one cannot do evil to achieve good, because evil by its very nature is destructive and corrupting. The soul knows that only repentance—not, as Lady Macbeth had said, a "little water"—can overcome guilt. When Macbeth cannot sleep, when he suffers nightmares or the torment of guilt, and when Lady Macbeth is afflicted with sleepwalking, these are the sufferings of the soul that the couple had dismissed as empty considerations. As the doctor explains, Lady Macbeth's condition is spiritual, not physical: "This disease is beyond my practice."

While Macbeth and his wife yield to the temptations of the witches and lose their souls, Banquo is not deceived by the wiles of the weird sisters. He is not "rapt" like Macbeth at the thought of kingship but suspects the false promises of the witches, calling them "bubbles." Banquo detects the cunning nature of evil, asking, "What can the devil speak true?" His wisdom recognizes the artfulness of temptation: "The instruments of Darkness tell us truths, / Win us to honest trifles, to betray's / In deepest consequence" (1.3.124–26). Banquo weaves no elaborate

Machiavellian plots or imagines that man must rape fortune to achieve his ambition. Unlike Macbeth, he does not welcome the insinuating suggestions of the witches or fantasize about dreams of power, and he never rationalizes that a moment of temptation is a decree of fate that will determine his destiny. Although the witches prophesy that Banquo's sons will be kings, he does not plunge into impetuous action to force his will upon circumstances. A man of integrity and incorruptible morals, Banquo senses the truth about Macbeth's plot to murder the king: "Thou hast it now—King, Glamis, Cawdor, all . . . and I fear, / Thou play'dst most foully for it" (3.1.1–3). This contrast between Macbeth's and Banquo's reactions to the witches illuminates the moral drama of the play. While Macbeth entertains the suggestions of the weird sisters and seeks them out several times to reassure himself of the kingship and his invincibility, Banquo doubts their words and dissociates himself completely from these dark powers. While Macbeth lets the witches tantalize him, Banquo rebuffs them. Banquo exemplifies man's power to resist temptation and subordinate passions to reason. His ears, unlike Macbeth's, which itched for what he wanted to hear, attend to the voice of conscience.

Thus, man's moral choices depend on recognition of self-evident metaphysical truths designed to give light to the mind. Man is a rational animal, not a fox with all its cunning or a lion with its brute strength. Man possesses a human nature endowed with moral knowledge, the natural law written on the mind and heart—not a godlike omniscience or infallibility. All sin produces guilt, troubles the conscience, and requires acknowledgment—not denial or rationalization. If the natural outlets of confession and contrition are suppressed, then guilt expresses itself in the unnatural forms of nightmares, sleepwalking, and sleeplessness. Because happiness follows from acting according to one's nature, human beings who renounce their moral nature suffer the consequences of inexorable natural laws. Nature will win. Truth will out. Either man respects his nature and lives a human life, or he abuses and debases his nature and suffers tragedy. Either man conforms his life to the truth and stops his ears against temptation, or he changes the truth and reinvents the meaning of good and evil to serve his own desires. The tragedy of Macbeth proves that man can no more invent a new morality than a new law of gravity.

Those who preach, teach, or counsel, then, are called to be a voice that exposes seductive words confounding good with evil. The blandishments that suppress the truth and tantalize with the lure of money, power, and pleasure must be opposed. The sophistry that states that the end justifies the means requires a Socrates to oppose it. It is the role of the parent, the pastor, the teacher, to proclaim the unchanging truths of moral laws in season and out of season, so that the Sirens' songs, witches' voices, and the tranquillizing propaganda of ruthless, modern pragmatism do not lead the soul into misery. Begin by asserting that "foul is fair," and you really will end with a life that signifies nothing.

XV. Gratitude:
The Rule of St. Benedict

Most of us know there is a theology of the word, which centers on understanding the Bible. Some have even learned about the theology of the body, laid out most fully by Pope John Paul II. Too few know that there is also a theology of food. The Bible's revelation illuminates the reality, mystery, and nature of God; the human body declares the glory of God's handiwork in its design for work, love, marriage, and children; and the goodness, abundance, and variety of food depict Divine Providence and God's copious generosity. Just as the Jesuit poet Gerard Manley Hopkins marvels at the loveliness and azure color of the bluebell ("I know the beauty of the Lord by it"), one can "taste and see the sweetness of the Lord" through an appreciation and gratitude for the gift of food. In Hawthorne's story "The Golden Touch," King Midas rediscovers the preciousness of food after his fatal gift changed trout, pancakes, eggs, and potatoes into solid metal. The heavy food, worth its weight in gold—"the richest breakfast that could be set before a king"—could not compare with the daily fare of "The poorest laborer, sitting down to his crust of bread and cup of water."[1] In Hawthorne's "The Miraculous Pitcher," Baucis and Philemon, practicing old-world

---

1   Nathaniel Hawthorne, *A Wonder-Book* (New York: Knopf, 1994), 85.

hospitality, serve their guests (Greek gods disguised as shabby vagabonds) the ordinary fare of bread, cheese, milk, honey, and grapes—a meal that reminds the visitors of heavenly food: "An honest, hearty welcome to a guest works miracles with the fare, and is capable of turning the coarsest food to nectar and ambrosia" (198). The taste, fragrance, color, abundance, variety, and nourishment of food testify to the profuse generosity of the God who provided manna in the wilderness, multiplied the loaves and the fishes, changed the water into the wine at Cana, and led the disciples to cast their nets until they were bursting.

George Herbert's poem "Providence" honors God's bountiful provision of food for all living creatures:
Thy cupboard serves the world: the meat is set,
Where all may reach: no beast but knows his feed.
Birds teach us hawking, fishes have their net:
The great prey on the less, they on some weed.[2]

As mentioned previously, in George MacDonald's *At the Back of the North Wind* the child Diamond also notices God's cupboard, which nourishes all creation. Even though hunger continues to ravage nations, agronomists agree that man has the resources to feed every mouth on earth—had we the political will and skills to distribute nutrition fairly.

God has not stinted us; it is we who fail each other.

---

2   *The Oxford Authors: George Herbert and Henry Vaughn*, ed. Louis Martz (New York: Oxford University Press, 1986), 105.

In Izaak Walton's *The Compleat Angler*, a falconer, hunter, and fisherman praise their favorite recreations, each marveling at the plenty of God's creations in the air, on land, and in the water. The falconer remarks, "Nay, more, the very birds of the air (those that be not Hawks) are both so many and so useful and pleasant to mankind, that I must not let them pass without observation: They both feed and refresh him; feed him with their choice bodies, and refresh him with their heavenly voices." The hunter then sings the praises of Mother Earth: "The earth feeds man, and all those several beasts that both feed him and afford him recreation." Praising the fruitful vine and the earth as a "bountiful mother," he marvels, "How doth the earth bring forth herbs, flowers, and fruits, both for physick and the pleasure of mankind?" The fisherman then further develops this theme of Mother Nature's abundance and God's plenty: "The Water is more productive than the Earth. . . . Nay, the increase of those creatures that are bred and fed in the water, are not only more and more miraculous, but more advantagious to man, not only for lengthening of his life, but fore the preventing of sicknesse."[3] All these examples from literature reveal the hand of God's Divine Providence and the goodness of the Lord when contemplating the fullness of His bounty, which David praised in Psalm 104:14–15:

Thou dost cause the grass to grow for the cattle, and plants for man to cultivate, that he may bring forth food from the earth, and wine to gladden the

3   Izaak Walton and Charles Cotton, *The Compleat Angler* (New York: Oxford University Press, 1982), 2, 28, 28, 34–35.

heart of man, oil to make his face shine, and bread to strengthen man's heart.

These generous, precious, life-giving gifts testify to God's overflowing will to give.

The theology of food not only acknowledges God's bountiful gifts of the abundant harvest but also illuminates His creation of infinite variety. In the course of a day, one savors the breakfast food of eggs, cereals, fruits, and breads, the luncheons of delicious salads and savory sandwiches, and the dinners consisting of sumptuous meats, flavored multigrained rices, and hearty potatoes. In the course of a year, perhaps one tastes Italian, Mexican, Middle Eastern, and various Asian cuisines. In the course of a lifetime, one can learn new recipes from the traditional dishes of countries from all over the world and constantly add to one's repertoire. In *The Idea of a University*, Newman cites the experience of a traveler going abroad into a foreign country and a student beholding the heavens through a microscope in awe, encountering the glorious variety of the world's largeness: "It brings a flood of ideas, and is rightly called an intellectual enlargement, whatever is meant by that term."[4] According to Newman, when a student explores the worlds of plant life and animal life, examines the breadth and scope of human history, and studies the entire range of philosophical and religious ideas, again he experiences a mental expansion and intoxication, a sense of wonder that follows this enlargement of mind in its

---

4   John Henry Newman, *The Uses of Knowledge* (Wheeling, IL: Harlan Davidson, 1948), 35.

discovery of the multiplicity and richness of reality. The world of food in its infinite variety also offers this sense of "true enlargement of mind" that leads to the existence of God. Hopkins reveled in the "pied beauty" of the world ("Glory be to God for dappled things") as it manifested God's love of art, color, and radiance—a pied beauty he also detected in the whole spectrum of tastes and flavors ("sweet, sour") in his reference to "[a]ll things counter, original, spare, strange." Marveling at "all this throng and stack of being, so rich, so distinctive," Hopkins in "Comments on the Spiritual Exercises of Saint Ignatius Loyola" compares each person's unique, original, and unrepeatable nature to the taste of food:

> [W]hen I consider my selfbeing, my consciousness and feeling of myself, of *I* and *me* above and in all things, which is more distinctive than the taste of ale or alum, more distinctive than the smell of walnutleaf or camphor . . . [n]othing else in nature comes near this unspeakable stress of pitch, distinctiveness, and selving, this selfbeing of my own.[5]

God's art of creation and nature's fruitfulness produce original masterpieces and extraordinary works that cannot be duplicated. This diversity of foods, the multiplicity of seasonings and spices, the unique tastes of ethnic foods, and the myriad of recipes from various cultures all express the mind of the Creator, who is the origin of both the one and the many.

---

5   Gerard Manley Hopkins, *The Major Works* (New York: Oxford University Press, 2002), 281.

The theology of food also teaches the virtue of hospitality and the charity of sharing the blessings of food, drink, and company with others. *Hospis venit, Christus venit* (A guest comes, Christ comes). As in the Benedictine tradition, all guests are to be received as if they were Christ. Feasts, banquets, and social occasions cultivate the joy of spreading happiness through a common meal that welcomes family and friends to partake of God's bounty and to enjoy celebrations that honor guests with courtesy and graciousness. In other words, the practice of hospitality instills a sense of appreciation for one another, confers dignity to both host and guest, and civilizes us. We learn to dress with propriety, to act with manners, and to converse with affability. Homer's *Odyssey* especially illustrates the humanizing function of hospitality as hosts provide for all the primary needs of the weary traveler. Bathed and anointed to feel refreshed in body, clothed in fresh garments to feel renewed in spirit, and served savory food to feel nourished in heart and soul, the traveler is reminded of what it means to "live well" rather than merely survive. Regaled with storytelling, music, and dance, the guest rediscovers that man works in order to play, enjoy the fruits of leisure, and appreciate the true, the beautiful, and the good. Invited to participate in the athletic events, Odysseus knows again the joy of participation in sports and the sheer pleasure of enjoyment for its own sake. All these refinements that the guest receives from the hospitable host, from "the feast, the lyre, the dance, clean linen in plenty, a hot bath, and our beds" to storytelling, sports, music, and dance, uplift the traveler's mind to a state of contemplation and wonder at the sweetness of life. Odysseus remarks, "I myself feel that there is nothing more delightful than when the festive mood reigns in a whole people's hearts and the banqueters listen to a minstrel from their seats in the hall, while the tables before them are laden with bread and meat, and a steward carries round the wine he has drawn from the bowl and fills their cups. This, to my way of thinking, is something very like perfection."[6] These rituals of hospitality, then, unite human beings in the common bond of their humanity and prefigure a vision of heavenly bliss in which each person's happiness increases the other's—the picture of Heaven in Dante's *Paradiso*.

This theology of food portrays the pleasure of eating as an occasion for friendship, conviviality, conversation, and brotherhood. In *The Compleat Angler*, a falconer, a hunter, and a fisherman explain their enthusiasm for their favorite recreation and exchange ideas and learn from one another. The delightful anticipation of the thrilling adventure of fishing is followed by the excitement of the catch. The great good fortune of the fishermen abounding with plentiful trout is followed by the pleasure of cooking and tasting their game and sharing it with others as they relax at an inn: "God speed you, good woman, I have been a-Fishing, and . . . having caught more Fish than will sup my self and my friend, I will bestow this upon you and your daughter, for I use to sell none" (80). Their day of fishing, recreation, and feasting ends on a note of mirthful songs that cheer the heart. The fisherman (Piscator) revels from the beginning to the

---

6 *The Odyssey*, tr. E.V. Rieu (New York: Penguin Books, 1985), 128, 139.

end of the day, his heart filled with the three parts of joy: the anticipation of the pleasure, the thrill of the sport, and the fond memories that follow. In this experience, then, of finding food by way of sport, preparing food by way of the art of cooking, and sharing food by way of friendship and hospitality, a person revels in the purest and most innocent of pleasures: "Welcome pure thoughts, welcome ye silent Groves, / These guests, these courts my soul most dearly loves." Piscator explains the laws that govern the ancient tradition of angling, namely, a rule of peace: fishermen are "fitted for contemplation and quietnesse; men of mild, and sweet, and peaceable spirits, as indeed most Anglers are" (227). This innocent pleasure of enjoying good food and cheer with friendly company in the practice of the golden rule is the purest of joys.

The theology of the word teaches God's love, justice, and mercy; the theology of the body illuminates the gift of self and the meaning of self-donation; so the theology of food instills many civilized virtues and Christian ideals. The Greek gods in "The Miraculous Pitcher" explain that the virtue of hospitality is a self-evident precept of the natural law that binds all men: "When men do not feel towards the humblest stranger as if he were a brother . . . they are unworthy to exist on earth, which was created as the abode of a great human brotherhood" (208). In the *Odyssey*, Menelaus reminds his servant of the moral obligation of all men to welcome weary travelers with kind hospitality: "Think of all the hospitality that you and I enjoyed from strangers before we reached our homes. . . . Unyoke their horses at once, and bring our visitors into the house to join us at the feast" (65).

The theology of food cultivates the virtues of kindness, gratitude, and charity and teaches that it is more blessed to give than to receive. It develops an awareness of the solidarity of the human race, a sense of the universal brotherhood and sisterhood of the human family, or an understanding of the members of the body of Christ. Chapter 53 of the Rule of St. Benedict enjoins the Christian obligation of hospitality: "All guests who present themselves are to be welcomed as Christ, for he himself will say: I was a stranger and you welcomed me" (Matthew 25:35).[7] In the sharing of a meal and the socializing between hosts and guests, everyone values the bonds of friendship, love, and family relationships, which unite people and provide a sense of belonging. While hosts practice liberality and guests show thankfulness, everyone is obligated to eat with manners, converse with congeniality, and take an interest in others, as the virtues of civility and courtesy create a tone that refines and elevates life. One learns in these occasions of hospitality and graciousness the distinction between living and living *well*—as the ancient Greeks taught—and also discerns the difference between living a meager life and a full, abundant life as Christ promised. The theology of food offers lessons in the primary purposes of life—sharing and spreading happiness, the giving and receiving of love, the inheriting and passing down of customs, traditions, and wisdom. While the host gives without expecting to receive, the guest in his gratitude feels the obligation to reciprocate. Menelaus reminded

---

7   *The Rule of Saint Benedict* (Collegeville, MN: The Liturgical Press, 1982), 73.

his servant of all the hospitality they had received, great gifts that they in turn were to transmit. While Baucis and Philemon give a hearty welcome to their visitors and offer all their provisions to accommodate their guests, the Greek gods are deeply touched by the pure hearts of the elderly couple and reward them with the miraculous pitcher that overflows with a continual supply of milk.

Thus, the eating of the meal creates an occasion to give thanks to God for the gifts of food and drink, moves the heart to welcome the stranger, delights in the simple pleasure of enjoying company and continuing friendship, and glimpses a hint of heaven, "something like perfection." It opens the mind to the law of love: to give with generosity, to receive with gratitude, to share the blessings of life, to spread joy and mirth.

The mind's road to God presents many paths. While the theology of the word glorifies God and His miracles, and the theology of the body declares His greatness ("For thou didst form my inward parts, thou didst knit me together in my mother's womb," Psalm 139), the theology of food also leads to the grandeur of God. While St. Thomas Aquinas logically demonstrates the five traditional proofs for the existence of God, the theology of food also declares His mind and heart. How can one eat three meals a day and not give thanks to God for this precious gift, which King Midas said is worth all the gold in the world? Tasting homemade bread, smelling apple pie in the oven, relishing the savor of coffee, finishing off a turkey dinner—any one of these can lead one to exclaim, "Taste and see the sweetness of the Lord." How can one enjoy all the tastes, flavors, smells, seasonings, spices, and combinations of foods from the cuisines of all the nations and not marvel at the wonderful variety and richness of God's plenty, a world of food that appears as infinite as the stars, plants, and animals that evoked the sense of "true enlargement of mind" that Newman identified with the discovery of God? One must be moved by the inexhaustible generosity of kind hosts and hospitable people and wonder at the infinite source of God's goodness that fills the human heart with its inexhaustible supply of love that keeps overflowing like the miraculous pitcher of Baucis and Philemon. At the table, peace, joy, gratitude, and laughter accompany friendship, play, conversation, and courtesy. All this points us to wonder and to the God who said, "And it was good." Think back on your most treasured meals, and you will know God—the generous Father who gave manna in the wilderness, the bountiful host who multiplied the fish and the loaves, the generous Lord who fed the four thousand and the five thousand, the miracle worker who changed water into wine and bread and wine into his own Body and Blood. The enjoyment of good food, an appreciation for the entire gamut of tastes and aromas, and the rejuvenation of body, heart, and soul that accompany good cooking and cheerful company naturally lead the mind to the contemplation of a Divine Providence reassuring man, "Therefore do not be anxious, saying, 'What shall we eat?' or 'What shall we drink?' or 'What shall we wear?' For the Gentiles seek all these things; and your heavenly father knows that you need them all."

XVI. Wisdom:
Samuel Johnson's *Rasselas*

We often bewail the decline of education, but in fact our society does a ruthlessly thorough job of teaching us certain things. It trains us to be hedonist consumers, to equate happiness with acquisition, fashion, and pleasure. It schools us to a bland and meaningless tolerance under the rainbow banner of "diversity." It forms us into citizens who jealously guard our own rights and maximize our own choices. If we keep to our lessons, we will indeed measure ourselves by how much wealth we collect, or how much prestige and power we can attain.

Amid this welter of passions and opinions, a universal truth about human happiness is forgotten. We can rediscover it in the work of Samuel Johnson. Imlac, the poet and sage in Johnson's short novel *Rasselas*, states, "[W]e grow more happy as our minds take a wider range."[1] He explains, "I am less unhappy than the rest, because I have a mind replete with images, which I can vary and combine at pleasure" (30). In other words, happiness is a particular state of mind, independent of one's material conditions or status in the eyes of others. A mind that takes "a wider range" transcends the narrowness of specialization, pedantry, and small-mindedness, and

---

1   *The History of Rasselas, Prince of Abyssinia*, ed. Gwin J. Kolb (Arlington Heights, ILL: AHM Publishing, 1962), 27.

a mind "replete with images" incorporates knowledge from many sources: experience and travel, books and learning, and encounters and conversations with people from all walks of life. Preoccupation with money, achievement, honors, or diversions does not expand the mind to a "wider range" or sense of the universal. The safe, "diverse" assumption that ultimate truths are relative (depending on "what works for you") discretely rules out as impossible an enduring, perennial wisdom. A mind that takes "a wider range" also transcends the bias of what C. S. Lewis termed "chronological snobbery"— the fashionable opinions and ideologies of the moment, which will vanish with next year's hemline.

In Johnson's tale, Rasselas, the prince of Abissinia, lives in a "happy valley" that appears to be a utopia. Physical comfort, pleasure, and luxury surround him:

> Every desire was immediately granted. All the artificers of pleasure were called to gladden the festivity; the musicians exerted the power of harmony, and the dancers showed their activity before the princes, in the hope that they should pass their lives in this blissful activity, to which only those were admitted whose performance was thought able to add novelty to luxury. (3)

Yet the prince is restless, melancholy, and bored in this narrow, confined world of the happy valley: "But, possessing all that I can want, I find one hour exactly like another, except that the latter is still more tedious than the former" (7). His mind enjoys neither a wide range nor a variety of images. Unoccupied and passive,

Rasselas lacks a goal and purpose. Having nothing to look forward to and needing "something to pursue," he cries out, "[G]ive me something to desire" (7). A healthy state of mind, then, that increases human happiness requires an enlarged view of the whole of reality; variety, contrast, and change to engage the mind and provide it with a new supply of images; and the anticipation of fulfilling some important goal. In the repetitious life of the happy valley, Rasselas's mind is jaded with the same stale images. Confined to a vale surrounded by vast imprisoning mountains, Rasselas does not participate in the wider world of the mainstream of life. Idling, the prince strives for nothing. This state of mind produces flights of fancy, what Johnson calls "the dangerous prevalence of imagination"—the fantasy that perfect happiness lies somewhere beyond the mountains, that an escape from the happy valley means heroic adventures and the triumph over evil.

A mind devoid of a plentiful variety of images lacks the raw material of thought, for nothing can come from nothing. Because humans spend much time in their own company and cannot always be diverted by pleasure, excitement, novelty, and adventure, a mind "replete with images" provides substance for reflection and contemplation. It allows for an interior life. Johnson writes, "But pleasures never can be so multiplied or continued, as not to leave much of life unemployed; there were many hours, both of the day and night, which he could spend without suspicion in solitary thought" (8). The antidote, then, to this solitary condition is an intellectual life furnished by the wardrobe of ideas that fills the vacuum of the mind. A mind replete with images consists of memories, ideas, and deposits from the multiple sources of knowledge that have left indelible impressions on the intellect. Imlac's own background encompasses broad travel from Persia to Syria, the experience of a merchant, sailor, and poet, and a life both in and out of the happy valley. From his pursuit of poetry, Imlac concluded that "he who knows most, will have most power of diversifying his scenes" (23–24). Ignorance, on the other hand, is the condition of an empty mind lacking the necessary images for a stimulating life of the mind. As Imlac remarks to Rasselas, "[I]gnorance is mere privation, by which nothing can be produced: it is a vacuity in which the soul sits motionless and torpid for want of attraction" (27).

Once Rasselas leaves the happy valley, he acquires a liberal education that counteracts the privation of ignorance and fills the void of an empty mind. Like Imlac, he acquires images from a variety of sources—from conversations with learned men such as philosophers and with simple laborers like the shepherds, from an exploration of the public life and high stations of powerful rulers to the humble circles of domestic life, and from studying all the various theories of happiness, from the Epicurean to the Stoic to the pastoral life. This multiplicity and variety of images from books, experience, travel, and conversation that Rasselas acquires in his journey outside the happy valley transform his whole state of mind. The boredom, restlessness, idleness, and melancholy vanish because Rasselas pursues a balanced life that alternates between activity and reflection, between social life and private life, and between familiarity and novelty. The enlargement of Rasselas's mind enhances his happiness, and the new images that fill the vacuity of his intellect overcome the emptiness of solitude in which the mind is prone to fantasize. Because nature abhors a vacuum, a mind that is not replete with images is soon overmastered by a disorderly imagination that recklessly daydreams: "The mind dances from scene to scene, unites pleasures in all combinations, and riots in delights which nature and fortune, with all their bounty, cannot bestow" (93–94).

What does the mind do with the images, and how does it think with the raw materials the images provide? As Imlac explains, a full mind allows a person to "vary and combine" the images, for "he, who knows most, will have most power of diversifying his scenes." When the mind is replete and when the varied images and memories of the past inform the experience of thinking, solitude does not mean tedium. Once the mind is indelibly imprinted with a sufficient number of images, it can compare and contrast them, using those parts of the intelligence that were known in Johnson's time as *wit* and *judgment*. The ability to see resemblances and discover analogies (wit) and the power of discerning vital, essential differences between similar things (judgment) distinguish a wise person. From his travels to determine his "choice of life," Rasselas encounters every possible version of happiness, from idleness to activity, from the single state to marriage, from a life of ignorance to the pursuit of learning, and from the "choice of life" to the choice of eternity. As the mind acquires the images necessary for the process of thought, its activity is essentially passive; it receives impressions, ideas, and memories from its interaction with the surrounding world. When the mind varies and combines the images, it is active as it discerns, weighs, compares, and distinguishes the variety of information. In this process of seeing resemblances and detecting differences, the mind generalizes and concludes. It arrives at universal truths—the strongest antidote to the fantasies invented by "the dangerous prevalence of imagination" and a cure to the restlessness and melancholy of Rasselas in the happy valley.

In this quest for "the choice of life," Rasselas rediscovers old truths about human happiness that others like Imlac have already acquired. For example, "Human life is everywhere a state in which much is to be endured, and little to be enjoyed" (27). The portion of life's happiness is not as great as Rasselas in his idealism expected when he anticipated the adventure of life outside the valley. Rasselas discovers another timeless truth when he visits the famous pyramids of Egypt: the vanity of human wishes. Nothing worldly can ever satisfy man's infinite appetite for happiness. Imlac explains to his fellow travelers that the erection of the pyramids testifies to "the insufficiency of human employments." Why did the pharaohs build such monuments? "It seems to have been erected only in compliance with that hunger of the imagination which preys incessantly upon life, and must always be appeased by some employment. Those who already have all that they can enjoy, must enlarge their desires" (69). No one is ever perfectly happy, and restlessness and the "hunger of the imagination" constantly devise imaginary wishes for greater schemes of human happiness. While Rasselas learns that no one is perfectly happy and discovers the inadequacy of human sources of pleasure, he also acknowledges that some states of life and conditions of mind offer greater degrees of happiness than others—a truth he could uncover only by first filling his mind with images and then comparing and contrasting those ideas.

After considering the images of idleness and busyness he recalls from his travels, Rasselas knows that idleness reduces a person's chances for happiness. In the happy valley, Rasselas lived an idle life with nothing to pursue and nothing to keep his life in motion. After considering the slothful young men of Cairo, "whose only business is to gratify their desires" and who live superficial lives, Rasselas concludes that "to act without a plan, and to be sad or cheerful only by chance," lies beneath the dignity of man (39–40). The Arab maids that Rasselas's maid Pekuah encounters impress upon Rasselas the misery of an idle life. Spending their entire day in needlework, the maids do not have enough activity to occupy their minds. "They ran from room to room as a bird hops from wire to wire in his cage" (84), or someone would pretend to be hurt or lost to alarm the others in order to produce some excitement to dispel the monotony of the day. In contrast to the idle who waste time or dissipate their lives, the busy, energetic individuals who live active, engaged lives enjoy a greater degree of happiness. Imlac has mastered the art of keeping his life in motion, for he has lived both in and out of the happy valley, and he has pursued the life of the merchant and the life of the poet, always learning and broadening his world. As Imlac explains to Rasselas, "To a poet nothing can be useless. Whatever is beautiful, and whatever is dreadful, must be familiar to his imagination: he must be conversant with all that is awfully vast or elegantly little" (23). The monks whom Rasselas meets instruct him in the art of living a happy life by their purposeful activity: "Their time is regularly distributed; one duty succeeds another, so that they are not left open to the distraction of unguided choice, nor lost in the shades of listless activity" (103). Thus Rasselas has no doubts that having "something to pursue" by way of a noble goal or useful activity increases a person's chances for happiness.

Another "choice of life" that Rasselas considers is between one lived in society and one as a recluse. After visiting a hermit and hearing the history of his life, Rasselas learns of the man's regret in abandoning human society for a life of peace and security. Disgusted by the turmoil of war and the decadence of the world, the hermit chose to remove himself from the temptations and vanities of the world, but he regrets his life of solitude and escape: "In solitude, if I escape the example of bad men, I want likewise the counsel and conversation of the good" (47). After the novelty of retirement faded, the hermit found himself unoccupied and unengaged, left to the riot of "vanities of imagination"—a condition similar to Rasselas's predicament in the happy valley, where he too found life "tasteless and irksome" because of the lack of variety. " 'Variety,' said Rasselas, 'is so necessary to content, that even the happy valley disgusted me by the recurrence of its luxuries' " (103). A social life and membership in a family provide this variety that enhances a person's chances for happiness. When Rasselas and his sister Nekayah discuss the nature of marriage and family life, Nekayah comments on the various miseries of marital life she has observed—"the diversities of temper, the oppositions of opinion, the rude collisions of contrary desire." Rasselas, however, objects: "I cannot be persuaded but that marriage is one of the means of happiness" (60). Despite the many sources of argument and conflict in marriage, Rasselas blames his sister for hasty generalizations, insisting that the "world must be peopled by marriage, or peopled without it" (61). Although Rasselas does not idealize or romanticize marriage, he argues that a comparison of the married with those in the single state always proves that marriage offers more sources of happiness. Regarding celibacy and marriage, Rasselas concludes, "Both conditions may be bad, but they cannot both be worst" (60). The unmarried hermit and the bachelor astronomer lament their situations because their loneliness leads to flights of fancy: "To indulge the power of fiction, and send imagination upon the wing, is often the sport of those who delight too much in silent speculation" (93). The eccentric astronomer, who "had never received any visits from women," behaves in a singular, strange manner. In short, marriage, like an active life, leads a person out of a narrow, confined, solipsistic world into a larger universe where the stimulation of new images, the experience of variety, and a life of purpose nourish the mind and improve a person's experience of happiness.

Because of the variety of images he has gathered from his travels and conversations, Rasselas clearly discerns the difference between ignorance and learning as a condition for happiness. The boorish shepherds "so rude and ignorant . . . that very little could be learned from them" disillusion Princess Nekayah about the fabled bliss of the pastoral life. The Arab maids who play childish games lack the mental resources for a healthy state of mind conducive to intelligent conversation: "[F]or of what could they be expected to talk? They had seen nothing; for they had lived from early youth in that narrow spot: of what they had not seen they could have no knowledge, for they could not read." The young men of Cairo pursue inane pleasures "in which the mind had no part," and their hollow laughter reflects that "their mirth was without images" (43, 84, 39).

On the other hand, Rasselas recognizes that Imlac, whose wisdom understands the true nature of human happiness and whose full life reveals the greatest resources for contentment, possesses a learning and an intelligence that reflect a liberally educated person. His mind, replete with images from books, travel, conversation, and experience, provides him an inner world rich with substantive food for thought. Imlac remarks, "I can amuse my solitude by the renovation of the knowledge which begins to fade from my memory, and by recollection of the accidents of my past life" (30). Because of this full mind, which he does not allow to become stagnant, Imlac can combat boredom, melancholy, restlessness, and daydreaming with the love of knowledge and the contemplation of the truth. With a mind full of varied images that Imlac can "combine," the ability to compare and contrast leads the mind to generalize and conclude—to discover the universal truths that govern the human condition. In his travels Rasselas also fills his mind with new images, fresh ideas, and a knowledge of men and manners that bestow repose and equanimity, for, as Johnson wrote in his "Preface to Shakespeare, "the mind can only repose on the stability of truth."[2] This possession of the truth dispels fantasies about

---

[2] "Preface to Shakespeare" in *The Oxford Authors: Samuel Johnson*, ed. Donald Greene (New York: Oxford University Press, 1984), 420.

utopia, since experience proves that no place is perfect. True wisdom cures restlessness through honest realism, the art of the possible—not the perfect: "Of the blessings set before you, make your choice and be content" (64). And this knowledge of the nature of things teaches that no panaceas exist to eliminate the recurrence of restlessness or "the hunger of the imagination," only the sound counsel of Imlac's common sense: "Do not suffer life to stagnate; it will grow muddy for want of motion" (75–76). It is self-evident to Rasselas that knowledge, truth, and wisdom increase a person's happiness.

However, it is not just any form of knowledge or type of learning that enhances human happiness. Throughout *Rasselas*, Johnson depicts many learned scholars and philosophers whom he satirizes as fools, characters Rasselas does not want to emulate. The flying artist, an accomplished mechanical engineer, proposes the idea of designing wings for humans to fly. Constructing a bat's wings for human use, "he waved his pinions a while to gather air, then leaped from his stand, and in an instant dropped into a lake" (15). Dominated by fantasy and imagination, the mechanic loses himself in the airy regions of speculation and loses contact with reality. His theory of flying is not based on facts, laws, or experience, and his knowledge amounts to vain philosophy—a knowledge that serves no human purpose. Likewise, the Stoic philosopher who proposes the rational control of passions and appetites as the secret of a happy life soon contradicts himself when his daughter dies of an accident: " 'Have you then forgotten the precepts,' said Rasselas, 'which you so powerfully enforced?' " When he is tested by life's tragedies, the philosopher's lofty doctrine of Stoic apathy and sublime reason amounts to nothing. Again, theory does not correspond with practice: "'Be not too hasty,' said Imlac, 'to trust, or to admire, the teachers of morality: they discourse like angels, but they live like men' " (42). In this example also, pretentious learning is exposed as useless knowledge that contributes nothing to human happiness. The same is true of the scholar who advocates a return to nature as the essence of human felicity, a doctrine he explains as "to act always with due regard to the fitness arising from the relations and qualities of causes and effects" (49)—high-sounding jargon that convinces Rasselas that "this was one of the sages whom he should understand less as he heard him longer" (50). Likewise, the astronomer's immense erudition exerts no influence on his happiness. As a specialist with a renowned reputation for his knowledge of the planets, the astronomer exaggerates his self-importance, imagining that he controls the weather and regulates the seasons. After enjoying the company and conversation of Rasselas, Pekuah, and Imlac, the astronomer confesses, "I have passed my time in study without experience. . . . I have purchased knowledge at the expence of the common comforts of life: I have missed the endearing elegance of female friendship, and the happy commerce of domestick tenderness" (100). In other words, mere formal learning, speculative theory, narrow specialization, and vain pedantry do not provide "the wider range" of universal wisdom that contributes to happiness. The "choice of life" Rasselas seeks as the source of happiness does not depend on factual information or advanced degrees but on the eternal truths and timeless wisdom that teach the art of living. None of these learned men possesses a mind "replete with images" from varied sources to form a balanced, realistic perspective on human life. The flying artist, the Stoic, the philosopher who counsels a return to nature, and the astronomer all formulate grand theories untested by experience, ideas that remain abstractions divorced from reality. Whenever knowledge precipitates the "dangerous prevalence of imagination" instead of leading to the truth, disillusionment follows instead of happiness. Only the knowledge of the truth offers happiness; only the "repose" that knowledge confers can dispel the restlessness of the mind.

At the conclusion of his journey, Rasselas faces a final important contrast: between earthly life and eternity. Recalling the pharaohs buried in the pyramids and discoursing on the nature of the soul, Rasselas reflects on the brevity of human life and the fact of death: "Those that lie here stretched before us, the wise and powerful of ancient times, warn us to remember the shortness of our present state" (108). In the light of this contrast between life and death and the difference between temporal forms of happiness and the immortality of the soul, Princess Nekayah concludes, "To me . . . the choice of life is become less important; I hope hereafter to think only on the choice of eternity" (109). When Rasselas left the happy valley, he fantasized that he could discover an ideal form of happiness somewhere on earth or in some philosophy of life. After his travels, he discovers that every form of human happiness and every way of life is flawed in some way. Everyone experiences some form of restlessness or daydreams about some impossibilities. No one is ever perfectly content, neither rich rulers nor poor shepherds, neither ignorant maids nor erudite astronomers, neither lonely bachelors nor married couples. To discover that restlessness is inherent in the human condition and to know that no form of human happiness is ideal is the beginning of human wisdom. This truth curbs the imagination of its flights of fancy and its tendency "to hope or fear beyond probability." This insight provides an honest, balanced, and realistic perspective on the limits of the human condition. Replete with all the diverse images of human happiness, the mind concludes that no happy valley, utopia, or paradise exists in the human world, and thus the imagination stops wandering. This fact about human happiness, then, allows the mind to contemplate the nature of eternal happiness and to "take a wider range" that transcends the limitations of temporal life. Rasselas's journey—unlike the travels of Voltaire's Candide—does not end in disillusionment, frustration, or cynicism, but in illumination. There is no need to look further or travel farther. There is no need to withdraw from the world and merely cultivate one's garden. The mind has collected enough images from a myriad of sources to understand the art of living and to grasp the general truths it finds: wisdom increases a person's happiness; everyone needs something to look forward to in life, "something to desire"; everybody needs to keep his life "in motion" and have "something to pursue"; the mind always needs to grow and acquire new images, lest "it grow muddy from want of motion"; a larger universe ("a wider range"), not a narrow world, enhances a person's possibilities of happiness; a human life requires variety and contrast and thrives on new stimulation; happiness is not a place but a cultivated state of mind, not the indulgence of pleasure but the possession of the truth; a knowledge of the truth cures a person of the madness of imagination; and God and eternity—not the happy valleys—are the ultimate sources of human happiness.

Places, things, theories, riches, and politics, for all their importance, do not bestow lasting joy. Only a healthy state of mind in touch with all of reality and desirous of truth in all of its integrity will possess the resources for living well. Indulgences that ignore the spiritual life and ideologies that distort the truth about human nature "send imagination out upon the wing" to search for some version of a utopian happiness or a happy valley that does not exist. Because the modern world disavows the reality of absolute universal truths—the natural law, the wisdom of the ages, the lessons of the past, divine revelation, and even common sense—it robs itself of the only real source of happiness. As Imlac states in *Rasselas*, the true thinker who wishes a fruitful life "must divest himself of the prejudices of his age or country; he must consider right and wrong in their abstracted and invariable state; he must disregard present laws and opinions and rise to general and transcendental truths, which will always be the same" (24).

XVII. Courage:
Huckleberry Finn

We are often prone to confuse two important concepts—that of the average and that of the normal. The normal signifies the way things *ought* to be according to a fixed moral or natural standard—the ideal or most excellent. The average frequently denotes not the golden mean but the lowest common denominator, the mediocre rather than the moderate. The average can designate the prevalent opinions of a large percentage of unqualified observers, or the fashionable trends of thought or conduct at a given time. Hence, in one century the "average" man approves of slavery; in the next he allows for abortion. The average in education often translates into the "dumbing down" of standards, the better to build up self-esteem. The appeal to the average is an insidious device that detracts from the ideal of the saintly, the heroic, and the noble, and makes these norms appear fantastical and imaginary. The aura of the average can absolve us of guilt, permitting popular consensus to replace exacting ideals of the normal, moral, or true. The best, the highest, and the most excellent examples of the human species lose their influence as the models for imitation. Instead, we comfortably pluck at the low-hanging fruit of the average—even when it entails abandoning true standards and unchanging principles.

Mark Twain's *Huckleberry Finn* portrays the universal truths about human nature and the human condition that reflect the timeless wisdom of the Great Books. In one of the violent episodes of the book, Colonel Sherburn gives an ultimatum to Boggs, a harmless old drunkard who has been insulting Sherburn before a large crowd, "calling Sherburn everything he could lay his tongue to, and the whole street packed with people listening and laughing and going on." Losing his patience, the irascible colonel warns Boggs that the insults must stop at one o'clock: "If you open your mouth against me only once, after that time, you can't travel so far but I will find you."[1] Blathering in his drunkenness, Boggs, known as "the best-naturedst old fool in Arkansas," cannot control his cursing of Sherburn and violates the one o'clock deadline. The hardhearted colonel calls Boggs by name on the main street and fires two shots that kill him. The townsmen, shocked at the cruelty and heartlessness of Sherburn's wanton murder of a harmless, foolish drunkard, form a mob and approach Sherburn's home to demand justice. Huck describes the scene: "Well, by and by somebody said Sherburn ought to be lynched. In about a minute everybody was saying it; so away they went, mad and yelling, and snatching down every clothes-line they come to, to do the hanging with" (223). When the angry mob arrives at Sherburn's home to punish the murderer, Sherburn confronts them with an intimidating double-barrel gun and insults their manhood: "[Y]ou think you had grit enough to lay your hands on a *man*? Why, a *man's* safe in the hands of ten thousand of your kind—as long as it's day time and you're not behind him." Sherburn

---

1 *The Adventures of Huckleberry Finn* (New York: The Penguin Group, 2008), 209.

terrifies the mob, which retreats when he denounces them as cowards: "The average man's a coward" and "The average man don't like trouble and danger. . . . Now the thing for you to do, is to droop your tails and go home and crawl in a hole" (225, 226). Throughout the novel, Twain excoriates the merely "average man," whom he portrays not only as coward but also as a sentimentalist, a fool, and a sluggard. Huck Finn, the unassuming, innocent boy who becomes the noble hero of the book, avoids all these vices of the average man.

Twain portrays the average man not only as a coward in a mob but also as a foolish sentimentalist. When the unscrupulous Duke and the King cheat gullible people, these two confidence men wear many disguises, posing as actors, missionaries, and beloved uncles from England. At the Pokeville camp meeting that the King and Huck attend, the people at the revival are rapt with religious frenzy. As the preacher flails his arms and shouts his words, the audience reacts with hysterical emotionalism: "And so he went on, and the people groaning and crying and saying amen." Noticing the agitated reactions of the audience, the King climbs on the platform and invents a farfetched tale of his miraculous conversion from pirate to missionary, boasting "he was a changed man now, and happy for the first time in his life; and poor as he was, he was going to start right off and work his way back to the Indian Ocean and put in the rest of his life trying to turn pirates into the truth path" (203, 204). As the King plays his part with the pretense of tears, compassion for the pagan pirates, and religious enthusiasm, a member of the crowd, gushing with sentimentalism, cries out, "Take up a collection for him, take up a collection!" (205). The scoundrel and imposter receives invitations to stay in Pokeville for a week, and everyone offers him hospitality in their homes "and said they'd think it was an honour." The average man, then, confuses true goodness with shallow kindness—or, in modern parlance, being tolerant and nonjudgmental.

Huck discovers this hard truth again when he is a guest in the home of the Grangerfords and treated with the most gracious hospitality. A genteel aristocrat and southern gentleman, Colonel Grangerford displays exquisite manners and dresses with impeccable good taste as he appears daily in a clean shirt and white linen suit. Huck observes that "[h]e was as kind as he could be," that "he didn't ever have to tell anybody to mind their manners—everybody was always good-mannered where he was," and that "he was sunshine most always—I mean he made it seem like good weather" (165). An affluent slave owner, Colonel Grangerford appears a cultured, respectable man who entertains frequently on his plantation with picnics and balls. The colonel and his family give the Bible a prominent place in their home and attend church as they hear a sermon on brotherly love. After church, however, Huck finds himself in a state of shock when the Grangerfords and Shepherdsons revive their ancient family feud, firing their rifles and even killing Huck's twelve-year-old friend Buck. Horrified at the violence of men ambushing and killing each other, Huck quickly realizes his naive illusions about the Grangerfords' hospitality, kindness, elegance, and religion: "I wished I hadn't ever come ashore that night, to see such things. I ain't ever going to get shut of them—lots of times I dream about them" (179). As Huck learns, the average man, trusting to first impressions and pleasant feelings, mistakes affected manners for good morals, judges character on the basis of clothes, and assumes that pious sentiments equal Christian charity. Huck's first impression of the Grangerfords and their home as the epitome of graciousness and culture changes dramatically when he discovers that what is "nice" is distinct from what is good. The boy who first observed, "It was a mighty nice family, and a mighty nice house, too. I hadn't seen no house out in the country before that was so nice and had so much style" (156), leaves the Grangerfords with a sense of disgust: "I was mighty down-hearted; so I made up my mind I wouldn't ever go near that house again" (179).

The average men in Twain's novel again let momentary feelings and reactions overcome common sense and prudence. They gullibly trust the claims of the Duke and Dauphin to be the British uncles of three daughters mourning the loss of their father, Peter Wilks. The crafty confidence men affect English accents, feign copious tears at the funeral, and shower their supposed nieces with effusive warmth to comfort them in their loss. Despite the testimony of eyewitnesses that the "uncles" from England did not arrive by steamboat from Cincinnati as they alleged but by canoe on the river, the average men act shocked when the imposters are told "it's a lie." They even kick against the truth: "Several of them jumped for him and begged him not to talk that way to an old man and a preacher" (304). When a doctor detects the affected accent of the liars and bluntly remarks, "It's the worst imitation I ever heard. You Peter Wilks's brother? You're a fraud, that's what you are!" (261), Wilks's three daughters do not believe a word—as Mary Jane, the oldest, gives the phony uncles a bag of gold to invest for them as proof of her absolute trust in their integrity. The mob approves: "Everybody clapped their hands and stomped on the floor like a perfect storm, whilst the king held up his head and smiled around" (262). The crowd melts as the sisters embrace the con men, who for their part gush with tender feelings for their mourning nieces. The average man's sentimentality avoids calling evil by its rightful name, just as the mourners at the funeral are repelled by the mention of "fraud" and "liars." How many current abuses of the moral law that present themselves as pieces of social progress does the average man approve? How many of us are cowed into silence on such uncomfortable subjects by the fear of deviating from what is average?

Huckleberry Finn also depicts the average man as a sluggard ruled by apathy and diverted by mindless, inane entertainment. In one of the towns, Huck notices a street where a crowd of "loafers" spend all their time whittling wood, chewing tobacco, and "gaping and yawning and stretching—a mighty ornery lot." Even their posture denotes sloth, as each one stands inactive with hands "in britches pockets, except when he fetched them out to lend a chaw of tobacco or scratch." Their speech, too, conveys the same listless drowsiness, for "they talked lazy and drawly, and used considerable many cuss-words." Their conversation is limited to comments on whose turn it is to lend the next "chaw" of tobacco:

"I wisht you'd len' me a chaw, Jack, I jist this minute give Ben Thompson the last chaw I had" (215, 216). The only stimulation that rouses the loafers from their idle sluggishness is the sight of curs attacking a sow or watching a dog fight—"unless it might be turpentine on a stray dog and setting fire to him, or tying a tin pan to his tail and see him run himself to death" (227). The average man, then, is lulled by apathy and thrives on the crudest forms of entertainment that appeal to the lowest common denominator, the "bread and circuses" demanded by the Roman mobs: violence, sensationalism, and animal pleasure. I leave it to the reader with cable TV and Internet access to identify the contemporary equivalents. On a less degraded level, a student of history might see an echo of such loafers in the affluent classes of Western nations who eschew the demands of rearing and educating children, bequeathing entire countries to those fertile immigrants who do society's heavy lifting.

The ugly embrace of the average is the enemy of the natural, the normal, the excellent, or the ideal. In Russell Kirk's words, modernity eschews all sense of "the normative consciousness" and substitutes for it what Twain depicts as "average." But such an ideal is not only ignoble—it is unstable. Statistics and opinions shift in the winds of propaganda, advertising, and unreflective media. The average is always fluctuating and variable, never fixed like the idea of the *nature* of things. *Average* is not a neutral word in Mark Twain's vocabulary but a term that signifies cowardliness, foolishness, sentimentality, and sloth. Human nature that remains average has not attained the status of virtue, which Aristotle called "the golden mean," but instead lacks its completeness. The cowardly need *more* fearlessness to attain the virtue of fortitude. The sentimental need *more* rationality to achieve the virtue of prudence. The lazy need *more* zeal, passion, and conviction to acquire the virtue of justice, of loving the good and hating what is evil. *Average* means deficiency, not normalcy. The modern sleight of hand that elevates the term *average* to a virtue has reduced human nature to a lower standard and robbed it of its content.

As Mark Twain shows in his novel, Huck Finn, that most typical, normal, unspoiled, and natural of boys, who loves to swim and fish in the river, dislikes "sivilization" and revels in his life of adventure on the raft; he is disgusted by the cowardliness of the mobs, the stupidity of the sentimentalists, and the laziness of the loafers. Unlike the average coward, Huck courageously said he would rather defy the law of the land and "go to hell" than betray his friend Jim the runaway slave to the authorities. Huck bravely risked harm when he took from the Duke and Dauphin's room the bag of gold they embezzled in their pose as uncles from England entitled to the inheritance of their "brother's" fortune. As Huck tells Mary Jane, "I stole it from them; and I stole it to give to you" (294)—a daring deed. Unlike the average sentimentalist, Huck is repelled by the cant he describes as "all full of tears and flapdoodle," "all that kind of rot and slush," and "all that soul-butter and hogwash" when he observes naive fools enabling the fraud of the Duke and Dauphin. Unlike the average loafer apathetic to good and evil, Huck passionately seeks justice, expending great effort in protecting Jim from slave hunters and defending Mary Jane and her sisters from being duped by the fabrications of imposters. Huck Finn, boy eternal and as natural as the river he calls his home ("It's lovely to live on a raft"), demonstrates that the natural is real, that it equals the moral and the just, the excellent and the heroic. It is not determined statistically by counting the upraised arms of a mob, or even the approved opinions of elites.

XVIII. Penitence:
The Canterbury Tales

In Chaucer's *The Canterbury Tales*, a merry company representative of all the classes and professions of medieval society is wending its way on a pilgrimage to the shrine of the martyr Thomas à Becket in Canterbury during the season of Lent. On their long trek the pilgrims agree to take turns telling stories to and from Canterbury, to avoid a tedious, humdrum journey in which they rode "dumb as stones."[1] The motley crew encompasses all the ranks, from knights and squires to monks and parsons, from doctors and lawyers to cooks and merchants. This cross section of medieval society embraces both men and women, young and old, and it includes human nature in its various temperaments (melancholic, choleric, sanguine, and phlegmatic) and in its various degrees of moral character, comprising heroic nobles and saintly religious, as well as rogues, swindlers, and drunkards. But these are more than mere travelers on a holy pilgrimage; the pilgrims serve Chaucer as a microcosm of the Church, the earthly body of Christ.

In the midst of their travels and storytelling, the pilgrims are joined by a man called the Canon's Yeoman—a wretched alchemist who has lost his health, debauched his mind, exhausted his nerves, troubled his conscience,

---

1   *The Canterbury Tales*, tr. Neville Coghill (Baltimore, MD: Penguin Books, 1967), 38.

and wasted his life by believing in the black magic of transforming base metals into gold. Pale in complexion from working underground in the darkness of cellars and smelling of chemicals and smoke, the Yeoman suffers ill health. Engaged in the criminal, forbidden practice of the witchcraft of evil and the deadly sin of avarice, the Yeoman has contracted a darkened intellect that believes lies and rationalizes sin. Bickering constantly with the Canon because their experiment never succeeds and their pots always crack, the Canon and the Yeoman hurl insults and blame each other for every failure to produce the magical elixir. Ashamed and guilty of sacrificing his mind, body, and soul for filthy lucre, the Yeoman feels the sting of conscience and laments the loss of his fortune. Disturbed by the weight of his sin in the diabolical hell of the alchemist's "holes and corners and blind alleys, / Places where every thief and robber rallies / By nature, fear stricken and secret places / Where those reside who dare not show their faces" (468), the Yeoman bursts with the urge to confess his criminal past and convert to a new life by joining the pilgrimage: " 'God save this jolly party! How fast I've spurred,' " he said, " 'all for your sake; I was determined I would overtake / Your happy crowd and ride in company' " (466).

This "jolly party" and "happy crowd" the alchemist joins represent the Church—the health and sanity the Yeoman's body and soul crave after his enslavement to alchemy. Smelling of brimstone, stinking like a goat, and leaden in complexion, the Yeoman escapes from the foul air of fires consuming base metals into the fresh atmosphere of a spring day. He rejects the demonic cave of black magic for the natural world of sunshine and the invigorating outdoors. Disgusted and disillusioned by the miserable company of the Canon, master of subtlety and "esoteric craft," the Yeoman welcomes the normal human society of the Canterbury pilgrims. Repelled by the madness and monomania of alchemy, the Yeoman escapes from the narrow world of dark alleys and partakes of the universal experiences of the human race. The tales themselves (medieval romances, beast fables, allegories, *fabliaux*, autobiographies, and a sermon) encompass the entire human drama of love and death, comedy and tragedy. Sullen and enervated from compulsive work and bickering, the Yeoman rejoices that he can associate with lighthearted, fun-loving companions who revel in storytelling contests and delight in leisure—jocund fellows like the Host: "a merry-hearted man" full of jokes. In short, the Canterbury pilgrimage with its jolly company, normal society, rich lore, and holy destination epitomizes the healing power of the Christian community on the body, mind, and soul. Ironically, alchemy not only professes to transmute metal into gold but also purports to discover the universal cure of diseases and to prolong life indefinitely. But, as the Yeoman learns, it is the Canterbury pilgrimage—its sacramental sensibility and Christian culture—that effects the true healing of his body and soul.

The Yeoman joins the pilgrimage in a state of sickness and physical deterioration: "And where my colour was a lively red / My face is wan and wears a leaden look; / . . . My eyes are bleared with work on preparations, / That's all the good you get from transmutations" (470). The all-consuming addiction to alchemy allows no leisure or rest and permits no balance between work and play. Alchemy is a waste of time and futile work and results in "empty money-bags and addled brains" (470). Alchemy is a grim, grave, deadly serious business that makes no allowance for relaxation or humor. Every time the pot breaks, "I've no idea why the thing went wrong; / Recriminations though were hot and strong" (478), the Yeoman recalls. The compulsion of the alchemist to discover the philosopher's stone that compels him to labor day and night illustrates the proverbial saying that "a man may go to heaven with half the pains it costs him to go to hell." While it is true, in St. Paul's word, that he who does not work does not eat, the Church has never idolized work as man's highest end. Men work in order to play, to enjoy beauty, friendship, hospitality, learning, and the contemplation of God. Because God rested on the seventh day, man too must pause from his labor to restore his soul and rejuvenate his spirit lest he feel dehumanized and a slave to work. The Canterbury pilgrims, engaged in such worldly professions as medicine, law, cooking, farming, carpentry, and business, have paused from their workaday occupations to revel in laughter, to expand their hearts, and to renew their spiritual life. The pleasure of conversation, the delight of stories, the convivial atmosphere, and the physical exercise of travel on horseback in the pleasant month of April, when Zephyrus with sweet breath "exhales an air in every grove and heath / Upon the tender shoots" as "the small fowl are making melody" (17), supply restorative, healthful medicine for a sick Yeoman.

The Yeoman has suffered a desolate life for seven years, oppressed by the surly Canon's unpleasant company. Lacking the pleasure of friendship, the Yeoman learned the misery of loneliness one might face in hell. Joining the Canterbury pilgrimage, he feels a sense of belonging instead of the alienation he has suffered in the sordid practice of alchemy. Chaucer's merry company represents, in John Dryden's famous phrase, "God's plenty"—characters from all the three estates of medieval society, from the Parson to the Knight to the Miller. The travelers not only exchange stories in their journey but also engage in honest arguments, debate the morals of marriage, and interact with lively conversation and strong opinions. All the sociability, banter, repartee, and wit the stories evoke dispel the gloom of the Yeoman's forsaken existence and enlarge his social world from one miserable partner in crime to God's infinite variety of human beings. Instead of associating only with a monomaniac obsessed by greed and gold, the Yeoman encounters a noble Knight who had loved chivalry, truth, and honor, generosity and courtesy; he meets a Parson "rich in holy thought and works," a priest "Who truly knew Christ's gospel and would preach it / Devoutly to parishioners, and teach it"; he discovers an honest Plowman pure of heart, "an honest worker, good and true, / Living in perfect peace and charity" (30, 31)—all men who live according to a sense of vocation that glorifies God and serves man. As a traveler joining the company to Canterbury, the Yeoman participates in the comedy and the revelry of the storytelling contest. He hears such rollicking tales as the Miller's and relishes the robust good humor of the Host. Thus the jolly company of the pilgrims cures melancholy and banishes loneliness. The camaraderie of the travelers recalls the original God-given purpose of a human society: mutual helpfulness and enjoyment.

The dreary world of alchemy hides in slums "[w]here those reside who dare not show their faces" (468); it dwells underground, in darkness and ignorance, better to carry out its hellish activity. The Yeoman confesses, "Although the devil didn't show his face / I'm pretty sure he was about the place" (475). The diabolical nature of the witchcraft of alchemy—its cunning, fraud, and dissimulation—darkens the mind and perverts the use of human intelligence. The alchemist's fantasy of finding the magical elixir always results in failure and frustration: either the fire is too hot or too cold, or the pot cracks: "We always failed, for all those tricks of his" (471). But the quest continues as the alchemist, "raving on in our illusion," repeats his experiments in vain and imagines that his black magic will produce the philosopher's stone—a total abuse of the mind. As the Yeoman remarks of his accomplice, the Canon: "Often enough a man with too much brain / Is likely to misuse it" (468).

By contrast the entire journey to Canterbury liberates the mind, illuminates the truth, and cures one of illusions. For example, the Wife of Bath obstinately argues that her five (failed) marriages qualify her as a greater authority on matrimony than the Church because of her "experience." According to the Wife's worldly wisdom, happiness in marriage follows when a man grants authority and headship to the woman. She summarizes the moral of her tale in terms of the answer to the riddle, "What do women desire most?" The married woman in "The Wife of Bath's Tale" answers: "A woman wants the self-same sovereignty / Over her husband as over her lover / And master him; he must not be above her" (302). The scholar of Oxford in his "Clerk's Tale," however, challenges her unorthodox views by depicting the humble patient Grisilda, who honors her marital vows for better and for worse and for richer and for poorer by her lifetime of fidelity—the epitome of an obedient wife who does not seek mastery over her husband. When the Pardoner resorts to the glib salesmanship of the confidence man to sell his fake indulgences to the pilgrims, the Host exposes the lie: "You'll have me kissing your old breeches too / And swear they were the relic of an old saint" (273). And when the Monk takes his turn to tell a tale and merely recounts tragic stories that illustrate prideful great men falling from high to low in example after example, the Knight protests, "Ho, my good sir, no more!" and "a little grief / [w]ill do for most of us" (229). The host also chides the storyteller: "Such talk as that's not worth a butterfly, / Gives no enjoyment. . . . I heartily beg you'll talk of something else" (229). The stories and characters on the pilgrimage check and balance each other so that the fullness of truth corrects heresy, exposes evil, and ridicules folly with the medicine of right reason and common sense—the virtues absent in the madness of alchemy. The Church always honors both reason and faith, seeing each as a royal road to the knowledge of God.

Guilty and ashamed, the Yeoman has joined the pilgrimage with a troubled conscience and a need to confess his crime and sin. When the Canon overhears the Yeoman divulging the alchemist's lie of borrowing money with the promise that "their money will be doubled or increased" and threatens him, the Yeoman defiantly continues to speak the truth: "Now I can talk, and I've a lot to tell. He's gone, the foul fiend carry him off to

Hell!" (469). Abandoning his hidden life of criminal vice and acknowledging all the lies of alchemy, the Yeoman joins a pilgrimage destined for a martyr's shrine in the holy season of penance and spiritual regeneration. On the journey he will hear "The Parson's Tale," a medieval sermon on the seven deadly sins that applies to all the travelers—each of whom, in some degree or another, struggles with one or several of these vices. In this sermon the Yeoman hears that the avaricious man has lost "the comfort of God" and searches for "a vain solace in worldly possessions," that he possesses "more faith in his possessions than in Jesus Christ," that he practices the sin of theft and resembles a wolf who devours the goods of the poor and the innocent, and that he is a "slave to idolatry." The Yeoman next hears of the virtues that counteract the deadly sin of avarice: mercy, pity, and generosity. "The methods of mercy are to lend and to give, to forgive and to set free, to have heartfelt pity and compassion for the troubles of one's fellow Christians, and also to chasten where it is necessary."[2] Thus the process of the pilgrimage itself serves as a teacher. It leads the Yeoman to the truth about the evil of alchemy and the vice of avarice, exemplifies for him the meaning of mercy and charity in the character of the Parson—"Giving to poor parishioners round about / From his own goods and Easter offerings" (30)—elicits from the alchemist the desire to confess his sins, and guides him to Canterbury to the sacrament of reconciliation. Like Augustine in the *Confessions*, the alchemist recognizes the uselessness of

---

2   *The Canterbury Tales*, ed. R. M Lumiansky (New York: Holt, Rinehart, and Winston, 1954), 428–29.

his life. Lost in debt and frustrated at the waste of seven years serving lies, the Yeoman knows that all the labor of alchemy amounts to nothing; the philosopher's stone will never be found.

While Chaucer's "General Prologue" includes many characters on the journey who are worldly, dishonest, hypocritical, or greedy, it also presents characters who spend their lives in a vocation of service to God and neighbor. The chivalrous Knight who follows the noble ideals of his order risks his life in many battles to serve God, king, and country. The Parson, true to his vocation as an *alter Christus*, never failed to practice love of neighbor: "Yet he neglected not in rain or thunder, / In sickness or in grief, to pay a call / On the remotest, whether great or small, / Upon his feet and in his hand a stave" (30).

The Clerk of Oxford, devoted to his vocation of learning, lives the asceticism of a scholar, spending his money only on books and never on worldly pleasures: "By his bed / He preferred having twenty books in red / And black, of Aristotle's philosophy, / To having fine clothes, fiddle, or psaltery" (25). And the humble Plowman performs his daily chores in the spirit of service and charity: "For steadily about his work he went / To thrash his corn, to dig or to manure / Or make a ditch; and he would help the poor / For love of Christ and never take a penny" (31). On the other hand, the Yeoman had lived and worked only for his own profit and sold his soul to worship gold. As a member of the pilgrimage he learns of martyrs and saints, associates with soldiers and priests who give themselves in self-donation to noble ideals, and hears stories about allegorical characters like

Constance in "The Sergeant of Law's Tale" who live out the Beatitudes and teach that it is more blessed to give than to receive.

In short, the Canterbury pilgrimage constitutes a Catholic society that reflects the culture, atmosphere, and truths of the Church, and so saves the soul of the degenerate alchemist. By leaving the diabolical world of black magic and joining the pilgrimage, he enters the natural world, the realm of light, sunshine, health, and beauty that restores the color of his complexion and rejuvenates his spirit as he once again learns the joy of play and the pleasure of friendship. The natural world is balanced and rhythmical, and Holy Mother Church, in tune with nature, recognizes the alternation of work and play, respects the union of body and soul, and teaches both the love of God and the love of neighbor. By means of the natural, the alchemist is led to the supernatural and the spiritual. Because the Yeoman lived an abnormal and unnatural life of overwork, physical exhaustion, lack of leisure, and absence of joy, he wandered into the underground realm of the devil's workshop. By leaving the hostile company of the Canon and joining the human society of jolly travelers, the alchemist participates in the family of mankind and learns the purpose of a social life as a natural order of giving and receiving, rights and duties, mutual helpfulness and mutual enjoyment. In this experience of a genuine social world ("God's plenty"), the Yeoman no longer identifies himself as an isolated individual or lonely stranger but as someone belonging to a family, a country, a tradition, a culture, and a universal church.

For the alchemist to travel with the pilgrims and hear their tales is tantamount to a liberal education, which broadens both his knowledge and his sympathies. "The Miller's Tale" is a comedy about a fool who believes Noah's flood will occur again; "The Monk's Tale" is a compilation of tragedies; "The Knight's Tale" is a chivalric romance; "The Franklin's Tale" portrays the adultery of courtly love; and "The Parson's Tale" is a sermon. In short, from his association with the Canterbury pilgrims, the Yeoman will gain knowledge of men and manners, a sense of the one and the many in human nature, and an understanding of the traditions of Western civilization and its Church. By joining a Christian pilgrimage to a holy shrine, the Yeoman acquires a new identity: he becomes a member of the body of Christ instead of a forsaken alchemist.

The Church is not a sect or a denomination but a universal sacrament of salvation; it is not a part, but the whole—the totality or fullness of truth in matters of morals and faith. The truth liberates and heals. The Yeoman renounced the small, dark room of the alchemist for the splendor of a glorious kingdom. He exchanged the madness of a monomaniac for the sanity of human wisdom. In *The Canterbury Tales*, fools deluded by their fantasies are brought down to earth, and scoundrels are humiliated. The stargazing philosopher, rapt in speculation, falls in a ditch; a simpleton imagines that someone's cry of "Water! Water!" after a burn signifies the coming of Noah's flood and falls from his roof in a bathtub. Both are literally brought down to earth and cured of folly by the medicine of truth, just as the Yeoman is healed of his obsession with gold after joining the commonsense world of the travelers. Experiencing the contrast between the earthy realism of the pilgrims and the "raving" of alchemy, the Yeoman escapes enslavement in a dark hell of robbers and finds the human freedom that corresponds to the dignity of persons. Treated with contempt and vilified with insults by the Canon, the Yeoman is welcomed with hospitality by the merry company of the pilgrimage. Listening to the Parson's sermon on the deadly sins and traveling to Canterbury for the purpose of confession and penance, the Yeoman confronts another perennial truth of the Catholic faith: the burden of guilt for sin must be confessed and forgiven, not rationalized or excused. As Chesterton explained, when one enters the Church or breathes the atmosphere of a Catholic culture or society, he discovers an estate in which one finds "everything in something" (all the parts of the whole) instead of "something in everything" (a part of the whole).[3] The Yeoman discovers this vastness and largeness of the "estate" in the Canterbury pilgrimage. He renews his health by returning to the natural world, liberates his mind by discovering universal truths, cures his loneliness by associating with joking companions, purges his soul by confessing his sins, and alleviates his conscience by repudiating his practice of alchemy. The hospitality of the Canterbury pilgrimage reflects the banquet to which the Church calls all men and women of every temperament and background, every degree of vice and virtue, every profession and social class, and every level of education and culture.

---

3   "The World Inside Out" in *The Wisdom of Catholicism* (New York: Modern Library, 1949), 857.

Outside the Church the lure of alchemy and magicians is tantalizing. The temptations of the world all operate with the same psychology, promising its victims what they will gain but never disclosing what they will lose; the real price is never stated. Magic in all its secrecy lures the gullible with the bait of instant gratification, a shortcut to happiness. Somehow dreams and desires will come true without effort, patience, and perseverance. The normal, natural, moral process of achieving an end can be circumvented, and some more sophisticated, ingenious, or innovative method can be applied. Such is the lure of alchemy and magic with its elixirs and philosopher's stones—to get rich quickly without work or to gain the fountain of youth without living a healthy life. This mentality is not limited to the superstitions of the Middle Ages but also thrives in the postmodern world, which uses the code words *science* and *research* for its belief in what is, essentially, magic—practices or techniques designed to circumvent the nature of things and defy the moral law so as to serve the escalating demands of the spoiled, imperial self. As the Canon's story demonstrates, that is no road to happiness. Only the buffer and balance of human society, the discipline of authority, the counsel of the wise, and the model of the holy can right the balance of a mind unhinged by desire. That balance is what we find in Christian community, in the Church.

XIX. Daring:
The Merchant of Venice and *The Great Divorce*

Christ told the apostle, "Follow me"— that is, take a chance, make a commitment, be loyal to the end, have faith. In his sermon "The Ventures of Faith," Cardinal Newman defines the true Christian as bold in his abandonment to God's Providence rather than ruled by comfortable security and diffident caution: "Our duty as Christians lies in this, in making ventures for eternal life without the absolute certainty of success." He cites the examples of Abraham's daring as he "went out, not knowing whither he went," and James and John's absolute commitment to the Lord in their promise "We are able," when asked if they could drink the cup of Christ's sorrows.[1] Every human life presents situations that require a person to take a chance—not foolish risks or reckless actions that defy common sense and prudence, but decisions that require a sense of adventure, a willingness to trust Divine Providence, and the courage of convictions. To take a chance means the abandonment of comfort, security, and certainty, and requires the daring to risk failure, disappointment, and defeat. "Nothing ventured, nothing gained" goes the old proverb. This confidence in taking chances often leads to turning points and milestones in a

---

1   *Realizations: Newman's Own Selection of His Sermons* (Collegeville, MN: Liturgical Press, 2009), 46–47.

person's life that fill it with marvelous surprises and the favors of luck. If "fortune favors the brave," as the proverb states, then the taking of chances invites the blessings of good luck that come only to an adventurous spirit fearless of the future. Without the taking of chances, life assumes the dullness of the grey town in C. S. Lewis's *The Great Divorce*, where the restless inhabitants are always moving and going nowhere as their lifeless faces—"some gaunt, some bloated, some glaring with idiotic ferocity, some drowned beyond recovery in dreams"[2]—reflect their uninspired lives.

The decision to take a chance is often not a simple matter of good or evil or an easy question between common sense or folly but a subtle choice that depends on discernment between two good, reasonable choices. In Robert Frost's poem "The Road Not Taken," the traveler compares two roads that seem virtually identical and ponders his options, as he wants to explore both paths: "And sorry I could not travel both / And be one traveler."[3] Comparing and contrasting the two roads that diverge in the wood, he notices hardly any difference between their inviting prospects. One road is "just as fair" as the other, and both paths are equally well traveled: "Though as for that, the passing there / Had worn them really about the same." These two roads in the poem do not pose the same choice that Christ presented when he contrasted the narrow way that leads to everlasting life with the broad road that leads to perdition. Wavering and indecisive,

---

2   *The Great Divorce* (New York: Simon & Schuster, 1996), 26.
3   *The Poetry of Robert Frost*, ed. Edward Connery Lathem (New York: Holt, Rinehart and Winston, 1967), 105.

the traveler finally commits to one of the two roads and consoles himself with the thought that in the future he will travel the other path: "Oh, I kept the first for another day! / Yet knowing how way leads on to way, / I doubted if I should ever come back." In retrospect, the turn in the road that seemed accidental or whimsical proved to be not a random choice at all but a major decision, a great crossroads or turning point that led to great good fortune and happiness: "Two roads diverged in a wood, and I— / I took the one less traveled by, / And that has made all the difference." Of course the traveler at the moment of choice did not determine that one road was "less traveled by," because they were indistinguishable: "And both that morning *equally* lay / In leaves no step had trodden black" (emphasis added). Some mysterious inclination or slight intuition disposed the traveler to select one of the roads. He does not carry on a debate that weighs the advantages and disadvantages of the two roads to reach a conclusion. Pondering the two options, he lets himself be led by a power he cannot exactly identify at the moment, but in retrospect he acknowledges the selection of the road as a wise choice, "the one less traveled by, / And that has made all the difference." Though the traveler wistfully takes credit for his intelligent decision—"And *I* / I took the one less traveled by" (emphasis added)—the mystery of good luck or Divine Providence deserves more tribute than the traveler's prudent judgment. Taking a chance, then, often leads to an astonishing journey filled with gifts, surprises, and accomplishments that one never anticipated at the beginning.

In Homer's *Odyssey*, the illustrious hero confronts a dilemma that also requires the taking of a chance.

Captured by the goddess Calypso on her island paradise of Ogygia and held for nine years, Odysseus has suffered exile, misery, and homesickness, and longs to return to his family in Ithaca. The lush enchantment of the island, the peerless beauty of the goddess, and a life of comfort, leisure, and pleasure do not fulfill the longing heart of the hero of the Trojan War who walks along the beach shedding tears. When Hermes, the god of luck, arrives on the island with the message from Zeus that commands Calypso to release Odysseus from captivity, Odysseus realizes his two choices. If he leaves the island to return to his family and home in Ithaca, he is not guaranteed a safe arrival or glorious homecoming. Poseidon, the god of the sea, harbors great hatred for Odysseus for blinding his son Polyphemus and so may destroy Odysseus's ship and drown him. Odysseus also recalls Agamemnon's victorious homecoming from the war—which ended in his being murdered by his wife, Clytemnestra. If Odysseus remains on the island paradise with Calypso, he escapes all the dangers of travel on the ocean, lives a life of security and pleasure, enjoys the beauty and love of a goddess, and gains immortality. As Calypso explains the two options that face Odysseus, "Yet had you any inkling of the full measure of misery you are bound to endure before you reach your motherland, you would not move from where you are, but you would stay and share this home with me, and take on immortality, however much you long to see that wife of yours, I know that she is never out of your thoughts."[4] For Odysseus to

---

4   *The Odyssey*, tr. E. V. Rieu (New York: Penguin Books, 1985), 93.

fulfill the deepest desires of his heart and return home, he must take a chance, risk the dangers of the sea, and hope that his beloved Penelope remained faithful during his absence—a chance that ultimately leads to Odysseus's glorious reunion with his son, wife, and father, who have mourned his absence for twenty years: "Penelope's surrender melted Odysseus's heart, and he wept as he held his dear wife in his arms, so loyal and true. Sweet moment too for her, sweet as the sight of land to sailors struggling in the sea, when the Sea-god by dint of wind and wave has wrecked their gallant ship."[5] As the figure of Hermes, who presides in athletics and wars, illustrates, taking a chance means seizing a golden opportunity that can lead to surprising escapes and victories that change the whole course of one's life.

In the ballad "The Wooing of Sir Keith" in Howard Pyle's *The Merry Adventures of Robin Hood*, an ugly crone—"a grewsome sight" and "the foulest dame"— appears at King Arthur's Round Table to ask a favor from a knight. For the curing of her painful disease, only one remedy will provide the healing: "Till Christian knight will willingly / Thrice kiss me on the mouth" (346–47). The woman explains that a married man cannot bestow the kisses, and no constraint can force a knight to grant this boon. But Sir Launcelot will not deign to kiss an old woman, Sir Tristram is repelled by the idea, Sir Kay feels embarrassed at the thought, and Sir Gawaine claims, "For sooner would I die." Sir Keith, however, takes a chance: "Now such relief as Christian can / I'll give to her, my lord" (102, 103). Thereupon the ugly hag undergoes

5   Ibid., 346–47.

a miraculous change from wizened crone to fair maid; red cheeks, sweet breath, and glittering hair suddenly transform her to a paragon of beauty. She offers her love and wealth to the knight whose "noble courtesy" broke the spell of her bewitchment. To be a chivalrous knight or a noble gentleman, a man must exert initiative and not be ruled by the pride, sloth, or respectability that inhibit the cowardly knights. Sir Keith wins the great gift of the lovely maiden, who showers him with her love and wealth because he ventured without counting the cost. This taking of chances—come what may—gives to life its mystery, poetry, romance, adventure, and unexpected rewards.

In Shakespeare's *The Merchant of Venice*, the three suitors who court Portia must solve a riddle and select the right casket to win her hand in marriage—a game of chance or a lottery. The first casket of gold reads, "Who chooseth me shall gain what many men desire"; the second casket of silver states, "Who chooseth me shall get as much as any man deserves"; and the third casket of lead says, "Who chooseth me must give and hazard all" (2.7.4–9).[6] The Prince of Morocco takes no chances as he follows the way of the world and chooses the golden casket ("what many men desire"). Prudent by worldly standards, he assumes he can gain the prize by reasoning according to monetary standards. The Prince of Aragon also refuses to venture, arguing after he looks at the leaden casket, "You shall look fairer ere I give or hazard" (2.7.22). He concludes that the gift of Portia's

---

6 *Shakespeare: The Complete Works*, ed. G. B. Harrison (New York: Harcourt Brace and Jovanovich, 1968), 594.

love depends on his merit, a reward he has earned by virtue of work: "I will assume desert" (2.9.51). When Bassanio makes his choice of the caskets, he does not calculate gain and loss by fantasizing about the wealth of gold or boast of his just deserts by focusing on his merit. He gives and hazards "all" and wins Portia's hand by selecting the leaden casket that contains her picture. A great prize demands a daring risk, the willingness to give without counting the costs, weighing the odds, or calculating self-interest. Shakespeare's play reveals that life's most precious gifts elude economic thinking and utilitarian logic. Bassanio understands this, refusing to view romance as a matter of cost, as a bargain, or as a fair price. And thus he wins the prize of love. To give or hazard all is to welcome adventure rather than to calculate a fixed profit or justified reward. To hazard all demonstrates an unconditional giving that inspires an unexpected gift that surpasses all one's costs. Portia's worth cannot be measured in ducats, gold, or silver— even though Bassanio borrowed from Antonio's fortune, and Antonio lost all his wealth in his ventures upon the sea. Taking a chance inspired by a high ideal wins the priceless treasure of love because it transcends the preoccupation of winning or losing money.

Shakespeare's Hamlet also takes a daring chance and wins a great prize (for his homeland, if not for himself). After discovering that King Claudius, the murderer of his father, has given orders for his own execution in England, Hamlet decides to return to Denmark to confront the king rather than escape with his life to another land. Even though his beloved and loyal friend Horatio, suspecting foul play, urges Hamlet not to accept the king's invitation to duel Laertes in court, Hamlet insists on taking a chance. On his voyage to England accompanied by his traitorous friends Rosencrantz and Guildenstern, Hamlet, in the middle of the night, narrowly escapes death by taking a chance—by unsealing the letters sent by the king for his beheading: "Our indiscretion sometimes serves us well," he tells Horatio (5.2.8–9). This "indiscretion" Hamlet demonstrates again when he chooses to duel Laertes despite Horatio's warning of treachery—a foreboding that is justified by Claudius's poisoning of Laertes's sword. When Horatio protests, "Nay, good my lord," Hamlet responds, "Not a whit, we defy augury. There's special providence in the fall of a sparrow. If it be not now, 'tis to come; if it be not to come, it will be now; if it be not now, yet it will come. The readiness is all" (5.2.224, 230–34). Hamlet risks death when he returns to Denmark from his journey and when he duels Laertes. However, by hazarding and venturing all, Hamlet exposes Claudius's plot, wounds him with the poisoned sword intended as Laertes's weapon, and cures Denmark of its violence and tyranny. To paraphrase Edmund Burke's famous statement, the only thing necessary for evil to triumph is for good people never to take chances, never to trust Divine Providence, and never to act with moral courage.

The hero ventures on a road that leads from way to way, and his choice culminates in a life of happiness. Odysseus sacrifices comfort and security on the beautiful island of Calypso, risks shipwreck and drowning on the sea, and rejoices in a blessed homecoming with his family. Sir Keith dares to serve an old woman with the magnanimous gift of three kisses that he does not relish and receives the favor of a beautiful maid's love and wealth. Bassanio hazards all and wins the prize of Portia, renowned for her "wondrous virtues." Hamlet risks his life by returning to Denmark and agreeing to duel Laertes, but he restores moral order to the "rotten" land of Denmark. As Bassanio explains the mystery of chance in his illustration of the lost arrow:

> In my school days, when I had lost one shaft,
> I shot his fellow of the selfsame flight
> The selfsame way with more advised watch,
> To find the other forth, and by adventuring both,
> I oft found both. (1.1.140–44)

To venture and hazard, then, is to invite surprises and wonders, to increase one's blessings and good fortune, and to let the mystery of providence play its part in human life. Man proposes, God disposes. The unforeseen outcomes that follow from this adventuresome spirit often exceed one's hopes and dreams as a single decision to take a chance leads to glory, gifts, and joys beyond measure. This wise abandonment to life's chances is ever present in the literature of epic, romance, heroism, and chivalry, and never reduces the glory of human life to getting and spending.

This sense of adventure, however, is a missing virtue in a modern culture that values control, security, and comfort more than chance. In C. S. Lewis's *The Great Divorce*, the inhabitants of the grey town journey to the bright world of the spirits, a heavenly world where truth, purity, beauty, joy, and the fullness of an abundant life of eternal happiness await them. While all have the choice of taking a chance and continuing in the bright transcendent world or returning to the prosaic grey town, many visitors decide to resume the old drab life rather than take a risk. When the narrator asks one of the passengers if the travelers actually *like* the dreary existence of the grey town, he receives this reply: " 'As much as they'd like anything. . . . They've got cinemas and fish and chip shops and advertisements and all the sorts of things they want' " (16). Upon arrival in the bright world of the heavenly spirits, the travelers from the grey town suffer pains and difficulties that persuade them not to take a chance and travel on this new road. They step on grass that feels as hard as rocks and diamonds, hear the sublime roar of a waterfall that terrifies them, behold golden apples too heavy to carry—sensations that provoke the travelers to complain, "Of course there was never any question of our staying. You can't eat the fruit and you can't drink the water, and it takes you all your time to walk on the grass. A human being couldn't live here" (54). At the suggestion that a new inhabitant of the bright world soon adapts to the new conditions and grows "acclimatised," the cynical traveler comments, "Same old lie," doubting that the habits of virtue reduce the hardships of the moral life: "All this poppycock about growing harder so that the grass doesn't hurt our feet, now!" (55, 56). The visitors from the grey town have other complaints. One murmurs, "What the hell would there be to *do* here?" Another is troubled that she is underdressed: "I'd never have come at all if I'd known you were all going to be dressed like that" (56, 60). Others resist every effort to teach them about the heavenly world of spirits and resent the spirits' rejection of their proposals "to dam the river, cut down the trees, kill the animals, build a mountain railway, smooth out the horrible grass and moss and heather with asphalt" (76), in other words, to remodel the bright world after the grey town.

Because the visitors from the city do not hazard or venture anything, they remain ghosts and participate only in the "Shadow of Life," never experiencing the truth come alive. The spirits, on the other hand, have become the Solid People because they did not fear the truth, resign themselves to sloth, or deny the gift of love and joy presented in the bright world at the cost of taking a chance, attempting a difficult task, and hazarding all. In daring to take risks, these bright spirits "drink the cup to the bottom" and behold the glorious majesty of a heavenly world of infinite joy.

This contrast between the ghosts of the grey town and the solid spirits of the bright world distinguishes those whose listless existence amounts to dreary lifelessness from those whose lives abound in the fullness of passionate love, joy, and truth. The ghosts will not abandon their attachments, vices, and bad habits to experience and taste the real world: "Their fists are clenched, their teeth are clenched, their eyes fast shut. First they will not, in the end they cannot, open their hands for gifts, or their mouths for food, or their eyes to see" (121). The heretical priest—attached to his "honest opinions, sincerely expressed"—prefers applause and popularity as he embraces the spirit of the age over the timeless truth of the Christian faith. He will not venture into the bright world because "I have to be back next Friday to read a paper" (42, 46). The fashionable woman—attached to her image of elegance in the mirror—feels out of style in the bright world and cannot remove her gaze from her reflection in the glass, provoking the Spirit's reproach: "Could you, only for a moment, fix your mind on something not yourself?" (62). The famous artist—attached to his reputation and interested only in paint—prizes the glamour of publicity more than knowledge of the author of Beauty itself: "I must be off at once. . . . I must go back to my friends. I must write an article" (82). The ghosts, then, go backward; they do not take a road that diverges in the wood and follow it to its terminus. The ghosts remain smug and complacent; they do not venture upon the risks of travel that Odysseus embraces so that he can live well rather than merely survive, and embrace wife, son, and father rather than continue on an island living an inhuman life with a goddess. The ghosts pander only to their appetites, self-interest, and ease; they do not serve others and cannot forget themselves as Sir Keith does in pleasing the ugly crone with chivalrous generosity. The ghosts are fearful and cautious, preferring lukewarm mediocrity to passionate living; they cannot hazard anything or take the slightest chance by leaving the monotonous grey town to seek the daring adventure of the bright world, which promises priceless treasure like that for which Bassanio sacrifices all. The ghosts become acclimated to sin and do nothing to dispel the greyness of their city or their lives; they do not dare to expose or confront evil in the way Hamlet challenges King Claudius and duels Laertes.

How grey is our day-to-day life today? How ghostly are the empty cradles and depopulated kindergartens of nations with plummeting birthrates? How loveless is the cool calculation of the man who does not ask a woman to marry him but allows her to split the rent? How dry and futile are liberal arts that are founded on a denial of objective excellence or truth? All these modern realities reflect the thinness of ghostliness and the pallor of death.

Like the people of the grey town, always moving from one part of the city to another in a constant whirl of restless, purposeless activity, we unstable inhabitants of contemporary culture do not commit to one of the roads in the wood and follow it to its natural destination. Instead, we act arbitrarily, driven by passions and whims, and when it suits us we overthrow moral laws and time-honored traditions, tossing perennial wisdom on history's trash heap. In *The Great Divorce*, one traveler describes the erratic constant activity of the grey town thus: "As soon as anyone arrives he settles in some street. Before he's been there twenty-four hours he quarrels with his neighbor. Before the week is over he's quarreled so badly that he decides to move away" (20). No natural purpose or divine end governs the activity of this city enamored of change for the sake of change. On the other hand, when the traveler in Frost's poem continues patiently on the road that leads to its natural completion, when Odysseus perseveres to return home to Ithaca, when Sir Keith serves a woman with magnanimous chivalry, when Bassanio hazards all to gain the prize of Portia, and when Hamlet commits to the moral cause of restoring justice, they cooperate with Mother Nature, Divine Providence, or moral law and reap a fruitful harvest. All these roads lead to a Bright World with Solid People surrounded by Real Things that are found by the man who will risk himself and take a chance.

XX. Kindness and the "Human Touch": The Short Stories of O. Henry

We all know the story of King Midas's golden touch, retold in Hawthorne's *A Wonder Book*. In that book, one of the children hearing of Midas remarks at the end of the tale, "But some people have what we may call 'The Leaden Touch,' and make everything dull and heavy that they lay their fingers upon." As the story indicates, Midas's own ability backfired on him, having turned his lively little daughter into a stolid statue. There are many kinds of touches that are dehumanizing, and only one kind that is truly human. Which manner of touch we use on each other makes all the difference in our lives. The short stories of O. Henry profoundly capture the nature of the human touch and illustrate its mysterious power to transform a person's life and uplift our existence.

In "The Last Leaf," a young artist struggling to earn her livelihood in Greenwich Village contracts a serious case of pneumonia that threatens her life. Johnsy, lying in bed and looking out the window in her state of weakness, counts out loud, remarking to her roommate Sue, "There goes another one. There are only five left now,"[1] meaning the leaves on the ivy vine she is watching. Because the doctor's prognosis offers her only a one-in-ten chance of surviving, she associates the falling of the leaves with

---

1   *41 Stories by O. Henry* (New York: Signet Classics, 2007), 33.

the ebbing away of her life: "I want to see the last one fall before it gets dark. Then I'll go too" (34). Resigning herself to her imminent death, Johnsy complains: "I'm tired of waiting. I'm tired of thinking. I want to turn loose my hold on everything, and go sailing down, down, just like one of those poor, tired leaves" (34). Sue tells this sad news to Behrman, an old artist with the dream of painting a masterpiece, a man who lives in the same apartment building as the two young artists. He is shocked to learn of Johnsy's passive acceptance of her inevitable death: "Is dere people in de world mit der foolishness to die because leafs dey drop off from a confounded vine?" (35). Gazing out the window the next morning, Johnsy sees that, despite a night of rain and wind, one last leaf remains on the vine against the brick wall. Even with the continuation of more rain and the gusts of the north wind during the course of the day, the one last leaf clung to the vine. This astonishing phenomenon becomes an unmistakable sign to the dying Johnsy, a message that death is not her fate and a reminder of her guilt in wishing for death: "Something has made that last leaf stay there to show me how wicked I was. It is a sin to want to die" (36). When the doctor checks on the improved condition of his patient, he tells Johnsy and Sue the shocking news that Behrman suddenly died of pneumonia in the hospital, the illness he contracted while painting on the brick wall the leaf that never fell. Sue explains to Johnsy, "Didn't you wonder why it never fluttered or moved when the wind blew? Ah, darling, it's Behrman's masterpiece—he painted it there the night that the last leaf fell" (37). In his sacrificial kindness, Behrman exemplified the human touch. He voluntarily performed the special favor without being asked. The idea came from his good heart without suggestions from others. He anticipated another person's need without any plea for help. His small deed had a wondrous effect in restoring to Johnsy her will to live.

The contrast between this sensitive human touch and other, harsher responses echoes through all of literature. In Robert Frost's poem "Love and a Question," an old traveler knocks on the door of a couple on their honeymoon: "He asked with the eyes more than the lips / For a shelter for the night."[2] The bridegroom looks at the sky and ponders the state of the weather, only to reply with evasive uncertainty: "Stranger, I wish I knew." As he looks within the house and sees his bride in the comfort of a glowing fireplace in the romantic atmosphere of this special night, the thought of spoiling the honeymoon with the interruption of a needy traveler blocks the response of the human touch. The bridegroom would gladly offer "A dole of bread, a purse, / A heartfelt prayer for the poor of God," but to invite the stranger into their abode and offer hospitality to a stranger on this night is not a duty he wishes to honor. The bridegroom's inhuman touch shows no kindness, no effort to extend a simple favor, and no recognition of another person's genuine need. His self-interested coldness reveals a lack of humanity. Sensing the plight of the old man who "asked with the eyes more than the lips," the bridegroom does not anticipate the request of the traveler but disowns any sense of obligation as he places his comfort and pleasure

---

2   *The Poetry of Robert Frost*, ed. Edward Connery Lathem (New York: Holt, Rinehart and Winston, 1967), 7.

before the suffering of another person. The human touch of Behrman provided for another person's happiness as he responded immediately, sacrificed his time, and endured foul weather to paint his "masterpiece." Conversely, the inhuman touch of the bridegroom feigns ignorance of another's unspoken request, hesitates and temporizes, and lets an old man suffer the inclement weather rather than offer shelter for the night. The human touch loves goodness for its own sake and does favors gladly or silently rather than invent excuses.

Shakespeare's Oberon is also a master of the human touch. In Shakespeare's *A Midsummer Night's Dream*, Oberon, the king of the fairies, encounters a lover's quarrel between Hermia and Lysander during the revels of the night. Because, according to the medieval saying, "pity runs quickly in gentle hearts," Oberon decides to reconcile the lovers with the medicine of the juice extracted from a flower that anoints the eyes while a person sleeps and casts a spell that will make him fall in love with the next creature he sees upon waking. Demetrius, who had declared his love to Helena and given every intention he would marry her, jilts her and turns his affections to Hermia, a woman in love with Lysander—a state of affairs that provokes Helena's stinging comments to her lover, declaring him to be a "hardhearted adamant" and insisting that the "wildest hath not such a heart as you" (2.2.197, 229).[3] The quiet, silent entrance of Oberon into the arguments of the lovers occurs in the darkness of the night, when the fairies frolic in the forest in their

3   *The Major Plays of Shakespeare*, ed. G. B. Harrison (New York: Harcourt, Brace & Jovanovich), 522.

invisible form. Although it is performed by a fairy, not a man, this gentle anointing epitomizes the human touch in all its tactful gentleness, unobtrusive manner, and refined thoughtfulness. Like Behrman in "The Last Leaf," Oberon has no special obligation to intercede, but compassion moves him to do this kind favor with a sense of playful gladness proper to good fairies—reveling in goodness for its own sake. Oberon's human touch embodies all the virtues that Demetrius's inhuman touch lacks. In fact, Helena protests to her lover: "If you were civil and knew courtesy, / You would not do me thus much injury" (3.2.147–48). Just as Behrman's human touch transforms the gloom of Johnsy's slow dying to hope and renewal, Oberon's magical touch changes the atmosphere in the forest from discord to harmony, from division to unity, and accomplishes the reconciliation that leads to happy marriages.

The workaday world of bureaucracy and big business is notorious for its inhuman touch. In Robert Frost's poem "Departmental," busy ants conduct their business with synchronized efficiency and dispatch as they march in order and obey commands with flawless perfection. A small ant that encounters a large dead moth on the table does not let this problem distract him from performing his function: "He showed not the least surprise. / His business wasn't with such. / He gave it scarcely a touch, / And was off on his duty run." The industrious worker cannot stop to perform a humane act toward the dead; he can only give signals to have the inconvenient body removed by a specialist, to "one / [o]f the hive's enquiry squad" whom "he would put . . . onto the case." When ants discover the dead body of one of their members, again they refer the matter to a bureaucracy rather than deviate from their assigned function: "One crossing with hurried tread / The body of one of their dead / Isn't given a moment's arrest—/ Seems not even impressed." The shock of death does not stop the flow of business as usual. In the most impersonal, perfunctory manner, an ant reports these accidents to any "With whom he crosses antennae, / And they no doubt report / To the higher up at court." The problem disappears when the order is communicated to an official branch of government, the office of the Janizary, whose trained members act with promptness to facilitate the harmonious operations of ant society. Organs of communication instantly spread the news ("Then word goes out in Formic"), the message is immediately received ("Death's come to Jerry McCormic"), the order is quickly given ("Will the special Janizary . . . [g] o bring him to his people"). The robotic ants with their instinctual automatic responses remove the dead with no disturbances or complications in their regimented lives. Finally, after the discovery, the report, and the orders ("This is the word of your Queen"), the mortician with his specialized instruments comes speedily to the scene and ends the temporary inconvenience of death's awkward appearance: "And taking a formal position, / With feelers calmly atwiddle, / Seizes the dead by the middle, / And heaving it high in air, / Carries him out of there." Here Frost satirizes the aspect of work, organization, bureaucracy, and technology that ignores the personal dimension, the human touch, which sacrifices humanity for the sake of efficiency and values abstract goals more than real, living persons.

Unlike Behrman and Oberon, who go out of their ways to extend kind favors to others at inconvenience to themselves, the ants have no time to stop, show pity, evince a gentle heart, or do good for its own sake. Their idea of action is purely utilitarian, never gracious or gratuitous. As functionaries, the ants send messages and receive and follow orders according to organizational charts with a chain of command. But they never initiate a thoughtful, spontaneous, playful, kind action on their own—the essence of the human touch. They lack the art of Behrman, whose "masterpiece" is the one remaining leaf he painted on the brick wall. They do not practice the magic of Oberon, whose imagination devised the love juice to cure the lovers' problems. The human touch is not the result of training or specialization but an expression of a refined heart cultivated by the practice of charity— what Edmund Burke in *Reflections on the Revolution in France* refers to as "the moral imagination" and "the unbought grace of life," qualities he associates with "the age of chivalry," which the French Revolution renounced. The human touch is a grace cultivated by the culture of the family, the manners of civilization, and the ideals of religion. As Burke remarked, "[A]ll the good things which are connected with manners, and with civilization, have, in this European world of ours, depended upon two principles; and were indeed the result of both combined; I mean the spirit of a gentleman, and the spirit of religion."[4] Both the ideals of chivalry and Christian charity inspire the love of virtue for its own sake and teach the joy of goodness, the blessedness of giving rather than receiving that shapes the human touch.

---

4   Edmund Burke, *Reflections on the Revolution in France* (New York: Penguin Books, 1986), 170, 171, 173.

The human touch reveals the unity of the human race and a common human nature as the basis of the natural moral law. The parable of the Good Samaritan and the ancient Greek custom of hospitality teach that all persons are human beings first and foremost before they are Jews or Gentiles, Greeks or barbarians. The Good Samaritan exemplifies Christ's definition of the second great commandment, "Love thy neighbor as thyself": "and when he saw him, he had compassion, and went to him and bound up his wounds, pouring on oil and wine; then he set him on his own beast and brought him to an inn, and took care of him" (Luke 10: 33). In the *Odyssey*, when Telemachus arrives in Menelaus's kingdom during a wedding feast, a servant announces the news to the king and asks, "Pray tell me whether we should unharness their horses for them or send them on for someone else to entertain." Menelaus's response demonstrates the unmistakable human touch: "Think of all the hospitality that you and I enjoyed from strangers before we reached our homes and could expect that Zeus might spare us from such pressing need again. Unyoke their horses at once, and bring our visitors into the house to join us at the feast."[5] Nathaniel Hawthorne sums it up in the story of Baucis and Philemon in *A Wonder Book*. This aged couple feels a moral obligation to practice hospitality to all strangers because it is not only a sacred law of the gods but also an act of human kindness needed by all persons: "a debt of love to one another, because there is no other method of paying the debt of love and

---

5   Homer, *The Odyssey*, tr. E. V. Rieu (New York: Penguin Books, 1985), 64–65.

care which all of us owe to Providence," Hawthorne writes. One of the Greek gods defines this custom as the quintessential human virtue: "When men do not feel towards the humblest stranger as if he were a brother . . . they are unworthy to exist on earth, which was created as the abode of a great human brotherhood."[6] In other words, the human touch always honors the dignity of other persons and responds to their most basic, immediate need. It is so profoundly appreciated that it creates a feeling of eternal indebtedness. The human touch develops from a sense of gratitude for the favors received from others—a sense of obligation to offer these same kindnesses in similar situations. The human touch, though simple, unspectacular, and humble, evokes wonder at the goodness of the human heart. In Hawthorne's tale, the Greek gods themselves are impressed and repay it with the gift of the miraculous pitcher that always refills after it is emptied. This pitcher is a symbol of the inexhaustible fountain of love reserved in the human heart.

Without the human touch, persons are left alone to commiserate and suffer the coldness of an impersonal world, one bereft of the thoughtfulness of a Behrman, the pity of an Oberon, and the hospitality of a Baucis and Philemon, whose masterpieces, magic, and miracles transform a gray world into a bright kingdom. Johnsy would be ignored and left to pine away and die. Old men with canes would not find lodging in the night. The machinery of business as usual would never stop and

---

6   Nathaniel Hawthorne, *A Wonder Book* (New York: Knopf, 1994), 189, 208.

recognize the leisure necessary to tend to the profoundly meaningful events of human life that supersede work. And human beings would behave and react like the ants in a column whose perfunctory movements lack the originality of Behrman's art, the spontaneity of Oberon's playfulness, and the sensitivity of Baucis and Philemon's graciousness. The human touch recognizes human suffering and attempts to relieve or end it, but the inhuman touch seems impervious to mercy or compassion. The human touch always acknowledges the humanity and dignity of other persons, but the inhuman touch considers others as inconveniences, burdens, or aliens.

The human touch does the utmost good and does all in its power to perform kind favors and make loving sacrifices, but the inhuman touch is ruled by the comfort of the fire, the machinery of bureaucracy, and the power of self-interest.

Modernity has lost the human touch. A culture that does not welcome children into the family or the world, a society that legalizes the violence of abortion, sexual mores that treat human beings as dispensable objects of pleasure, a hardhearted ethos that disregards the suffering inflicted upon the victims of divorce, and power-hungry governments that wage unjust wars with wanton violence, ignoring the cost of human life for the sake of ideology and empire—all need the correction of the human touch to make life more humane. Burke explained that the moral sentiments that cultivate the human touch originate in chivalry and religion, but these ideals do not inform a world suffering from fatherless families and from secularism that relegates God to the realm of private opinion and moral relativism. Burke's "spirit of a gentleman" that honored the duty of service to others—especially women and children—and Burke's respect for religion as a pillar of civilized society need to recover their influence in refining the consciences and the feelings of fathers, mothers, lawmakers, physicians, educators, and employers. If this happens, men and women will honor marriage; parents will protect their children whether they are "wanted" or not; lawmakers will conform to moral reality rather than replace it with ideology; physicians will obey the Hippocratic Oath and "do no harm" to their most vulnerable patients; teachers will transmit truth and wisdom rather than sway with every trend; and employers will respect the human dignity of all workers with just wages and safe working conditions. These human touches, always gentle and sensitive, can transform an otherwise brutal world.

XXI. Love:
The Divine Comedy

The rhythm of love is reciprocal and mutual, the alternating of giving and receiving in constant, varying, and surprising ways. The Holy Trinity models this paradigm of love as the Father loves the Son and the Son loves the Father—a love that is endlessly generated and issues in the Holy Spirit, the third person of the Trinity, who also circulates and returns the love He has received in His continuous activity of outpouring, fruitful love. In the *Paradiso*, Dante depicts this mystery of love's ongoing rhythm of generating, circulating, giving, and receiving of love's eternal procession:

The light supreme, within its fathomless
Clear substance, showed to me three spheres, which bare

Three hues distinct, and occupied one space.

The first mirrored the next, as though it were
Rainbow from rainbow, and the third seemed flame
Breathed equally from each of the first pair.[1] (canto 33, 115–20)

---

1   Dante Alighieri, *The Divine Comedy 3: Paradise*, tr. Dorothy L. Sayers (New York: Penguin Books, 1973), 346.

The Nicene Creed (in its Western form) acknowledges that the Holy Spirit "proceeds from the Father and the Son" (*filioque*), and St. Augustine in *On the Trinity* explains that the "Holy Spirit proceeds from the Father as the first principle and, by the eternal gift of this to the Son, from the communion of both the Father and the Son" (*Catechism of the Catholic Church*, #264). This reciprocal communication of Father, Son, and Holy Spirit always produces the responses of love—always giving, constantly passing on what one receives, eternally outpouring the riches of generosity. This movement of eternal responsiveness in returning the love received only to receive more of the bounty of love to perpetuate and distribute its inexhaustible riches in never-ending motion is the paradigm of Trinitarian love that also reveals its quintessential human quality. Man, too, is created to give and receive love, to respond to a voice, to acknowledge a gift, to answer when called, to speak in return, to accept an invitation, and to give glory to God. This is the circulation of love that the Trinity models for human imitation.

So often in human experience, however, love does not receive its proper response. Just as a gift frequently does not receive its expression of thankfulness, good deeds often go unacknowledged and unrewarded. If gratitude is lacking when love is received but not returned, the rhythm of love does not run its course. A person writes a letter but receives no reply, or a person leaves a phone message that is never answered. An invitation is sent but is not accepted, or an invitation is accepted but never reciprocated. A person initiates a conversation and extends friendliness only to be greeted with silence or indifference. A teacher poses questions in the classroom, but no students participate or are sociable enough to speak. In all these examples love does not follow its natural progression, because one person initiates an action that soon loses its momentum or energy when the other party shows no interest and fails to do his part in maintaining the alternating rhythm. In Shakespeare's *King Lear*, Lear bemoans the fact that his two ungrateful daughters, Regan and Goneril, give nothing in return, not even gracious hospitality to their father and king for his lifetime of care and love. "I gave you all," Lear laments, only to be denied his simple request of visiting their castles with his attendants. Without the water of gratitude, love dies and bears no fruit.

Robert Frost's poem "Two Look at Two" illuminates this antiphony of love's music and rhythm. A couple in love walking in the woods prepare to return as they sigh, "Good-night to woods," only to be surprised by a deer: "A doe from round a spruce stood looking at them / Across a wall, as near the wall as they" (229). As the couple turn to retrace their steps, another surprise captures their attention: "A buck from round the spruce stood looking at them / Across the wall, as near the wall as they." As the buck fixes his gaze upon the loving couple, his quizzical look implies a question: "Why don't you make some motion? / Or give some sign of life?" Friendliness, charity, and love invite and expect exchange and interaction. Both the doe and the buck have the same reaction to the sight of the human couple: after their stare of quiet concentration on the figures, they pass "unscared along the wall" because they sense an exchange of love that dispels their instinctive fear: "She [the doe] seemed to think that, two thus, they were safe." The buck's gaze also reflects a natural affinity between man and animal and between the two couples—a perfect kind of communication that invites a handshake of friendship as the buck "had them almost feeling dared / [t]o stretch a proffering hand." When two look at two, each pair responds and communicates across the wall: the human couple's bond of love evokes an answer from the union of doe and buck that replies to the message they receive from the loving couple's companionship: "As if the earth in one unlooked-for favor / Had made them certain earth returned their love." When two look at two, love's initiative awakens love as the glances are exchanged and reciprocated. The love of man and woman reflected in the attraction of the doe and buck communicates affection between man and animal. As the two couples occupy opposite positions with the wall of separation between them, they look, as it were, into a mirror that sends back their reflection. Thus proceeds a love between man and woman, an attraction between doe and buck, and an exchange from human to animal and animal to human that captures love's fruitful, life-giving nature. In the three successions of glances and reactions, Frost shows the bountiful effects of love: "This is all," "This, *then* is all," "This *must* be all." When love's responsive rhythm of giving and receiving is set in motion, there is always "more." The first time, when the couple imagine that their walk has ended ("This is all"), they are surprised: "But not so; there was more." The second time, when they conclude that their brief glimpse of the doe has faded ("This, *then*, is all"), they are again astonished: "But no, not yet." The third time, when the

man and woman and the doe and buck exchange looks ("This *must* be all"), they remain spellbound in wonder: "It was all." They discover the law of love's perpetual alternating and ongoing rhythm of mutual giving and receiving. This sense of "more" is always one of love's fruits when its rhythm moves naturally.

Gerard Manley Hopkins's poem "Hurrahing in Harvest" also captures this rhythm of love's music. In the poem the completion of the harvest that marks the end of summer leaves rows of corn stalks at irregular, uneven heights—a scene of the abundance of the earth that reflects God's plenty in nourishing human life:

> Summer ends now; now, barbarous in beauty, the stooks rise
> Around; up, above, what wind-walks! what lovely behaviour
> Of silk-sack clouds! Has wilder, willful-wavier
> Meal-drift moulded ever and melted across skies?
> (31)

The rolling, fluctuating, unsymmetrical heights of the stalks depict a wavy pattern that clouds and heaps of grain ("meal-drift") also form when gathered—a scene of Mother Nature's bounty that evokes wonder at the riotous exuberance of God's goodness, "barbarous in beauty" in all its wild splendor. This beauty, abundance, and generosity reveal God's handiwork that manifests his goodness and Divine Providence. The harvest that declares the glory of God's great love is a form of communication, a speaking that evokes a listening. Thus the narrator responds:

I walk, I lift up, I lift up heart, eyes,
Down all that glory in the heavens to glean our
Saviour;
And, eyes, heart, what looks, what lips yet gave you a
Rapturous love's greeting of realer, of rounder replies?

The rhythm of love's antiphony moves from God's goodness to man's gratitude, from God's beauty to man's wonder, from God's glory to man's contemplation, from God's speech to man's reply, from God's giving to man's receiving. This response of lifting up the heart and the eyes to God in profound awe and thankfulness recalls of course the lifting up of the mind to God in the Christian Eucharist: "V: Lift up your hearts. R: We lift them up to the Lord." God's statement of love does not go unacknowledged or unappreciated but receives "[r]apturous love's greeting of realer, of rounder replies" as man's eyes behold the splendor of God's heavenly glory reflected in the "barbarous" beauty of the cornfield, as man's heart surges with joy not only at the earthly gifts of grain that he gleans from the field but also at the heavenly food of the Eucharist, and as man's lips sing praise and resound with the happiness of love. Throughout this poem, God speaks and man answers, God gives and man receives, God performs miracles and man beholds in contemplative wonder. Again, the course of love yields a bountiful harvest.

In the scene of the harvest depicted in Hopkins's poem, only two actors or speakers interact, but the exchange is harmonious, complementary, and perfect. The beautiful human and heavenly gifts that flow from the liberal outpouring of God's inexhaustible generosity are cherished and honored. Because of the alternating responses of this antiphony, the action of love is completed and reciprocated when God gives, man receives, and man in turn offers thanksgiving:

These things, these things were here and but the beholder
Wanting; which two when once they meet,
The heart rears wings bold and bolder
And hurls for him, O half hurls earth for him off under his feet.

For vision to occur, the world needs sunlight and man needs eyes. For knowledge to occur, the world requires intelligibility and man needs reason. For love to happen, the splendor of beauty must shine and man must contemplate the miracle. The union of the beholder and the beheld, designed and intended for one another, generates the drama and excitement of vision, knowledge, and love that inspire the passionate energy that gives unending joy to these relationships. "The heart rears wings bold and bolder / And hurls for him, O half hurls earth for him off under his feet." This thrill and ecstasy of beauty created, proffered, and prized, of love given, received, and returned, of truth uttered, comprehended, and shared, lies at the heart of a creation that is rhythmic in its movements: wavy, wild, undulating, and fluctuating. This movement produces the cornucopia of love's harvest.

This responsiveness of love's rhythm fills Christ's teaching in the Gospels. When Peter, Andrew, James, and John heard Christ's words "Follow me and I will make you fishers of men," they responded to the invitation without any reservations and received the power of the apostles to work miracles: "Immediately they left their nets and followed him" (Matthew 4:19–20). Before Christ cured two blind men, he asked them, "Do you believe I am able to do this?" Their simple response of "Yes, Lord" moved Christ to perform the miracle: " 'According to your faith be it done to you.' And their eyes were opened" (Matthew 9:29–30). In these examples, Christ invites or initiates, and man cooperates. When Christ pitied the crowds and told his disciples to feed his followers, they protested that five loaves and two fish were not enough food, only to hear Christ's request: "And he said, 'Bring them here to me' " (Matthew 14:18). Because the disciples honored Christ's wishes, they beheld the miracle of the multiplication of the loaves and fish that fed five thousand. In the marriage at Cana, Christ commands the servants to "fill the jars with water" and then utters, "Now draw some out and take it to the steward of the feast." When the servants respond to Christ's request and respect Mary's wish when she asks them to "[d]o whatever he tells you" (John 2:5, 7–8), they marvel at the miracle of water changed into wine. And of course, Mary's fiat, "Be it done to me according to thy word," says yes to God's invitation to become the mother of God and welcomes the miracle of the Incarnation. Man's response to God's commands, invitations, and actions always inspires greater love, unexpected gifts, and astounding miracles on God's part. The movement of love flows, circulates, and travels back and forth between man and God in the cycle of unending mutual giving and receiving.

The Eucharist and all the other sacraments illustrate this perpetual exchange of love between God and creature. In the Eucharist the bread and wine that God first gave to man as the fruits of the earth are offered to God in thanksgiving for these blessings. These gifts of bread and wine, then, miraculously become the body and blood of Christ, as God receives man's simple gifts and first fruits only to change them into more precious heavenly gifts, the food of eternal life. First, God gives man grain and grapes. Second, man gives God bread and wine. Then God gives man the heavenly manna, the body and blood of Christ, "the medicine of immortality, the antidote for death, and the food that makes us live forever in Jesus Christ," in the words of St. Ignatius of Antioch. In this sacrament, as the *Catechism of the Catholic Church* explains, *"we offer to the Father* what he has himself given us: the gifts of his creation, bread and wine which, by the power of the Holy Spirit and by the words of Christ, have become the body and blood of Christ" (#1331, #1357). Likewise, in the other sacraments the matter that man brings or uses (water, oil, the body) are God-given gifts that man then offers and incorporates into the sacramental actions (baptism, confirmation, matrimony) that will confer divine graces in the exchange of gifts. First God gives to man, then man makes offerings to God, next God blesses man's gifts with supernatural powers that bestow divine life to the soul. In all the sacraments, then, the rhythm of love's antiphony unites man and God as beholder and beheld in an exchange of mutual giving and receiving in which God always gives increase.

This flow of love's rhythm of life-giving energy, however, ceases when exchange does not occur because of the absence of response or barriers that prevent interaction. In Robert Frost's poem "Mending Wall," two neighbors meet annually in the spring to reconstruct a stone wall that has collapsed because of winds, storms, and ice. While one neighbor firmly holds to his father's proverb "Good fences make good neighbors," and reasons that walls establish privacy and ensure justice because they eliminate arguments about "mine" and "thine" and promote peaceful neighborly relationships, the other neighbor finds the custom antiquated and impractical: "There where it is we do not need the wall: / He is all pine and I am apple orchard." The day each spring when they meet to mend the wall, which he considers a silly custom, "just another kind of outdoor game," he insists, "Something there is that doesn't love a wall." This neighbor desires a higher form of relationship than legal justice, respect for property, privacy, and perfunctory obedience to the letter of the law that the wall signifies. The presence of the wall inhibits the natural responsiveness of friendship—the easy coming and going between friends and the spontaneous interplay of conversation and good will that flows in alternating responses. As long as the walls are rebuilt and good fences make good neighbors, the waves of love's rhythms do not come and go to bless and beautify human life. As Aristotle writes in book 8 of the *Nicomachean Ethics*, "For without friends no one would choose to live, though he had all other goods."[2]

---

2   *Introduction to Aristotle*, ed. Richard McKeon (New York: Modern Library, 1947), 471.

The art of living well, then, demands this exchange of sentiments, conversation, and companionship that makes life abundant rather than merely moral or law abiding. Perhaps the neighbor who insists that "[s]omething there is that doesn't love a wall" had in mind Aristotle's statement that "when men are friends, they have no need of justice, while when they are just they need friendship as well, and the truest form of justice is thought to be a friendly quality" (471–72). The fulfillment of living an authentic human life comes from this cooperation, union, and harmony between persons united in the bonds of love and friendship that perpetuate the continuous cycle of giving and receiving that is modeled in the Trinity.

Throughout the *Paradiso,* Dante portrays the communication of love's goodness as musical, rhythmic, and antiphonal movement. For example, Dominicans and Franciscans practice this law of love as they form an inner and outer circle in which St. Thomas, a Dominican, praises the life of St. Francis, and St. Bonaventure, a Franciscan, honors the life of St. Dominic, thus achieving the harmonious balance of love's movements. In response to the Dominican's recognition of St. Francis, St. Bonaventure replies: "The love that makes me beautiful / bids me proclaim that captain who praised mine / With such fair words, and him in turn extol" (12.31–33). Throughout Paradise, Dante observes movements causing movements as each planet in the Ptolemaic universe influences the motion of the other planets, and as words and acts of love beget more words and acts of love among the various orders of the blessed in Heaven. When Dante asks Piccarda to recite her story, she answers immediately and cheerfully: "Our love would no more turn a rightful claim / Back from the door, than He who is indeed / Love's self, and will have all His court the same" (3.43–45). In Dante's conception of Paradise, then, the rhythm of love consists of its instant, spontaneous, glad responsiveness, with no delays, doubts, hindrances, or walls. Love is always coming and going in the way that light constantly diffuses light and planets move in circles—a rhythm Dante compares to bees traveling to flowers and then returning to their hive: "As bees ply back and forth, now in the flowers / Busying themselves, and now intent to wend / Where all their toil is turned to sweetest stores" (31.7–9).

Thus love's growth, fruitfulness, and harvest depend on this eternal wave of coming and going that rejects barriers and walls. If one receives love but does not return it, benefits from a gift but never acknowledges a debt of gratitude, is blessed by God but never offers praise or worship, then the dynamic potential of love's energy is never released and life remains static or dormant. The fecundity of love is frustrated. God created man for friendship, marriage, and union, which depend on the constant exchange of receiving, returning, receiving more, and returning more, in an eternal cycle of love's infiniteness. It is this explosive power of love that Gerard Manley Hopkins captures in "God's Grandeur" when he writes, "The world is charged with the grandeur of God. / It will shine out, like shining from shook foil; / It gathers to a greatness like the ooze of oil / Crushed." The rhythm of love needs continuation for its miracles to happen, for its fruitfulness to yield its abundance, for God's blessings to flow, and for the greatness of God to charge and recharge the world and, in Hopkins's words, release "the dearest freshness deep down things" to renew the face of the world. Frost's famous line reflects the timeless wisdom of the Church: "Something there is that doesn't love a wall."

Related Reading

Robert Royal
Dante Alighieri: Divine Comedy, Divine Spirituality

Robert Royal gracefully guides you through this rich and evocative work, offering a careful and reader-friendly exploration of the text as well as a fine biographical portrayal of Dante — the man, the writer, the spiritual lover extraordinaire. Robert Royal holds a B.A. and an M.A. in Italian studies from Brown University as well as a doctorate in comparative literature from Catholic University. He is President of the Faith and Reason Institute in Washington D.C., and author of the acclaimed *The Catholic Martyrs of the Twentieth Century,* and *The Pope's Army. Dante Alighieri,* 246 pages, paperback, ISBN 978-0-8245-1604-8

*Support your local bookstore or order
directly from the publisher by calling
1-800-888-4741 for customer service.*

*To request a catalog or inquire about
Quantity orders, please e-mail
info@CrossroadPublishing.com*

The Crossroad Publishing Company

Related Reading

David Robinson
The Busy Family's Guide to Spirituality
Practical Lessons for Modern Living From the Monastic Tradition
ISBN 978-08245-25248

"Families would be enriched both spiritually and humanly if they read and applied the wisdom of St. Benedict as distilled by the author. *The Busy Family's Guide to Spirituality* is a rich book with many spiritual nuggets for the reader to mine and profit from."

—John O'Connell,
editor, *The Catholic Faith Magazine* ."

Hectic schedules and competing interests chip away at the sense of community and support that family members need to thrive. David Robinson synthesizes his rich experience as a father, pastor, teacher, and member of a monastic community to help families address modern-day challenges and cultivate a sense of togetherness and spiritual nurture. Drawing on timeless principles of monastic communal living, this spiritual guide for families offers effective tools to meet challenges and counteract the divisive forces that can splinter a healthy home.

Each chapter of this book includes a practical lesson from the Benedictine traditions that have been cornerstones of Western Christian monastic life for millennia. Spiritual practice, making time, discipline, sharing, hospitality, and changing family dynamics are some of the topics addressed in this wise and wide-ranging handbook, while exercises, checklists, and ideas for family activities are included at the end of every chapter.

Support your local bookstore or order
directly from the publisher by calling
1-800-888-4741 for customer service.

To request a catalog or inquire about
Quantity orders, please e-mail
info@CrossroadPublishing.com

The Crossroad Publishing Company

Related Reading

Stratford Caldecott
The Power of the Ring:
The Spiritual Vision Behind *The Lord of the Rings*
ISBN 978-08245-22773

Stratford Caldecott reveals the spiritual undercurrents in *The Lord of the Rings*. In this illuminating reflection on Tolkien's profound vision, Caldecott examines the influence of the author's faith, and considers Tolkien's craft in the light of thinkers like C.S. Lewis, Carl Jung, Rudolf Steiner, Owen Barfield, Joseph Chilton Pearce, and G.K. Chesterton. Caldecott also points to Nordic, Greek, and Roman mythology as well as Plato, Blake, and Goethe to shed light on the moral and spiritual ethos that pervades the Tolkien canon. Caldecott's book contextualizes and enriches our understanding of the beloved storyteller who continues to enchant readers and audiences today.

Support your local bookstore or order
directly from the publisher by calling
1-800-888-4741 for customer service.

To request a catalog or inquire about
Quantity orders, please e-mail
info@CrossroadPublishing.com

The Crossroad Publishing Company

Related Reading

Robert Barron
Heaven in Stone and Glass
Experiencing the Spirituality of the Great Cathedrals
ISBN 978-08245-19933

"Besides what a feature symbolizes—for instance, the cathedral's interior space represents the womb of Our Lady, a place of safety and comfort—Barron explains the doctrinal rationale and implications of the feature's significance. He does the latter so literately and congenially that the little book makes fine devotional as well as informational reading."

—*Booklist*

Like a mystical tome waiting to be deciphered, gothic cathedrals hold many secrets about Christ, the Christian life, and the soul's yearning for God. This book gloriously unfolds the stories of light and darkness, and the labyrinth of life. Barron teaches us how to understand the language of the great cathedrals, exploring the effects of elements such as rose windows, cruciformity, gargoyles, and vertical space. Whether you are preparing for a pilgrimage to York Minster cathedral in England or Notre Dame in Paris or looking ahead to bedside reflection on sacred space, this book is the perfect guide.

Support your local bookstore or order
directly from the publisher by calling
1-800-888-4741 for customer service.

To request a catalog or inquire about
Quantity orders, please e-mail
info@CrossroadPublishing.com

The Crossroad Publishing Company